T0204693

The Tactics
Of End-Games

Jenö Bán

DOVER PUBLICATIONS, INC.
Mineola, New York

Bibliographical Note

This Dover edition, first published in 1997, is an unabridged
republication of the work first published by The Corvina Press,
Budapest, in 1963. It was translated from the Hungarian (original
title, *A Vegjatekok Taktikaja*), by Jenö Bochkor.

Library of Congress Cataloging-in-Publication Data

Bán, Jenö.
 [Végjátékok taktikája. English]
 The tactics of end-games / by Jenö Bán.
     p.   cm.
 Originally published: Budapest : Corvina Press, 1963.
 Includes index.
 ISBN 0-486-29705-5 (pbk.)
 1. Chess–End games.   I. Title.
 GV1450.7.B353   1997
 794.1'24–dc21   97–22514
                                                          CIP

Manufactured in the United States of America
Dover Publications, Inc., 31 East 2nd Street, Mineola, N.Y. 11501

CONTENTS

PREFACE

The development of chess in its present form dates back to an age in which the secret of the philosophers' stone was still the chief concern of medieval alchemists. The first masters of the royal game were thus looked upon as occult magicians who owed their victories to a knowledge of some mysterious secret. A host of amateurs tried to unearth this secret and, by so doing, laid the foundations of the theory of chess. More and more notes were collected. as to the o p e n i n g m o v e s preferred by this or that outstanding player, and the first "theoreticians" claimed to have found in these the clue of success. Long centuries passed and their "theory," their scientific research into chess play, still got no further than cramming a great number of opening variations into the heads of the studious, while completely ignoring the intricacies of the middle-game and the subtleties of the endings. And the result? Pitiful, indeed! As a matter of fact, the problem of which opening is best is still undecided, and no one opening can claim to be indisputably better than the rest.

Yet the standard of chess play has risen tremendously and is still improving. Why? Because wealth of experience has now turned the attention of theoreticians to the later stages of the game: to the middle-game and the endings. Their systematic work has made it considerably easier to survey the requirements of correct play. The bibliography of modern chess already lists many an excellent theoretical work on middle-games and endings, vying in importance with the books on openings. For all that, there still is one aspect of chess play which, cloaked in mystery, has defied theoretical treatment with no small success. This is the world of tactics.

Tactics in chess play are like the salt in the soup or the plums in the pudding. The tactical motifs add flavour and spice to the game, the combinative turns delight player and onlooker alike. But the very kaleidoscopic variety of tactics, the frequent defiance of set rules and laws makes it difficult to impart a knowledge of tactics to the novice or to the average player in the same way as general principles of strategy or the theory of openings.

The present book ventures to attempt what has been considered virtually impossible: it endeavours to systematize and, by reducing them to their elements, to classify the tactical motifs that constitute the foundation stones

7

of each and every combination, from the simplest to the most deeply calculated. As the title shows, our purpose is to examine the tactical motifs in end-games. These are in no way different from those which may also occur in the middle-game; it is only for the sake of better understanding and clarity that the illustrative examples chosen are relatively simple positions with a minimum number of pieces on the board. The reader will be surprised to note how many interesting points, finesses and subtleties are concealed in even these apparently simple positions.

If you simply turn over the pages of this book, casting a glance at the diagrams here and there, you may get the impression that it is a mere selection of end-game studies. In a sense this is true, and if you have a fancy for the artistic demonstration of chess endings, you will find here many an outstanding composition by the most brilliant authors. But as soon as you give some attention to the introductory remarks at the head of each chapter and to the comments on the diagrams, you will agree that the book has been designed primarily for the actual player and not for the enthusiast of chess compositions. Its intention is to teach you the tactics of end-games and to increase your all-round playing powers. The only reason for our having taken the illustrative material from the world of studies instead of from grandmaster practice is that we have endeavoured to combine the pleasing with the useful, while trying to give you an insight into the deeper aesthetic beauties of endings. The ideas expressed in the artistic examples in so crystal-clear and brilliant a way, very often appear also in the actual finish of an over-the-board game, though in a less polished form. One would describe the finish of such a game as a "study-like" ending.

The author hopes that, after a careful perusal of this book, the reader himself will more often be able to create such "study-like" endings in the course of over-the-board play.

Jenő Bán

TRANSLATOR'S NOTE

The reader will certainly find that this book contains many new, one might say revolutionary, ideas explained by the author from an entirely new aspect. Consequently the expressions and phrases coined by Mr. Jenő Bán had not only to be translated but also "recoined" in English. I wish to express here my thanks to Mr. Peter H. Clarke and to my friend Mr. Raymond B. Edwards for their valuable suggestions and help.

Jenő Bochkor

FUNDAMENTAL CONCEPTS

Our object is to examine the methods of leading from the most diverse but relatively simple positions that arise on the chessboard during the progress of the game to the most favourable termination, namely a victory or, failing that, a draw. Before going into details it seems necessary to clarify the concepts to be dealt with later in this connection.

THE CONCEPT OF END-GAMES

The end-game is the last phase of a game of chess. The starting-point of an end-game is, accordingly, an "initial position" that has been reached from the basic position after an unspecified number of normal moves. **The content of an end-game** is that series of moves which leads from this "initial position" to the actual termination of the game, i. e. to the palpable demonstration of its ultimate outcome. **The form of the end-game** is determined by the pieces that are on the board in the "initial position", or after each move of the series of moves leading to the actual finish.

The end-game is characterized by its content and by its form. Any closer definition of the fundamental concept must derive from one or other of these attributes. As a matter of fact we only know where the "last phase" ends, it is uncertain and disputable where it begins.

It is generally believed that in an end-game there are only a "few" pieces on the board. This definition is, however, very loose, nor is it necessarily supported by the tendency of theoretical textbooks to deal mostly with positions comprising 4 or 5 (and very rarely 6) pieces. Others again maintain that it is not the exact number of chessmen but the number and type of the pieces that determine an end-game. In this light any position where one or both of the players have only 1 or 2 pieces left might, irrespective of the number of pawns present, be regarded as an end-game.

Many theoreticians hold that the end-game begins with the moment when the role of the kings changes, i. e. when the position has been so simplified that there is no danger of a direct mating attack and the king can appear as an active factor on the scene. But we can rarely assume that both kings will be **equally** active at the same time; indeed, the intervention of one king may suddenly strengthen the mating threat to the other.

One often hears, moreover, that "the outcome has already been decided in the middle-game—or even in the opening." This in fact amounts to saying that some games have no end-game. Not only would such an assumption obscure our definition but it would be in flagrant contradiction to it.

For this reason let us approach the question from another angle. What is the difference between the opening and the middle-game on the one hand, and the end-game on the other? Any analysis of the opening and middle-game can lead only to estimated and probable results. The result of an end-game, on the other hand, admits of a concrete, tangible and verifiable demonstration based on an objective analysis.

In this we may already have a clear-cut definition of the concept at issue, indicating as it does, irrespective of the varying number and position of the pieces, the exact moment at which the ending phase occurs in any particular game. Accordingly, the transition to an end-game has been completed as soon as the player to move has an opportunity of demonstrating, by a sequence of forcing moves in all variations, his unquestionable victory or the absolute futility of his opponent's efforts to win.

Consequently, the "initial position" of an end-game already implies the elements of the final position, including the outcome; the shorter or longer chain of moves connecting the two is made up of links, each of which is amenable to an objective, scientific analysis.

Of course, this premise might as well be extended to make the concept of the end-game cover that of the whole game, the basic position itself being regarded as the "initial position". Theoretically and logically there is nothing against it, but the limited scope of our knowledge and the immensity of the field of research would thwart any attempt to do so. One may encounter many a position with a mere 5 or 6 pieces which, though simple in form, is of a content that cannot be fully explored even by the most thoroughgoing research; and again, there are many apparently complicated "full board" positions in which evident and concrete moves lead to a calculable outcome—the final position.

All positions—irrespective of the number of pieces—the appraisal of which does not lead to an irrefutable result, should be classified as **middle-game positions,** while positions (again disregarding the number of pieces) from which the outcome may be objectively deduced by sequences of best moves on both sides, should be regarded as **end-game positions.** The borderline between the two is that area of incessant research where fresh ground is being reclaimed by degrees from the impenetrable jungle of the middle-game to give free passage through the ever widening glade of end-games.

THE FINISH AND THE STUDY

As we have said the end-game is the last phase of a game. Since even the shortest game has its last phase, it follows that every game, including those which, in form, actually terminate in the middle-game or the opening, must have a phase which may be designated as its end-game.

The shortest game conceivable consists of only two moves:

1. P—KN4, P—K4 2. P—KB3??, Q—R5—mate!

"Where is here the end-game?" one might ask. Well, in the light of our previous definition, the end-game position arose when the player to move was able to demonstrate irrefutably his ability to reach the "final position". This followed White's gross blunder on the second move and Black had merely to make one single, but fully convincing, move in order to meet the requirement: "Black wins".

The shortest match-game known in chess literature went along very similar lines:

Gibaud—Lazard (Paris, 1927).

1. P—Q4, N—KB3 2. N—Q2, P—K4 3. P×P, N—N5 4. P—KR3? N—K6!! and White resigned.
The final position:

1.

Of the moves played here the last one only belongs to the "end-game", but inherent in it are two variations demonstrating victory. One of them is, in fact, the same mating position as we saw in the previous example: 5. P×N, Q—R5 ch, 6. P—KN3, Q×P (N6)—mate. The other variation leaves White a queen down (against a knight).

In the latter alternative to prove the continuation to the actual mate would undoubtedly be a laborious task, but Black's material superiority (without any positional disadvantage!) is so convincing that we can rightly accept it on the principle of an "adequate logical basis."

A striking feature common to both end-games—apart from the unusually large number of pieces still on the board—is that the majority of the pieces play no part in the final outcome.

If someone wished—for the purpose of instruction or entertainment—to show simply the forcing motif by which it is possible to mate a king (walled in by his own pieces) with a queen or even a bishop, or else wished to demonstrate how mate or loss of the queen was inevitable after the sacrifice of a knight, be could remove quite a number of pieces from both the White and the Black armies and still leave the means of achieving his final aim or the character of the final result unchanged.

The mating position in the first game can be shown most economically as follows:

2.

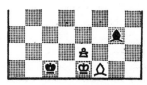

Thus by removing the "superfluous" pieces an "initial position" created in a very early stage of the opening can be transformed and simplified—with its content left intact—so that the residual position will at first glance give the impression of an "end-game."

Not only is such a transformation possible but it is in fact desirable from the didactic point of view. The ways and means of winding up a game can be shown more clearly and decisively if we retain only those pieces which play an actual part, active or passive, in bringing about the final result.

Theoretical books on end-games therefore mostly employ examples which are not positions from actual play but positions intentionally designed, transformed or simplified for the purpose. These positions meet the requirement that they can be legally derived from the basic position by a series of regular moves but the manner of derivation is extraneous and therefore unimportant.

The use of artificial end-games instead of actual game-endings as examples has several advantages: (1) An artificial end-game may in a simple condensed form comprise all the practical lessons to be drawn from numerous game-endings of similar character. (2) The artificial ending presents its motifs divested of all irrelevancies, motifs which might otherwise get lost among the many alternative variations of actual play or which will occur but seldom. (3) The artificial ending may actually fill gaps in practical experience and draw attention to possibilities which so far have not occurred in actual play. (4) Exploration of the content of an artificial end-game opens up a field of impersonal, objective research, because it is not bounded by any sequence of moves actually made by the two players.

An artificial end-game may simply be an instructive demonstration of some typical end-game technique, or else a truly artistic study demonstrating some quite extraordinary or unique termination of an imaginary game.

Grandmaster Richard Réti (1889—1929) who was among the best both as a chess player and as a problemist gave the following concise definition of the study: "A simple position of extraordinary content." Subscribing to Réti's opinion, we cannot but acknowledge the merits of the study both as a source of aesthetic pleasure and as a useful didactic medium.

For this reason most of our examples have been chosen from among studies that are simple in form but rich in content.

THE CONCEPT OF TACTICS

Tactics are the art of handling forces in battle. In terms of the chessboard this means the art and science of correct direction and effective execution of local skirmishes and minor but fierce actions. In real warfare there is generally one battle among the many which decides the fate of the whole war. The British have often been said "to lose every battle except the last." So on the chessboard, where in the last phase of the game, i. e. in the end-game, the last encounter may decide the outcome of the whole fight.

This last encounter may in fact radically change the situation and reverse the course of events. Therefore, it is especially important to make ourselves familiar with the details of the tactical methods which may come in handy during end-games.

Tactical changes in a game of chess are characterized by ingenuity, cunning, surprise attacks, traps and the like. Under the microscope of objective research such elements as cunning and surprise become transparent and disappear, but sufficient remains in view to lead us inevitably to the conclusion: **Forcing is the principle of tactics!**

In pursuing this principle there can be no fastidiousness about means. It is the end which is all-important and towards that end every available means may be utilized.

What are the **forcing motifs** in chess?

(a) **Capturing.** The capture of a piece forces the opponent to recapture a piece of the same value, failing which the balance of power is upset.

(b) **Attack.** Attack on an important piece forces the opponent to organize the defence or rescue of the attacked piece, or possibly—if his king is not involved—to launch an immediate counter-attack against a hostile piece of the same value.

(c) **Threat.** This means an imminent attack which—according to its gravity—compels the opponent to make provision against it. Thus the threat limits the opponent's freedom of action.

Beside these three factors **the move itself**—irrespective of its content—can be regarded as a forcing motif, because according to the rules it compels the opponent to make his own move. In certain cases this obligation can be very unpleasant. (See: **Zugzwang.**)

The sequence of moves comprising the motif of forcing is called **tactical operation.** The main feature of tactical operations is that of the three elements of chess play: material, space and time. **Time** is here the most significant.

There is not always an opportunity in a game for effective forcing. Such opportunities must be carefully prepared and established by means of methodical play. The establishment and preparation of the play and the alignment of the forces before the decisive battle constitute strategy. The strategically established possibilities or the unexpected chances resulting from some particular move by the opponent are exploited by tactical means.

The time factor which underlies all tactical possibilities makes it necessary that in a **momentarily given position** immediate and prompt measures are taken and in the process we must keep harassing our opponent by a continual succession of forcing motifs without, as it were, pausing for breath. Promptness and vigour are of even greater importance if our opponent is also using tactical weapons and, in reply to our **attack,** launches a **counter-attack.**

It is in this sense that we must stress the priority of the time factor, adding that this priority also applies to endings with a few pieces when the board is nearly "empty" although **space** and its importance will increase in proportion with the number of empty squares. In tactical operations also space plays a not altogether insignificant part which, however, always plays second fiddle to time.

The third element, **material**—i. e. the total value of pieces at one's disposal—will **during tactical operations completely lose the importance** it is normally given on a relative or exchange value!

The general value of a piece is determined by its "ability" to exercise direct control over a certain area, to **occupy** certain ranks, files, diagonals or squares and to move in that area with the aim of **capturing** other squares. A queen is "more valuable" than a rook, because it keeps more squares under control from its post and being able to move in all directions, it will be ready to conquer many more in a single move.

When, however, the situation is ripe and the concrete aim is within reach, the **role of the pieces will be limited** to the **accomplishment of the task** on hand, hence their value will be exclusively determined by their ability to accomplish that end.

Let us now, by way of example, take a position where White has the opportunity of capturing a queen by giving a simultaneous check to Black's king and queen but where the square making this double attack possible is controlled by one of Black's knights. It is obvious that at this juncture our attention is drawn to Black's knight, which is standing in our way and our primary task will be to drive away or "kill" this knight. It will not make any essential difference whether we simply attack the knight with a pawn move or capture it prosaically with, say, a bishop, or else annihilate it by the more elegant sacrifice of a rook or even a queen! As a result we may not be a full queen ahead but the advantage accruing from the capture of the knight will for all practical purposes be nearly as important.

It follows that the piece thrown into action will often be utilized—for tactical reasons—without any consideration of its "exchange value". Therefore, the execution very often takes the form of a **sacrifice.**

By sacrifices are meant those deliberate, voluntary, and hence "unforced" moves and captures which lead to the opponent having a net material advantage. Consequently, every move is a sacrifice which, at first glance, so far from conforming to elementary ideas of common sense in chess play, namely to the effort to secure an advantage, actually appears to fly in the face of it.

Of course, such voluntary munificence is unreasonable unless it is only apparently in contradiction with the effort to win. In reality a correct sacrifice is nothing but an organic introductory part of a well-knit tactical operation, designed not only to offset the temporary setback but to transform it into an advantage.

The tactical operation preceded by a sacrifice is called a **combination**: This term aptly expresses the basic principle of correct chess thought, namely that it is not single, isolated moves which should be the subject of our "evalution" but a whole sequence of them linked together by a unity of content. It is only the ultimate balance of the combination that needs to be favourable, and it would be just as unreasonable to evaluate any of the intermediate phases on their own merits as it would be to say during the course of a game that "White is a queen ahead," when Black on the next move is actually going to recapture.

It is in the course of a combination that the principle of forcing is given its widest scope. The player taking the initiative may so effectively curtail his opponent's freedom of manoeuvre that throughout a shorter or longer sequence of moves he is able to direct the course of play. In this way he will significantly reduce the number of possible alternatives, because the opponent, more often than not, has only some **forced move** at his disposal. This permits the developments to be calculated to the last degree. This calculation—i. e. foreseeing the final aim and searching for a route to it—is the **process of combination** or, in other words, the methodical examination and utilization of tactical possibilities.

THE ELEMENTS OF COMBINATION

Before proceeding to examine what can be achieved by combination, and in what way, we must be aware of our own purpose, we must know **what we want to make the opponent do.**

In the last resort, our aim is **to give mate** by building up a position in which we can ensnare the opponent's king. But practically equivalent to this is the creation of such positions as will enable us to acquire a **decisive material superiority** (e.g. winning a queen or a rook, or queening a pawn).

No matter how infinitely great the number of possible situation on the board, the possibilities of obtaining material advantage can be divided into a few, exactly defined groups.

If for simplicity's sake we temporarily disregard qualitative considerations, then the conceivable **general possibilities of capturing and gaining a piece are as follows:**

(a) Double attack. A situation in which one or two pieces make their offensive effect simultaneously felt by two hostile pieces which are either unprotected or of greater value. It results in winning one of the attacked pieces.

A double attack can be a **fork** when the aggressive piece can exercise its effect in two directions at the same time (e. g. fork with a pawn, or check to both the king and the queen with a knight), it can be a "skewer" when two hostile pieces on the same file, rank or diagonal find themselves in the sphere of action of a rook, bishop or queen (geometrical motif), and finally it can be a **discovered attack** when the aggressive move of one piece gives way to the attack of another against a second hostile piece.

The diagrams below exemplify the mentioned varieties of the double attack:

3.

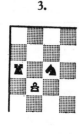

4.

Fork with a pawn; and with a knight.

5.

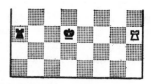

Rook skewer. The rook exerts its effect "through the body of the king." After the king's move Black's rook is lost. (Geometrical motif.)

6.

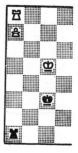

Discovered attack. After 1. R—QB8!, R×P White has 2. K—N6 at his disposal giving "discovered check" to the king and attacking the rook at the same time.

(b) Tying down. A situation in which a piece cannot escape an attack because of some other threat. All attacks against **pieces pinned** previously or pieces warding off some threat belong here. Also the **threatening attack** or double threat (similar to the double attack) comes under this heading. For example:

7.

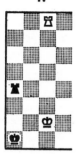

1. K—N3! threatens R—B1 mate. The king attacks Black's rook at the same time. Result: winning the rook.

(c) **Ensnaring.** A situation in which a piece cannot escape an attack because of lack of space, or restriction of movement. Essentially it is the concept of mate though with reference to some piece other than the king.

In ensnaring, the edge of the board and the self-blockade of the pieces play an important part. Examples:

8.

1. K—N7 "ensnaring" the knight.

9.

"Mate" to the rook.

10.

Ensnaring the queen.

The **pawns** with their restricted movement will usually fall victim to ensnaring, since they are unable to escape the attack.

If a **fixed** piece—which we want to trap—is adequately **defended** by the opponent, we can gain material advantage by **multiple attack,** i. e. we have to concentrate more pieces than the number of those in defence. The same applies for defended pinned pieces.

(d) **Encirclement.** A situation in which every possible move of the opponent leads to a material loss. From the point of view of the weaker side this position is called **Zugzwang.**

In the position created by encirclement there is no direct attack or threat, or rather, the pieces under attack are sufficiently protected. Yet the very circumstance of having to move, the **Zugzwang,** compels the player to leave one of his pieces unprotected or even offer it for slaughter without any compensation. For instance:

11.

Encirclement. After Black's move the knight is lost.

12.

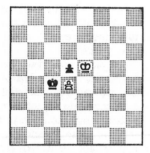

Zugzwang *The player to move loses his pawn ... and the game.*

(e) Queening. A situation in which the promotion of a pawn cannot be prevented or if so only by the sacrifice of a piece. It follows that the player queening his pawn will gain material advantage either by an increase of his own forces or by a decrease of those of his opponent.

If we regard the mate as a special instance of "gaining material advantage" by trapping the opponent's king, then we have already defined the concept of all theoretical **winning positions** that may result from double

attack, tying down, ensnaring, encirclement and queening. These positions may well be given the common designation **target positions** so that we have a single term to describe the ultimate situations we have in mind when embarking upon a combination.

Of course there are certain **conditions** for bringing about such "target positions" and obtaining an actual advantage.

The combination is the creation of the conditions necessary for attaining a certain target position.

Let us take for example the simplest form of the double attack. What is needed for such a position?

There must be two hostile pieces on two definite squares of the board, exposed to the same attack.

There must be a piece of our own standing by for carrying out the double attack.

The starting point of the attack must be open for the offensive piece.

Further conditions of making the double attack efficacious are that

(i) the two pieces under attack should not be adequately protected,

(ii) they should not be in a position to organize mutual defence,

(iii) neither of the two pieces should be able to dodge the attack by launching a counter-attack or gaining a tempo.

In order to secure these conditions we usually have to remove numerous obstacles from our path by energetic, prompt and forcing measures. The most frequently employed means of liquidating obstacles is the sacrifice. It should be emphasized, however, that the sacrifice is only **a form** of forcing and is merely indicative that all available means are being utilized. In principle we could equally attain our end without a sacrifice if we had the proper means at our disposal. (Let us recall our previous theoretical example: if we intend to capture a knight, it makes no difference if we take it with a pawn or sacrifice our queen for it.)

The sacrifice—as the most energetic form of forcing—is designed to remove some or all of the obstacles in the way of achieving the target position.

Let us examine, for instance, the possible obstacles to a successful double attack:

(1) The two hostile pieces are not in the requisite position. Therefore, our task is to force these pieces (or at least one of them) to the appropriate square. This may be called "driving on" (Hinlenkung).

(2) Our aggressive piece is not in a position to attack because

(a) it is pinned,

(b) its way is blocked,

(c) it cannot reach its "base of operation" in one move.

What is to be done? We have to speed up the movement of our piece and to secure the starting point of the attack by way of (a) **diversion** (driving off) of the hostile piece (which pins down ours), (b) **opening of a file**, (c) **gaining of tempi** (e. g. by giving check to the hostile king).

(3) The opponent defends the square which serves for a possible starting point of our attack. In this case we must **liquidate** the defending piece or **divert** it from its post.

(4) The pieces attacked by us are adequately defended. We find ourselves again confronted with the task of liquidating or diverting the defending piece.

(5) The two pieces can mutually defend each other. In this case we have to disrupt their co-operation by way of **closing a file or erecting a blockade.**

(6) The piece under attack might escape by gaining a tempo or launching a counter-attack. Now we must **close a file** in order to cut the way of refuge or counter-attack.

Having enumerated the possible obstacles we have also pointed out the general features of the elementary tactical operations which define the aim of the sacrifice in a given case.

"Driving on" and **"driving off"** (diversion) are, however, such basic concepts that they must be marked from the very outset as the most characteristic motifs of **directing** the course of a game. They have a significant part to play not only in the double attack but also in achieving any of the listed target positions. Let us look at two simple examples illustrating these concepts.

13.

DAMIANO, 1512.

Driving off.

1. Q×P ch, Q×Q
2. N—B7 mate.

14.
SCHEME.

Driving on.

1. Q—N8 ch!!, R×Q
2. N—B7 mate.

The two diagrams demonstrate two typical instances of engineering the well-known "smothered mate". In the first White diverts Black's queen from the square B7, in the second he drives Black's rook to N8, thus paralysing the hostile king.

The latter case—the role of Black's rook in the mate—calls our attention to the fact that some pieces may be not only of positive but also of negative "value". A piece which in a certain situation has a damaging effect on its own camp, is a **"harmful"** piece.

15.
SCHEME.

Driving off.

1. B—B5!, B×B
2. P—N8 queens and wins.

16.
SCHEME.

Driving on.

1. N—N7 ch!, N×N
2. P—R6 and wins.

Here we see typical examples of the exploitation of a passed pawn in a bishop and in a knight end-game. The sacrifice of White's bishop serves for the diversion of Black's bishop which commands the square N8. The sacrifice of White's knight purposes to force Black's knight to N7 where it blocks the way of Black's king (after N—N7 ch!, N×N 2. P—R6, K—B1 3. P—R7! Black's king cannot occupy the square N7).

Now we have seen that both the driving off and the driving on forcibly determine the movement of the opponent's pieces. The difference between the two lies only in the direction of movement. In case of a diversion (driving off) the **"wherefrom,"** and in case of the driving on the **"where-to"** is the essential thing. Of course, in a combination both motifs may occur successively, or at the same time for that matter.

The following study demonstrates both concepts in an elementary yet attractive form:

17.

A. A. TROITSKY, 1924.

White wins.

After 1. P—R7! Black has two alternatives to choose from, to prevent the queening of White's pawn. In both variations White gives a check to Black's king and drives it on to the file or rank of Black's rook. Then—by a double attack—White diverts Black's rook, and prevents it from guarding the promotion square:

(A) 1. P—R7, R—Q1 2. R—B4 ch, K—Q7 3. R—Q4 ch! and wins.

(B) 1. P—R7!, R—KR7 2. R—B1ch, K—Q7 3. R—B2 ch! and wins.

Almost every complicated, surprising or even astounding combination is based upon such simple elements. Its progress—if it does not consist of only 1 or 2 moves—simply "forces" on us the comparison with the process of sowing, ripening and harvest, since on the peaceful battlefield of the chessboard the same thing happens (taking a metaphor from agriculture) as on the fields from autumn to spring. After properly "tilling the soil" we can sow the seeds by sacrificing 1 or 2 pieces, then the position ripens for launching the decisive attack and finally we can gather in the rich crop.

* * *

We are now familiar with the concept of winning target positions and we have outlined the tactical elements. We might from this proceed to discuss the details of end-game tactics.

It would be logical first to examine the simplest operations (of one or two moves) and then to pass on to the more complicated ones. But there is a rub. Beyond the concepts, elements and motifs we have already discussed, there are further tactical possibilities of a quite different kind.

The possibilities in question are those whose purpose is to secure only a **draw,** by means quite removed from the general principles of tactics. We refer to **stalemate,** the less known **virtual stalemate** and **perpetual** attack. These too may be considered **target positions,** if we modify the original concept insomuch as our aim now is to achieve a draw instead of a victory.

In order to create such situations we must have a good grasp of the theory of tactics. The adoption of tactical methods demands also a knowledge of these situations, because it is evident that the player at a disadvantage will take up tactical arms against the opponent striving for victory, with the purpose of achieving at least a draw.

For this reason, we shall introduce first of all the various forms of "special draws" without going into the details of the tactical methods to be adopted.

In the first part of the book our primary purpose is to demonstrate the possibilities, while the second part deals with the tactical methods, their elements, and their use in end-games.

I. FIGHT FOR A DRAW

THE STALEMATE

The stalemate is a special case of winding up the game. Some might even say that it is a case occurring very rarely in practice, a misconception which should, however, be dispelled at once. The fact that a match-game ending in a draw is very seldom labelled with the word "stalemate," hardly means more than the equally rare occurrence of "mate" at the end of a game actually decided. Admittedly, the number of games terminating in actual stalemate is small, but in a high percentage of draws it is the possibility of stalemate, after all, that frustrates the victory of the stronger side.

Why is it a futile effort to try to mate an unsupported king with two knights? Why cannot a queen win against a pawn advanced to B7 or R7? Why is it often impossible to promote a RP supported by a bishop (or sometimes by a knight)? Why cannot we force a win with an active rook and king against the opponent's cornered king and bishop? And, as is often shown in everyday practice, why is there no hope of crowning a well-supported pawn when the hostile king has managed to occupy the square right in front of it?

In each of these cases there is only one answer: Because of stale-mate. It will appear, therefore, that the peculiar character of stalemate is by no means attributable to its rare or unusual occurrence, but rather to a valuation founded on the rules. As the rules of chess will have it, the complete immobilization and encirclement of the opponent's forces, the deprival of mobility to all his pieces is in itself not worth a straw!

This seemingly illogical rule gives logical content to tactical operations that also appear illogical in handling end-games. It permits a heaping up of sacrifices without striving for compensation either in material or in position. Indeed, our objective now becomes the intentional increase in the opponent's forces and the widening of their scope, while at the same time restricting the mobility of our own pieces. As soon as total immobility is reached and we have no legal move available, we have achieved our purpose.

Tactical means of achieving stalemate:

(i) Forcing sacrifice of the mobile pieces;

(ii) "Walling in" of the mobile pieces by self-block or blockade;

(iii) Encircling one's own king by

directing the opponent's pieces or by a royal march to the "stalemate nest."

These operations can be made more effective if connected with threats that can only be warded off or prevented by the opponent at the cost of some other disadvantage-equalization of the game or even defeat. Often stalemate is combined with perpetual chase, i. e. we offer our mobile piece for sacrifice again and again after each refusal on the part of the opponent.

In the majority of over-the-board games stalemate is only an obscure variation among the many ways leading to a draw, though it has a decisive role in the developments. Therefore, in order to get a clear picture of the relevant concepts, it is best to examine such artistic studies as will bring into focus the tactical possibilities of achieving stalemate as their main theme. Thus we shall be spared the mistake of reading "brilliant" stalemate combination into end-games in which their occurrence is not necessary but purely accidental.

Let us now look at the possibilities of stalemate in various types of endgames.

STALEMATE POSITIONS IN PAWN END-GAMES

A king forcing its way through the pawns of the opponent may easily run into a blind-alley, the defensive forces stopping it in its tracks. In such a case one might try to bar the way of retreat instead of a "switchback." Motifs: square-blocking, self-block, pawn blockade—eliminating a square vacation by directing the opponent's pawn.

Very often the Zugzwang is also of great importance.

18.

H. RINCK, 1911.

Draw.

1. K—N3, P—R4 2. P—K4, K—N8 3. P—K5!, P×P—stalemate.

This is an elementary example but —in its simplicity—it clearly illustrates (1) the forced move, (2) the Zugzwang, and (3) the typical "driving-on" pawn sacrifice.

19.

F. LAZARD, 1916.

Draw.

A textbook example giving a fine demonstration of the theme mentioned above. Solution:

1. K—Q6, K—Q1 2. P—B5!, K—K1 3. P—B3!, K—Q1 4. P—B4, K—K1 5. P—B5, K—Q1 6. P—B6, P×P—stalemate.

20.

A. SELESNIEV, 1918.

Draw.

In this situation White's king cannot, even by the most accurate manoeuvring, avoid the Zugzwang and the eventual loss of its pawns. But the stalemate nest on his KR5 offers an escape:

1. K—B6!, K—Q1 2. K—Q5!, K×P 3. K—K4!, K—Q3! 4. K—B3, K—K4 5. K—N4, K—B3 6. K—R5!, K×P—stalemate.

* * *

In the next situation Black is compelled to stalemate White's king at the edge of the board because of Zugzwang.

21.

V. HALBERSTADT, 1929.

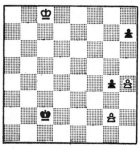

Draw.

1. K—Q7, K—Q6 2. K—K6, K—K6 3. K—B5, P—N6 4. K—N4!, K—B7 5. K—R3! and Black has no better continuation than 5. ..., P—R4 with stalemate as a result.

In the event of other winning attempts White would bring about a theoretical drawing position by winning Black's KRP, e. g. 3. K—B5, P—R4 4. K—N5, K—B7 5. K×P, P—N6 6. K—N6!, K×P 7. P—R5, K—B6 8. P—R6, P—N7 9. P—R7, P—N8 (Q) ch 10. K—B7! and draws. Forcing White's king in front of its pawn would create a stalemate; consequently Black cannot gain time for advancing his own king.

This variation shows how a pawn is able to draw against a queen. It is a well-known fact that a **BP** advanced to the seventh rank and supported by its own king can put up a successful fight if the hostile king is far away. Motif of the draw: sacrifice of the pawn by withdrawing the king into the corner. If the opponent's queen captures the BP, the king is immobilized.

Since the stress is upon this particular stalemate position, it should not seen surprising that even a central pawn may secure a draw, should its fall, under certain favourable circumstances, result in a similar stalemate. Such a possibility is shown by the next study:

22.

A. A. TROITSKY, 1899.

Draw.

Black's distant RP is very menacing. It is hopeless to seek defence by a back-pedalling circular tour of White's king because the RP and the KP would then fall prey to Black. There is only one way left: active counterplay.

1. K—N6!, K—B1 (otherwise P—R6, P—R7 etc. would follow) 2. P—R6, K—N1! 3. P—R7 ch!, K—R1 4. K—B7, P—R4 5. K×P (Q6), P—R5 6. K×P, P—R6 7. P—K5, P—R7 8. P—K6, P—R8 (Q) 9. P—K7, Q—Q4 ch 10. K—B7, Q—K3 II. K—Q8, Q—Q3 ch 12. K—B8!!, Q×P—stalemate.

Here the cornered position of Black's king has the effect of moving the edge of the board one file in to

White's benefit. In this situation White's KP has the same role as the BP would have in the customary case. It may be added that Black cannot make capital out of his king's close proximity because e. g. 12. K—B8, Q—B3 ch 13. K—Q8, K—N2 would be followed not by 14. P—K8 (Q)?? (14. ..., Q—B2 mate!!) but first by 14. P—R8 (Q) ch!—forcing the king's return and then 14. ..., K×Q 15. P—K8 (Q).

WALLING IN

The fact that pawns move one way only is apt to lead to a completely mechanical restriction of moves and a total immobility of pieces.

This motif calls our attention to the fact that a stalemate can be achieved also by walling in, by way of building up a self-blockade. Sometimes it is enough to build a wall of fixed pawns around the king, but sometimes it is necessary to do so also around other pieces. Examples:

23.

J. BERGER, 1889.

Draw.

Since Black's RP cannot be overtaken, White must also try to establish a distant passed pawn. The preparatory 1. P—N3 is too slow, for Black catches up with White in time; the result would be the same also after 1. P—R4, P×P 2. P—B4, K—B2. This leaves us 1. P—B4! as the only alternative with a promising break-through (1. ..., P—R4? 2. P—B5, P×P 3. P—R4!). What are we to do, however, if 1. P—B4! is met by 1. ..., K—B2!? Then comes the unexpected turn, inevitably leading to a stalemate:

1. P—B4!, K—B2! 2. P×P!, P—R4 3. K—N3, P—R5 4. K—R4, P—R6 5. P—N3!—and the **walling in** is complete.

24.

I. C. CAMPBELL, 1855.

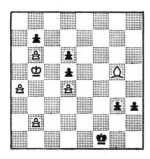

Draw.

At first glance it is hardly conceivable that White can put up a successful fight against Black's connected passed pawns, but it soon becomes obvious that any continuation on Black's part leads to a stereotyped case of "walling in," whereby we secure a draw—if only we have an eye for it! It takes but three moves: 1. B—Q2!—2. B—R5!—3. P—N4! —with a frozen stalemate position, irrespective of what Black has done in the meantime.

* * *

It is much harder to conceive the walling in of a piece without the presence of pawns on the board, with the significant exception of a cornered bishop, which can in fact be paralysed by merely blocking a single square.

25.

A. and K. SARYTCHEV, 1929.

Draw.

White's chief concern is how to rescue his endangered bishops, because the continuation 1. B—B1 ch, K—N6 threatens the pin R—N8 and even 2. B—K4 is no salvation on account of 2. ..., R—K1 with an indirect threat of mate. The bad position of White's king is accordingly the main source of trouble. But it is just

27

such a siege that usually offers the possibility of a stalemate combination.

Here is how it goes:

1. P—N3 ch!, B×P (. . ., K×P? 2. B—K5 ch) 2. B—B1 ch, K—N5 (otherwise 3. K—N2) 3. B—R1!!, R—N8 4. K—N2! and after R×B **the stalemate is achieved.** Any other continuation would permit White to bring his bishop into safety.

THE QUEEN AS A FACTOR IN STALEMATE

The queen may menace too many squares at a time, make too large an area "forbidden land" for the hostile pieces, and her power cannot, therefore, always be regarded as an advantage. We all remember the unpleasant experiences of our tyro days when, a queen ahead, we triumphantly massacred the steadily dwindling forces of an opponent on the brink of defeat only to wake up to the sad truth that the game had suddenly ended in . . . **stalemate!**

More often than not the queen is the "hero" of the simplest stalemate combinations, though naturally in a passive sense. A queen responsible for stalemate looks on the board like some clumsy Cyclops outwitted and mocked by Ulysses, a case of "more brawn than brain!"

What are the tactical elements of utilizing this lesson in practice? (1) Driving the opponent's queen to the square from which it immobilizes our king. (2) Annihilation of the rest of our mobile pieces by their forcing sacrifice. These two aims may be realized simultaneously by way of a **directing** (driving-on) **sacrifice.**

First of all let us examine how the immense combined strength of two queens may turn—to a disadvantage.

26.

F. J. PROKOP, 1925.

Draw.

White offers a rook sacrifice by which he either captures one of the queens or brings about various stalemate positions, making the circle complete round the "loosely" posted king.

The first stalemate position:

1. R—QR1!, Q×R 2. Q—K4 ch!, Q×Q—stalemate!

The second:

1. R—QR1!, Q—Q1 ch 2. K—B2!, Q×R 3. Q—Q5 ch!, Q×Q—stalemate!

The third:

1. R—QR1!, Q—K6 ch 2. K—B2, Q×R 3. Q—QB8 ch, K—R2 4. Q—N7 ch!, K×Q—stalemate!

And finally a fourth possibility:

1. R—QR1, Q—K6 ch 2. K—B2, Q—K7 ch 3. K—N3!, Q×R and now 4. Q—K4 ch! (4. Q—R5 ch?, Q—R3!) result in **a stalemate position demonstrating the enormous scope of two queens.**

27.

L. I. KUBBEL, 1925.

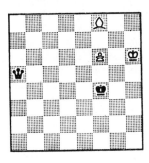

Draw.

Our first impression is that this is a typical instance of **the BP on the seventh rank securing a draw** against the queen. We are not far out, but an ordinary approach to the desired goal would be cause for disappointment. 1. P—B7? would not do because the continuation 1. ..., Q—N4 ch 2. K—R7, K—B4 3. B—N7, Q—N3 ch 4. K—N8, Q—K3 is a sure win for Black.

The solution:

1. B—Q6 ch!, K—B4! 2. P—B7, Q—Q7 ch 3. K—R7!, Q×B 4. P—B8 (Q) ch!, Q×Q—stalemate!

A truth worth remembering: even the simplest positions often hide a surprise!

28.

L. I. KUBBEL, 1922.

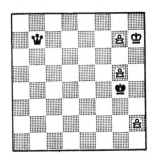

Draw.

1. K—R8, Q—QN7 2. P—R4!, K×P 3. K—R7, Q—B7 ch 4. K—R8, Q—B6 5. K—R7, Q—B2. [Since Black is unable to give check on the KR file, he endeavours to reach the square K2 (White's K7) by gaining tempos, and posting the king on KR3 (White's KR6) whereafter he can easily win against White's promoted pawn. To serve this aim he may also choose the manoeuvre Q—Q6—Q5—K5—K4 etc.]

6. K—R8, Q—K4 7. K—R7, Q—K2 8. K—R8, K×P 9. P—N8 (Q) ch, K—R3! (This Zugzwang position is generally regarded as a typical winning position of queen endings. Black would easily win if all the pieces were posted two or more files to the left, but now . . .)

10. Q—K6 ch!!, Q×Q—and White is stalemated!

In these examples the annihilation of the White pieces, which were

29

jeopardizing the stalemate, is carried out by brutally forcing active sacrifices. This method can generally be applied if we want to liquidate a queen, or, less frequently, a rook. It is far more difficult, for instance, to sacrifice a knight so that the opponent has no alternative to capturing it. A mere attack, an orgy of checks to the king will, of course, not meet the case; the move aiming at the annihilation of the knight should also contain some real **threats**.

The stalemate combinations carried out with a knight occur as a rule not in a distilled form, but mixed with motifs aimed at winning the queen (pinning, geometrical positions, simultaneous check to king and queen) and at achieving perpetual check. These motifs are shown in the following masterpiece of remarkable beauty:

29.

L. I. KUBBEL, 1921.

Draw.

1. N—Q4!!

Opens up the third rank, **closes**—at the same time—the bishop's long diagonal and also endangers the squares QB6 and K6. White threatens R—R3 ch followed by R—QN3, and R—K6 (winning the queen at once) as well. Black cannot parry these threats by moving the king or the bishop, and the queen is in danger both on the QR—N—B files and the sixth rank. One might make an attempt at 1. . . ., Q—Q1, but in this case the dominant knight would make its effect felt:

1. . . ., Q—Q1 2. R—R3 ch, K—N2 3. R—N3 ch, K—B1 (K—B2? 4. N—K6 ch) 4. R—N8 ch!, K×R 5. N—B6 ch—and draws.

So the "quiet" knight move, in fact, is a forcing sacrifice. First it appears as if the aim were to achieve perpetual check . . .

1. — —	Q×N
2. R—R3 ch	K—N4
3. R—N3 ch	K—B5
4. R—B3 ch	K—Q4

. . .but this attempt to escape reveals an unexpected point:

| 5. R—Q3!! | Q×R |

—and White is stalemated. It is worth noting how many-sided the final rook move is: it directs the queen, annihilates the rook and blockades the pawn. All this by means of a pin which incidentally parries the mating threat that has also been in the air all the time (Q—N7).

In an over-the-board game many would call this "blind luck." But only those who blindly pass by their luck . . .

THE FIGHT AGAINST THE PASSED PAWN

It often happens in an ending that one is willing to offer major material sacrifices in order to pave the way for a passed pawn. In such instances positions may come about in which one of the players is a piece, or even two pieces, ahead and still not able to prevent within a move or two the promotion of the opponent's passed pawn.

If the appearance of a new queen is going to turn the scale, there may be no other saving course than to seek combinative stalemate possibilities.

To attain stalemate we should strive for the annihilation (or possibly pinning or blocking) of the pieces on the board and for the appropriate directing of the opponent' s new-born queen. Compared with the cases already examined (when the fight was carried on against an already existing queen), our task now is that much easier since the opponent's manoeuvring freedom is more restricted during the introductory moves, owing to his lack as yet of a queen—and we also know which square will be the birthplace of the prospective queen. On the other hand, our calculation is complicated by the fact that the opponent has every right to promote the advancing pawn not only to a queen but to any other piece. Consequently, this circumstance precludes, for instance, the possibility of sacrificing all the pieces in the hope of achieving a stalemate after the queenly promotion.

30.

F. AMELUNG, 1905.

Draw.

At first glance it seems that White's advantageously posted king might be the source for a mating threat or perpetual check. But a few attempts will convince us that there is no salvation after 1. R—B8 ch?, B—Q1 2. R—B1, P—K7! (3. K—B5, B—N3!). White's king instead finds a "suitable" place on a much "worse" square:

1. K—B5!, P—K7, 2. K—N4!, P—K8 (Q) 3. R×Q, B×R 4. K—R3!

Queening or a rook promotion would stalemate White, and an underpromotion would not lead to a win either, for another bishop would obviously be useless, while after 4. ..., P—N8 (N) 5. K—N2, N—K7 6. K—B1 there would remain insufficient force to mate.

* * *

The simple motif of the former ending may come in good stead even in more complicated cases, as shown by the following study:

31.

M. PLATOV, 1905.

Draw.

On this situation we can make three observations:

(i) A rook by itself is helpless against two outside passed pawns; (ii) Black's KRP cannot be advanced to coronation even if supported by the bishop; (iii) The knight might overtake Black's NP via KB4 because of the possible check to the king from K2 (secondary range!).

It would seem logical from this to conclude that a draw might be reached in sacrificing the rook for the QRP—forcing the bishop away from control of the KB4 square—and annihilating the other would-be queen with the knight (1. R×P ch, B×R 2. N—B4, P—N8 (Q or R) 3. N—K2 ch).

But this seemingly simple method fails if Black chooses to reply 1. R×P ch, K—N7 and now the pawn promotion cannot be prevented! Clearly, salvation lies in another direction which is by no means easy to find, although the two introductory moves are the same, but in the reverse order and with different aims. The solution:

1. N—B4!!, B×N 2. R×P ch, K—N7! 3. R—KN3!!, B×R ch 4. K—R3!—and in case of 4. ..., P—N8 (Q or R) the well-known stalemate pattern arises. An under-promotion (B or N) would be followed by 5. K×B and the loss of the RP, and any other move by 5. K×P with a "book" draw.

* * *

Though it takes only one move, the "co-operation" on the part of White's king is extraordinarily effective and surprisingly forcing in the next study:

32.

H. MATTISON, 1914.

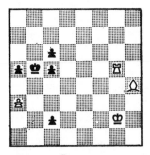

Draw.

Because of the rook's awkward position the bishop cannot obtain control of the queening square, and the king's interference prevents the rook from doing so. The prevention of queening or the liquidation of the pawn when promoted calls for substantial sacrifice.

The alternative 1. B—B2, P—B8 (Q) 2. R×P ch, Q×R 3. B×Q, K×B would result in a lost position for

White, nor is the bishop able to put up a successful fight against Black's pawns after 1. R×P ch, K×R 2. B—N5, K—B5 3. K—B3, K—N6 4. B—B1, K—R7. The only way out, absurd as it seems in view of the completely loose position of White's king, is a stalemate combination again.

1. P—R4 ch!, K—N3 2. B—B2, P—B8 (Q) 3. R×P, Q×R 4. K—R1!!

The startling point! The capture (..., Q×B) results in **stalemate,** otherwise Black is compelled to give up his queen for nothing because of the perfect Zugzwang.

★ ★ ★

The role of **Zugzwang** and the various forms of pawn promotion are demonstrated in reciprocal stalemate variations by the following study:

33.

F. LAZARD, 1902.

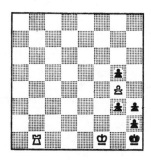

Draw.

1. R—K1!, P—N7 ch 2. K—B2 ch, P—N8 (Q) ch 3. K—B3!, Q×R and White is stalemated!

2. ..., P—N8 (B) ch 3. K—B3 and Black is stalemated!

2. ..., P—N8 (R) 3. R—KB1!, R×R ch 4. K×R and Black is stalemated again. The same result would spring also from the knight promotion, only a single rook tempo is needed on the first rank.

★ ★ ★

Sometimes the winning combination is bound up with the directing of the king. In this case the defence may attempt to combine the unpleasant with the useful so that the compulsory detour of the king should coincide with its approach to the stalemate nest.

34.

F. LAZARD, 1912.

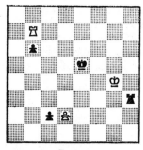

Draw.

The passed pawn cannot be stopped by 1. R—QB7, since Black would conveniently close the file by ..., R—QB4! after ..., R—R4 ch. A roundabout way by 1. R—N7 ch intending to take control over the square KN1 would only be practicable in case of 1. ..., K—R5, but would lose after 1. ..., K—B6! because Black's king could rush to the aid of his pawn.

Who would ever think of looking for a stalemate possibility to extricate White from his plight, if this natural position cropped up in an over-the-board game? Yet the stalemate becomes a reality after a reciprocal driving of the kings!

1. R—N7 ch, K—B6 (..., K—R5 2. R—N1, R—R7! 3. R—QB1, R×P 3. K—K4 is drawn too) 2. R—QB7!, R—R4 ch 3. K—Q4!, R—QB4! 4. R×R, P×R ch 5. K—Q3!! and White is stalemate after 5. ..., P—B8 (Q or R).

Black is able to prevent stalemate by 5. ..., P—B8 (B), but a drawn position will arise also from the continuation 6. K—B4!, B—R6 7. P—Q4!

Let us, accordingly, analyse some positions where White's king stays put and it is up to the rest of his pieces to build up by active play and purposeful manoeuvres a comfortable stalemate nest around him.

Here is the motif in its simplest form:

35.

E. B. COOK, 1864.

Draw.

1. R—N7 ch, K—B1 2. R—N5!, P—B8 (Q) 3. R—B5 ch!, Q×R—stalemate!

Let us look now at this old and familiar pattern elaborated as an end-game theme in a composition of later date.

36.

F. J. PROKOP, 1943.

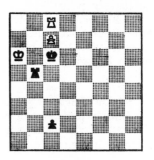

Draw.

1. R—N8!, K×P 2. R×R, R—Q3 (2. ..., P—B8 (Q) would be met immediately by 3. R—B5 ch!) 3. R—N6 ch, K—Q2 4. R—N7 ch, K—B1 5. R—N5!, P—B8 (Q) 6. R—B5 ch! with the same stalemate.

Should Black make an active rook sacrifice, then a **"twin" stalemate pattern** might arise:

1. R—N8!, R—R4 ch 2. K×R, K×P 3. R—N4!, P—B8 (Q) 4. R—B4 ch!, Q×R.

* * *

The directing, driving power of the rook is characteristically shown in the next example:

37.

L. I. KUBBEL, 1925.

Draw.

1. R—B4 ch! (1. R—N4? does not suffice, since Black's victory would be a cinch after ..., B—R7 ch 2. K—Q5, P—N8 (Q) 3. R×Q, B×R.)
1. ..., K—K1! 2. R×P ch, K—Q1 3. R—R4! (Either 3. R—N4 or 3. R—K1 would be a blunder because of ..., B—R7 ch 4. K—B5, P—N8 (Q) 5. R×Q, B×R 6. K—N6, K—B1. But now White threatens mate, therefore 3. ..., B—R7 ch? fails against R×B.)
3. ..., B×P! 4. R—N4!, P—N8 (Q) (..., P—N8 (R) 5. R×B drawn) 5. R—N8 ch!, Q×R—stalemate!

* * *

If the rook has another companion, the preliminary annihilation of the latter is mostly effected in the form of a **sacrifice threatening an extension of its scope.** In other words; its capture would result in a stalemate; but without capture the piece offered for sacrifice will overtake the passed pawn or win the promoted queen, as the case may be.

38.

F. J. PROKOP, 1923.

Draw.

It is obvious that after 1. R—K4 ch Black's king may not go to the KB file for fear of 2. R—B4 ch and 3. R—B1. On the Q file again, the king and the prospective queen will be in geometrical alignment, thus making possible the rook's directing intervention. This directing in the first instance paves the way for a double attack on king and queen by the knight, in the second it gives rise to the desired stalemate.

1. R—K4 ch, K—Q2, 2. R—K3!' P—Q8 (Q) 3. R—Q3 ch!, Q×R 4. N—K5 ch!, B×N—and White is stalemated.
The other variation:
1. R—K4 ch, K—Q1 2. N—K5!, P—Q8 (Q) (2. ..., B×N 3. R—K3 etc. leads to the former path). 3. R—Q4 ch!, Q×R 4. N—B6 ch and 5. N×Q draws.

* * *

It goes without saying that the **directing and suicide manoeuvres,** referred to in this chapter, may arise

35

in various situations in a diversity of combined forms.

An especially multifarious **concerted action** may be expected from **minor pieces** in their struggle against passed pawns. Let this point be here illustrated by a truly colourful combination in which the stalemate position is the product of a quadruple forcing sacrifice.

39.

L. I. KUBBEL, 1909.

Draw.

  1. B—B5 ch   K×P
if 1. ..., K—B3 then 2. P—R7, K—N2 3. N—B7!
  2. B×P   P—Q7
  3. N—B5 ch   K—R4
3. ..., K—N4 would be followed by 4. N—K4, P—Q8 (Q) 5. N—B3 ch
  4. P—N4 ch!   K×P
  5. B—K1!!
This typical directing pin clears the ground for an effective knight intervention.
  5. — —   P×B (Q) or (R)
  6. N—Q3 ch!   N×N
—and White is stalemated!

SELF-PINNING

In order to achieve stalemate it is not explicitly necessary to annihilate one's own pieces, it is sufficient to immobilize them, to have them pinned. A conscious recognition of this possibility is especially important in the fight against passed pawns, since we can considerably increase the usefulness of the piece chasing a passed pawn. How this can be done is best illustrated by some simple examples.

40.

A. W. DANIEL, 1908.

Draw.

Here the pin is purposely invited as a kind of sacrifice. Since the rook is unable to stop both pawns, it "throws away its own life" as a last resort, instead of resorting to a protracted yet-hopeless defence:
  1. R×P!, B—B7 2. K—R8!, B×R —stalemate!
This is the simplest form of the combination.

What would happen, however, if Black—instead of capturing the rook —decided to play 2. ..., P—R7!? 3.

R—K1 looks unsatisfactory because of the line interference B—N8. Another attempt at self-pinning would only be successful in case of 3. . . ., P—R8 (Q)?, but fail against 3. . . .,P—R8 (R)! eliminating stalemate, since Black easily wins after 4. R—B5 ch, K—N3!

To avoid these dangers we must elaborate the saving combination in a subtler way by decreasing the scope of the offensive pieces first:

1. R×P!, B—B7 2. K—R8!, P—R7! 3. R—K1!, B—N8 4. R—K5!, P—R8 (R) (4. . . ., P—R8 (Q)? —stalemate!) 5. R—QR5!—and draws, because the capture leads to another form of stalemate, and also 5. . . ., B—R7 serves no purpose since White's reply 6. R—R7 ch does away with the mating threat.

41.

L. I. KUBBEL, 1916.

Draw.

Here we see a typical demonstration of self-pinning as a motif in stalemate, rounded off by the pointed frustration of all attempts at unpinning.

1. P—N4! (Threatening 2. K—N2 and 3. B—N3 mate.)

1. . . ., K×P 2. K—R1!, P—R7 3. B—N1!

Now 3. P—R8 (Q) or P—R8 (R) would lead to stalemate; and 3. . . ., K×P would allow time for White's bishop to catch the passed pawn. Knight promotion is ineffective because of 4. B—N6!, but promotion to a bishop may give cause for concern. Even so, White's bishop manages to save the day, not now by remaining passively under pin, but by the exercise of its active directing powers: 3. . . ., P—R8 (B) 4. B—Q4!, B×B —stalemate!

* * *

The stalemate position by self-pinning is, also in the next study (No. 42), a decisive element of the knight manoeuvre undertaken with an attack on the queening square in view:

1. P—B7, K—K2 2. N—K6!, K×P 3. N—N5 ch, K—B3 4. N×BP!, P—B7 5. N—N1! and in case of 5. . . ., P—B8 (Q or R) White is stalemate.

42.

H. RINCK, 1908.

Draw.

otherwise 6. N—K2 assures a draw.

In this example White's passed pawn has been responsible for directing the king in the introductory phase. Now we propose to examine such positions in which the directing force of a passed pawn is the basic motif of the stalemate combination.

DIRECTION WITH PASSED PAWNS

A passed pawn is not only a potential means of increasing our material superiority by its promotion, but also a convenient means of **forcing direction,** of driving the opponent's pieces to a desired point of the board. The advancing passed pawn has a kind of magnetic effect on part of the hostile forces and, as a crowned sacrifice, it is apt to lure the hostile piece lying in ambush for it to a definite square. This motif, which, as will be discussed in a separate chapter, underlies many other combinations aimed at securing a draw, comes in handy for creating a stalemate position, since the driving manoeuvre is combined at the same time with the self-annihilation of a mobile piece.

Among the over-the-board types of end-games we may refer here to the case when we send into battle our **BP on the seventh rank** against the opponent's queen. In Diagram No. 27 we have already come across an unusual instance of this familiar situation. A similar stalemate pattern may spring from the **fight of a NP against a rook.**

43.

A. COZIO, 1776.

Draw.

This old "textbook example" is not a study, presenting as it does no exceptional possibility, but the down-to-earth, technical method of achieving stalemate in similar positions.

1. K—R7, K—B3 2. P—B8 (Q) ch!, R×Q 3. P—N7, R—B2 4. K—R8!, R×P—stalemate!

That is the shortest way; in the last instance also the attempt beginning with 1. K—N7 leads to this channel, the same applies for the variations with Black to play first. (E. g. Black to play: 1. ..., K—B3 2. K—R7, R—KB1 3. P—N7!, R×P 4. K—R8! etc. or 1. ..., K—B1 2. K—R7, R—R1 3. K—R8!—3, K—R6? would lose because of R—R8.)

44.

A. SELESNIEV, 1920.

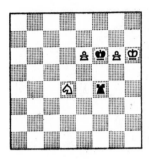

Draw.

The knight cannot be saved on account of the mating threat; hence the balance of material seen in the former example is reached after White's first move. Nevertheless, the knight has this advantage, that it can drive either the king or the rook to a less favourable place, and thus White gains time for advancing his pawn.

1. N—B5!, K×N (after 1. ..., R×N 2. P—N7, R—B8 3. P—N8 (N) ch! draws).

2. P—K7, R—K5 3. K—R7!, K—B3 4. P—N7! and now the continuation 4. ..., R×P 5. K—R8!, R×P leads to the stalemate already known, and the alternative 4. ..., R—R5 ch 5. K—N8, K×P results in a new stalemate position.

45.

L. I. KUBBEL, 1916.

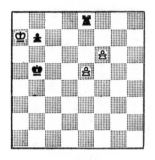

Draw.

The united passed pawns alone would win against the rook—in case of a more favourably posted king. But White's king is too badly posted, or rather "badly enough" to find refuge in a stalemate.

1. P—B7, R—KB1 2. P—K6, P—N3! (Preventing P—K7 because of R×P pinning the pawn on the king.)

3. K—N7, K—B4. (Now the seemingly natural continuation 4. K—B7?, K—Q4 5. K—Q7 would lose after K—K4! etc.)

4. P—K7!!, R×P 5. K—R6, R×P —stalemate!

* * *

The directing power of a passed pawn and a knowledge of the stalemate possibilities resulting from it is of considerable practical importance also in bishop endings.

46.

J. BEHTING, 1893.

Draw.

This simple-looking position calls for careful and profound analysis.

I. K—R6!!	K—B1

If 1. . . ., B—K6 2. K—N5!, P—B6 3. K—B4, B—Q7 4. B—B2!, P—B5 5. K—N3!, P—B6 6. B—K4, P—KB7 7. B—N2 White will keep his own pawn while stopping Black's BP's and securing a draw. After the text, however, the king alters his course:

2. K—R7!	B—K6
3. K—R8	B×P

3. . . ., B—B5 would fix the KBP again making 4. B—B2 possible.

4. B—N3!!—drawn,

because the capture would result in a stalemate (4. . . ., P—B6 5. B—K6 ch and 6. B×P).

* * *

Finally, let us look at a classical example demonstrating the enormous directing powers of a pawn:

47.

L. I. KUBBEL, 1921.

Draw.

I. B—K5

Obviously the only way of saving the pawn, otherwise Black would easily win, being a rook ahead. But now the bishop falls also!

1. — —	R—N5 ch
2. K—Q5!	R—N4 ch
3. K—B6!	R×B

White has only a single pawn against two pieces! But his king stealthily approaches its distant goal. Black—in order to stop the pawn—is compelled to keep on chasing it in the desired direction.

4. P—Q7	R—K3 ch
5. K—N7	R—Q3
6. K—B8!	

Not K—B7?, because R—Q7 ch! 7. K—B8, R—B7 ch would allow the bishop to control Black's QB2.

| 6. — — | R—B3 ch |
| 7. K—N7 | R—B7 ch |

Now even the pawn must fall! But a price has to be paid after all!

| 8. K—R8!! | R×P |

—and White is stalemated!
Who would have expected this in the initial position? . . .

* * *

This brings us to the end of our analysis of stalemate possibilities. We have by no means discussed all the motifs, only the most characteristic ones.

Of course, we do not expect the reader, if he has got thus far, to think that he has acquired "a wealth of practical experience" and that, from now on, he will be able to save all his hopeless games, or every second one, by a stalemate . . .

We are very much gratified if these model patterns have helped the reader to **see more,** or at least to **consider more possibilities** than he did before. The stalemate combination is only a minor weapon in the tactical armoury of chess, but the **forcing motifs** involved will also prove useful in many other instances.

For this reason, we need not memorize the positions quoted in this book, much less reckon with the infinitesimal chance of their exact recurrence in practice, but should remember the methods that help us—often with very inferior forces—to take the initiative, to direct the course of events and to move the **opponent's** pieces as if they were mere marionettes.

VIRTUAL STALEMATE

In the preceding chapter we have become acquainted with the pursuit of stalemate as an effective method of saving a game, even against heavy odds. We have stressed, however, that in order to achieve stalemate we have to adopt manoeuvres that are diametrically opposed to the general "reasonable" principles of play, i. e. we must actually rather than apparently and definitively rather than temporarily strive for the complete annihilation or immobilization of our forces.

Clearly, whenever our end in view is a draw, there is, in principle, nothing against our abandoning this topsyturvy method, and reaching our goal by **immobilizing the opponent's forces instead of our own.** There is the rub, however, that in practice we are but very rarely offered this option, for in most cases we are confronted with the opponent's **superior forces** whose complete stalemating by our weaker army may hardly be reckoned with.

Yet, there is such a case, or at least a very similar one. Let us take first a very simple example which is, however, of considerable importance in over-the-board play:

48.

SCHEME

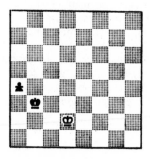

Draw.

Here White naturally wants to get in front of Black's pawn by 1. K—B1!, and if Black replies 1. . . ., P—R6, 2. K—N1 and 3. K—R1 leads to stalemate.

If Black, however, bars the approach of White's king by 1. . . ., K—R7, White can no longer adopt the defensive method consisting in **selfstalemate,** but he may seize another opportunity: 2. K—B2! **restricts Black's manoeuvring freedom** so that his king would be **stalemated** after further advance of the pawn.

The same idea may for instance be realized in a forcing manner in such types of practical end-games as those where a bishop has to hold the balance against a knight and an outside pawn.

49.

SCHEME.

(After S. Loyd, 1860.)

Draw.

Black threatens to close the diagonal by N—N7 and queen his pawn. The only remedy against this is:

1. B—R1!	N—N7 ch
2. K—Q2!	K×B

And now it has still to be decided whether and how Black's king can be kept permanently stalemated in the corner. If we are aware of the knight's inherent inability to gain tempi and to attack a square of the same colour on which it stands, then it will not be difficult to find the correct solution. **We are to move our king to a square of the same colour as the one the knight is posted on.** (The same course ought to have been followed if Black had captured the bishop on his first move.)

3. K—B1!!	—and draws,

because the freely moving knight is unable to prevent White's king from repeating the moves K—B2—B1 etc. (You may convince yourself by trying.)

What kind of a situation has been arrived at here? Though we cannot speak of a stalemate, we may observe a **partial** stalemating of the stronger side's forces! Black—even in possession of an extra pawn and knight—cannot count on the assistance of his king, since White has managed to paralyse it and shut it out of the play.

A game can very often be saved even against heavy odds if we partially immobilize our opponent's forces in the manner shown above, for, as is well known, even the mightiest piece, the queen, lacks the ability to force mate if unsupported by "her royal consort!"

Those exceptional drawing positions, where an existing measurable material superiority cannot be exploited owing to a lasting restriction of the mobility of some piece or pieces, are called **positional draws.** The term refers to the fact that the material balance, considerably upset as it is, can only be re-established in a given situation, under given circumstances, through the greater scope and mobility of inferior material.

50.	51.
J. MENDHEIM, 1832.	A. A. TROITSKY, 1908.

Draw.	*Draw.*

Well over a hundred years old, this problem aptly illustrates the underlying idea. Black's pawn is out of reach and therefore White makes preparations for static warfare against the prospective queen.

    1. N—Q7!   P—R7

After Black's king move 2. N—B5 and 3. N—QN3 would neutralize the pawn.

    2. QN—B6!   P—R8 (Q) ch
    3. K—K6 (or B5)

—and **draws** because the king can easily move about while the cavalry keeps Black's king stalemated.

At times the joint efforts of a knight and bishop may be as effective as that of two knights in shutting off the king and offering stout resistance to the queen.

    1. B×P ch!   K—B1

After 1. . . ., K×B 2. P—N7 White too will promote his pawn.

    2. N—Q4!!   P—R8 (Q)
    3. N—K6 ch!   K—N1
    4. B—K8!

From here the bishop protects the knight in an indirect way, so that White secures the draw against a single remaining pawn as in the following possible variation: 4. . . ., Q—R7 ch 5. K—N3!, Q×N 6. B—B7 ch, Q×B7. P×Q ch, K×P 8. K—B3!, K—B3 (or K3) 9. K—B4 (or K4)! etc.

    4. — —   K—R1

5. B—B7! with a draw as a result.

It should be pointed out, however, that here the draw is not the inevitable outcome of the ultimate structural situation but much rather of the threat P—N7 ch, permanently in the air. Strictly speaking, the shutting off of the king would only be perfect if we posted (in the final position after 5. B—B7) another Black pawn onWhite's KN7.

In that case, however—and that is what we should like to show through this example—the situation **would not be a draw!** Why? Because the idea of immobilizing the king could be realized also by Black by way of queen manoeuvres and eventually White would be in Zugzwang. If now either the protecting bishop or the protected knight were forced to move, it would soon fall victim to the mobile queen after a series of checks. For instance (continued from the final position, and supposing that Black has an additional pawn on his N2): 5. ..., Q—R6 6. K—K2, Q—QB6! 7. K—B2, Q—Q6 8. K—N2, Q—K6 9. K—R2, Q—KB6 10. K—N1, Q—K7! 11. K—R1, Q—KB7!—and the virtual stalemate becomes mutual, leaving Black with a material surplus that decides the issue.

* * *

Hence, we have arrived at the conclusion that a **queen by herself cannot mate the king but she can stalemate him,** if he fails to find refuge near a friendly piece.

52.

G. N. ZAKHODJAKIN, 1930.

Draw.

White's minor pieces stand their ground even against a queen and a knight because the partial stalemate can be extended to cover Black's whole army except the queen.

1. P—N7 ch   N×P
1. ..., K—N1 would be followed by 2. N—N4! winning Black's BP; the threat is: N—B6 ch and P—N8 (Q).

2. N—B7 ch	K—N1
3. B—B5!	P—B8 (Q)
4. N—R6 ch	K—R1
5. B—Q6!!	and draws,

because White's knight defends the KN5, K5 and Q6 squares indirectly. As a result, it is always open to White, even if Black's queen should stalemate his king, to resort to perpetual tempo-wasting by way of B—K5—Q6—K5, etc., and he can always repel Black's knight by B—K5 ch, if it tried to jump into freedom. A possible Q×B would also result in a draw, because

45

N—B7 ch would restore the balance in material.

* * *

In the examples shown the decisive factor of an effective defence against heavy odds was the shutting off of the opponent's king. The total immobilization of one's own king and other pieces we have already discussed in the chapter dealing with stalemate. To complete our account of the king's role in achieving a draw against superior forces, reference should be made also to a third possibility.

This is in fact a type of positional draw which is in some ways analogous to the stalemate, with the weaker side building up a hedgehog position that can safely hold out against all attacks. We are confronted here with something closely related to stalemate yet different enough from it to deserve a special name. For want of a better term we propose to call it "pupation" and give this artistic end-game study for a clearer understanding of the underlying idea.

53.

F. SIMKHOVITCH, 1926.

Draw.

In face of Black's unstoppable RP White finds himself in great straits. The more so as the only conceivable saving course offered by the situation is not satisfactory in the simple form it first presents itself.

Our first thought evidently is to play P—B6, then K—B8—N7 and hold the fort by simply tempoing with king and knight behind the solid wall of mutually protected pieces. But it is not as easy as that:

1. P—B6, P—R7 2. K—B8, P—R8 (Q) 3. K—N7, K—Q2 4. B—N4 (If 4. B—B8 then 4. ..., Q—R1! 5. K—N8, K—K3 6. K—N7, K—B4 7. K—N8, B—B5—a tempo move to prevent the reply B—R6—8. K—N7, Q—KR8! followed by queen sacrifice —Q×N—with a sure win.) 4. ..., K—K3 5. B—Q2, K—B4 6. B—K3, Q—B6 7. B—Q2, Q—K7 8. B—B1, Q—K5! with this queen manoeuvre Black forces the bishop off White's QB1—KB4 diagonal, and after 9. B—N2 (R3) Q—KR8! now inevitably leads to Q×N ch and K×P, and Black's new passed pawn triumphs.

This attempt shows that the knight alone is no sufficient protection for White's NP, while the bishop cannot defend it from QB1. Conclusion: the game is lost unless White's bishop can be posted on R6!

The quick way to this fails on 1. P—B6?, P—R7 2. B—B8, P—R8 (Q) 3. B—R6,? Q—R1 ch 4. K—K7, Q—Q8 mate.

These deliberations point to the direct tactical measure to be taken before the implementation of the ultimate strategic plan, viz. the elimination of the queen's quick intervention; in other words, **Black's king must be driven on to the long diagonal!** A suitable means of realization is the **threat of scope extension** on the KR2—QN8 diagonal, that is, an immediate attempt to stop Black's pawn.

1. B—B6!!　　　　K—Q3

After any other move 2. B—K5 would solve the problem.

2. B—K7 ch　　　K—K4

If 2. ..., K—Q4 or K—B3, then White will reach his partial aim: closing of the long diagonal. Black must soon resign himself to this to avoid a draw by repetition of moves.

3. B—Q8!　　　　K—Q3

The best Black can do for fear of the threat 4. B—B7.

4. B—K7 ch　　　K—B3

And now the time is ripe for the manoeuvre of "pupation":

5. P—B6!　　　　P—R7
6. B—B8!　　　　P—R8 (Q)
7. B—R6!　　　　and draws,

because 8. K—B8 and 9. K—N7 cannot be prevented and thereafter White is free, in an inaccessible defensive position, to keep tempoing perpetually by N—B8 and K—N8—N7.

We have deliberately chosen a difficult but fascinating example to demonstrate a possibility that is rarely thought of in over-the-board play. It would be a mistake, however, to assume that we have wandered too far from the realities and practical probabilities of over-the-board play. Even the simplest everyday games can offer plenty of similar cases, if in less beautiful and less complicated form.

* * *

Let us analyse now some other cases of virtual stalemate. Not only the king but occasionally also some other piece can be permanently shut off from the play and in this way a drawing position against superior forces arrived at.

At first glance, the diagram below exemplifies the imprisonment of a rook; inreality, however, it is an instance of how a queen (!) should be shut off:

54.

F. SIMKHOVITCH, 1927.

Draw.

With his two minor pieces against the rook White would not be at a material disadvantage if Black did not have the threat of obtaining a passed pawn up his sleeve after ..., R—N8! and ..., R×P. Something must be done to counteract this.

1. B—N4 ch	K—Q3

The continuation is similar after other moves of the king.

2. B—B5!	R—R7!

The rook maintains the threat even so. The prospective queen can, however, be actually cornered on the QR file!

3. N×R!!	P×N
4. K—B1	P—R8 (Q) ch
5. B—N1!	and draws,

because the queen cannot extricate itself from the trap and White can manoeuvre with K—B2—B1—B2 etc. unhindered.

* * *

The next example shows how a positional draw can be reached by putting a **rook** on ice.

55.

C. J. de FEIJTER, 1941.

Draw.

1. P—N7	R—K8 ch!

After 1. ..., R—K1? 2. B—R7! Black should give up the rook for the promoting pawn. But now it is White's turn to be cautious since his king move would be to Black's advantage after ..., B—K4! e. g. K—R2?, B—K4! 3. P—N8 (Q)?, R—R8 mate! therefore:

2. B—Q1	R—K1!

2. ..., R×B ch? would be followed by 3. K—B2 and Black would not be able to prevent queening because of his own bishop barring the way of the rook.

3. B—R5!	R—KN1
4. B—B7!	R×P
5. P—N6	and draws,

because the rook is permanently caged. (Black cannot reckon on stalemating White now with his king and bishop, that is he cannot bring his opponent into Zugzwang because White's bishop can also intervene if needed. We refer, for example, to the possibility 5...., K—B6 6. K—R2, K—B7 7. K—R1, B—R6 8. K—R2, B—N7! 9. B—N3 ch!)

* * *

If both sides have several pawns on the board the rescue of the imprisoned rook by way of sacrifice is always a latent possibility. In the next example, White must, after having achieved a positional draw, wriggle himself out of threatened Zugzwang (see Diagram No. 56).

At a moment of temporary material equilibrium White has both pieces "en prise." The loss of the bishop would be fatal, therefore he chooses to renounce his rook, and hope against hope for a virtual stalemate.

56.

J. H. MARWITZ, 1942.

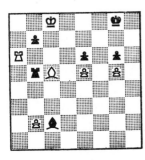

Draw.

1. R—B6!!	P×R
2. P—N4!	

This shuts the door on the rook and the peculiar situation at the same time prevents all co-operation between Black's king and bishop. White can mark time now, merely playing K—B8—B7, until "something happens".

2. — —	K—B2
3. K—B7	K—K1
4. K—B8	B—Q6
5. K—B7	

Without some sacrifice Black cannot get any further. Therefore:

5. — —	R×B!
6. P×R	B—N4

Aiming not to defend the pawn—whose capture would indeed bring grist to Black's mill—but to try and gain the tempo needed for squeezing out White's king, White would counter the immediate 6. . . ., B—R3 7. K—N6!, B—B1 8. K—B7, B—Q7 by 9. K—Q6!! and after 9. . . ., K—Q1 he is stalemated!

Later on, a similar stalemate position saves White from being squeezed out. It is a remarkable structural peculiarity of the position that the control of the squares QB1 and QB2 requires Black's bishop to penetrate to Q2; in this section of the board, however—from Q2 to QR2!—it has no opportunity to gain a move. Consequently, the final struggle is marked by oppositional considerations.

Here is the finish resulting in a "strategic stalemate":

7. K—B8, K—K2 8. K—B7, B—R3! 9. K—N6!, B—B1 10. K—B7, B—Q2 11. K—N8, K—Q1 12. K—N7, B—B1 ch 13. K—N8!, K—Q2 14. K—R8!!, K—B2 15. K—R7! and draws, since after 15. . . ., B—N2 White would be **stalemated!** Accurate tempoing is very essential here because e. g. 14. K—R7?, K—B2 15. K—R8, B—N2 ch 16. K—R7, K—B1! 17. K—N6, K—N1 18. K—R5, K—R2! 19. K—N4, B—R3! 20. K—R4, B—K7 21. K—R5, B—Q8! 22. K—N4, K—R3 would have led to an easy win for Black despite the complicated procedure of forcing a decisive gain of space.

* * *

In addition to shutting off, walling-in and stalemating there is still another possibility of immobilization: **pinning.**

In the game, the pin is usually of a momentary or transitory occurrence, therefore it has a prominent part mostly in sudden tactical turns. (This is by the way the subject of a separate chapter.) It may happen, however, that a pin becomes lasting and unbreakable. Such a **perpetual pinning** is a very suitable means of achieving a positional draw. A case in point is the parrying of the Black knight's intervention in end-game No. 52.

The concept of the positional draw is closely related to that of the "theoretical" draw. The relationship between the two arises from the fact that "theoretical" draw as a definition is not used in practice as an absolute idea; it is not applied to every self-evident drawing position, but mostly to exceptional situations where at first glance it seems reasonable to except—because of the unbalance in material—that victory will go to one side; yet where theoretical research has proved beyond a doubt that the materially stronger side has no prospects of winning.

There are some absolute types of theoretical draw which are defined by the balance of material alone, regardless of the given position. A familiar instance of this is the fight of a king and two knights against an unsupported king, where there is practically no arrangement of the pieces that will lead to an enforceable mate. Another case in point is the struggle between a lonely king and an adverse RP supported by a bishop which cannot take control of the queening square. Here, however, an additional positional condition must also be met, namely the king on the defensive must manage somehow to get in front of the pawn.

In other cases there are more rigid positional restrictions. An unsupported king can put up a successful fight also against a RP and a knight, but only if the pawn is forced to the seventh rank and the king can occupy the square in front of it. If we come to other positions again in which the support of an extra piece fails to usher even some other pawn to victory, we shall reach a point where the borderline between the concepts of "virtual stalemate," "hedgehog position" and "book" draw (in the wider sense) disappears.

By way of illustration, let us now look at the best known type of stalemate quoted in the textbooks as a characteristic form of the theoretical draw:

57.

SCHEME.

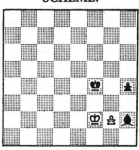

Draw.

White's defence against the bishop and the RP lies in his getting rid of his own bad pawn. 1. P—N4? would be a blunder because of the reply 1. ..., P—R6! 2. P—N5, K×P 3. K—B3, K—B4! and Black **wins.** Far sounder is the continuation

1. P—B3 ch!   P×P
2. K—N2

for although Black's RP has turned into a NP, his bishop is now a frozen asset and the game is **drawn.**

* * *

Some help is needed against a NP and a freely moving bishop. This is shown by the next example:

58.

L. I. KUBBEL, 1934.

Draw.

Once the bishops of the same colour are removed, there is a glimmer of hope: perhaps a kind of hedgehog position might be arrived at if only Black's pawn could be made to ad-

vance to N6 (White's N3) and White's king posted on his QB1. If we realize this, the job is as good as done!

1. B—N6 ch   K—Q2
2. B—R5!   P—N6

After 2. ..., B×QNP 3. B×P the extra piece is of course of no real value. Now White's king can safely approach his pawn.

3. K—Q2   B×KNP
4. K—B1!

4. B—B3?, B—R3 ch! 5. K—Q1, B—R4 ch! 6. K—K1, B—B8! and Black's king walks to his QB7 and wins.

4. — —   B—R3 ch
5. B—Q2!   and draws,

because the pawn is inaccessible after the exchange; otherwise White's bishop can undisturbedly move along the diagonal Q2—R6.

* * *

Artistic and at the same time game-like examples of attaining theoretical draws by forcing means are to be found among the studies of the eminent Soviet end-game composer L. I. Kubbel. In the first study one side is two knights to the bad.

Against an opponent two knights ahead we must concentrate our efforts on liquidating the rest of his forces. In most cases the tactical means of forcing are the driving-on manoeuvre the restriction of movement of the main force by line interference, and later its elimination by exchanges.

The same idea can be realized also with a bishop:

59.

L. I. KUBBEL, 1929.

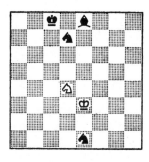

Draw.

60.

L. I. KUBBEL, 1930.

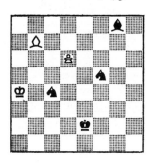

Draw.

White's only task is to exchange his knight for the bishop. Therefore he makes preparations for restricting the mobility of the bishop by driving Black's knight from White's K1 to KN6.

1. K—K2!	N—N7
2. K—B3!	N—R5 ch

2. ..., N—K8 3. K—K2 leads to a repetition of moves.

3. K—N3!	N—KN3
4. N—N5!	and draws,

because 6. N—Q6 and 7. N×B cannot be prevented. The knight, so to speak, mates the bishop which is restricted in its movement.

The passed pawn comes in handy here to force through the driving-on manoeuvre.

1. P—Q7!	N—N3 ch
2. K—N4!	N×P
3. B—B8	B—K3

The bishop is in the stocks. But any other move would have lost a knight.

4. B—R6 ch	K—K6
5. B—B4	and draws,

because Black's bishop cannot avoid being exchanged.

* * *

For the sake of completeness let us see how a rook is exchanged off in an analogous way.

61.

L. I. KUBBEL, 1931.

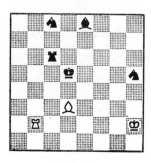

Draw.

The exchange of the bishops is at hand but it is not enough. The rooks must then be exchanged off or a knight won. (Rook against rook and knight is a theoretical draw.)

1. B—N5!	R—KR3!

1. ..., R—K3 2. B×B, R×B 3. R—N5 ch would lead to the loss of the knight (on the R file). The sacrifice of the exchange would get Black nowhere, because White—playing accurately—could sacrifice his own rook back for the bishop. (Against two bishops and a knight the rook would be much worse off. In such cases the superior forces prevail.)

2. R—Q2 ch!	

Naturally, the immediate capture of the bishop would not be worth a farthing because of 2. ..., N—B3 ch and 3. ..., N×B. Backed by the "surviving" rook, Black's two extra knights would do the job.

But now Black has not many choices left for on 2. ..., K—B4 White threatens, after exchanging the bishops, R—B2 ch and R×N. In the case of 2. ..., K—K4 (5) the same developments ensue, with the scene shifted to the K-file. Therefore:

2. — —	K—K3
3. B×B	N—B3 ch
4. K—N1!	N×B

And what now befalls Black's rook? Since the king has been driven to K6, it cannot escape being exchanged off or, at best, being exposed to perpetual attack.

5. R—KR2!	R—N3 ch
6. R—N2!	R—B3
7. R—KB2!	with a
	draw as a
	result.

* * *

By comparatively simple instances of manoeuvre we have endeavoured to show that in many a complex-looking position there lurks a familiar pattern as its nucleus though slightly thrust to the background amidst a few "superfluous" pieces.

Of course, there are numerous more unusual, more startling end-game positions, in which the situation arising after the show-down confronts us with a "clear" material superiority on one side—which is "theoretically" enough for the win—without any prospect of the weaker side putting up a lasting, "positional" resistance ...

yet the scales remain in equilibrium. The secret of this "miracle" is nothing else than the greater activity of the outnumbered side offsetting the superior forces which are temporarily in a passive or self-restricting position.

At this point the active intervention of the king comes to the fore, when the agile monarch finds it not beneath him to thin out the enemy's superior forces with his own royal hands.

62.

A. A. TROITSKY, 1896.

Draw.

If this situation arose in an over-the-board game, White would in all probability try to play 1. P—B6! (other moves are out of consideration in view of the threat ..., B—B6). After 1. ..., N—K3 (?) he would continue to play 2. K—N6 with a sigh of relief, even if he saw that 2. ..., B—N5 3. P—B7, N—Q5 4. K—N7, N—N4! indirectly prevents the promotion (the threat is ..., N—Q3 ch), for, instead of queening, 5. P—B8 (N)! is enough for a draw.

If Black, however, replied 1. ..., B—N5! 2. P—B7, N—N2! White would certainly resign without hesitation because ..., B—B1 or ..., N—Q3 and ..., N—B1 cannot be prevented. Yet it would be premature to give up either the game or hope!

Pondering a little longer over the situation, we shall find that the N—N2 —B—B1 formation seems to be a tight "bottleneck" for Black. White only has to muscle in among Black's pieces by K—B7! If only his BP were not in the way! Away with it then! But how? Black would not capture it at once if White played 3. P—B8 (Q)?, but would interpolate ..., N—Q3 ch! Therefore we must be accurate down to the last detail:

3. P—B8 (N)!!   B×N
4. K—N6!

..., and here is the exception to the rule: the bishop and the knight **cannot win** against the unsupported king because one of them will fall within a move or two. In reply to 4. ..., N—Q3 or 4. ..., K×P, 5. K—B7 will wind up the game with a double attack. It is a positional draw—but in a dynamic and not a static interpretation.

Of course, from the point of view of the final situation one is not justified in including this in a separate chapter, under a separate title. It is in fact that most ordinary type of draw—however exceptional it appears to be in form—which arises as a result of **equalization of forces**. This simply means that, though no perfect equilibrium is achieved, neither side has the material superiority required for giving mate.

But if gaining a material advantage takes the form of a **threat** and if the opponent's resistance to this threat can be renewed repeatedly, we come across a special case of draw in which we cannot speak of the complete success of either attack or defence. Nor can this be considered complete failure on either side. This mutual "half success" is manifested in a **repetition of moves** or in **perpetual attack.**

The "perpetual check" is a very common instance of the draw. This concept, however, covers only some of the cases which are in principle fully identical; therefore its extension under the heading "Perpetual Attack" seems desirable.

This "terminus technicus" is perhaps not the happiest, and the concept might be more realistically described as "uninterrupted chase," but the attribute "perpetual" is generally accepted in international usage so that we prefer to stick to it. "Attack" too is a well-known chess term and seems to be—even in the given case—more expressive of the idea contained than the word "chase" which also implies the "motif of consequence."

A precise definition of perpetual attack may clarify what we mean by it.

A perpetual attack is an interminable series of moves—resulting sooner or later in a repetition of position—in the course of which one of the players attacks (and threatens to capture) a certain adverse piece move after move, and the other side replies, move after move, by taking the piece in question out of the danger zone.

Such a chain of moves leads—according to the rules—at the latest after 50 moves but in most cases also much

earlier (after the third recurrence of a position) to a draw. Thus the achievement of a position giving an opportunity for perpetual attack already contains the possibility of securing a draw.

Any piece can be exposed to perpetual attack (except a pawn, because it has only a limited route of escape), but the usual target is the king, in which case we speak of **perpetual check.**

63.

H. WEENINK, 1927.

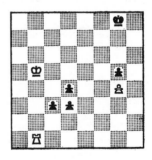

Draw.

In this situation White cannot fight effectively against the dangerous passed pawns despite his extra rook. Any attempt at stopping the pawns would be courting disaster. E. g. 1. K—B4, P—B7! and . . ., P—Q7! etc.

The only escape is offered by the not altogether obvious recognition that Black's king is to a certain extent restricted (!) in its movement, and the united forces of White's king and rook can be utilized for hatching some kind of "plot" against him.

1. K—B6!!   P—Q7

After the more agressive 1. . . ., P—B7, the continuation 2. R—K1!, P—Q7 3. R—K8 ch, K—B2 4. K—Q7! would lead to the target position. Even an attempt to escape would make no difference since after 1. . . ., K—B2 2. K—Q7!, K—B3 3. R—K1! or 2. . . ., P—Q7 3. R—B1 ch and 4. K—K7! the roads leading to freedom would be blocked.

2. K—Q7!   P—B7

If 2. . . ., K—N2 then 3. K—K7!, P—B7 4. R—KB1! etc.

3. R—N8 ch   K—B2
4. R—K8!   and draws,

because White can keep Black in perpetual check (R—K8—K7—K6), whatever the latter's move.

In this example the possibility of perpetual check was virtually handed up on a plate; Black was quite helpless against it. For all that, White's first move has a startling effect, clearly demonstrating that the perpetual check is explicitly a tactical success.

* * *

Indeed, besides stalemate the perpetual check is the weapon most likely to secure a draw, even against enormous odds. The chance of an orgy of sacrifices forcibly leading to perpetual check mostly occurs in middle-game-like positions. Yet it may also crop up where there is the smallest conceivable force.

64.

J. BRENEW, 1934.

Corrected by J. BÁN.*

Draw.

Who would guess that the completely stalemated knight will be able in

* In the original study White's king is posted on KR5, Black's pawn on Black's KB5. The opening moves are: I. K—N4, P—B6. We had to drop the first moves, however, because—in the original position—also the by-play: 1. N—B7!, P—B6 (. . ., B×N? 2. K—N4) 2. N—Q6, P—B7 3. N—B5, and 4. N—K3, etc. would lead to a draw.

this situation to carry on an effective fight not only against the bishop but even against a queen (!)? Certainly no one who would look for the solution in some book of endings, under the heading "Bishop and pawn against a knight" . . .

1. K—N3!	K—N8
2. N—K6!	P—B7
3. N—B4!	

Threatening N—R3 ch. If Black parries it by 3. . . ., B—K3! then 4. N—K2 ch, K—B8 5. N—B4, B—B4! 6. K—B3!! secures the draw.

3. — —	P—B8 (Q)
4. N—R3 ch	K—R8
5. N—B2 ch	K—N8
6. N—R3 ch	and draws

on account of perpetual check.

However surprising the finish may be, the moves leading to perpetual check were here, too, more or less on hand and the result was due to the cornered situation of the king and its mechanically restricted mobility.

In the restriction of the king's movement lack of space proper is often combined with other factors. During the flight certain squares may be forbidden to the king because their occupation would jeopardize the safety of the rest of his camp. A frequent case in point is the indirect restriction of movement by a threat of scope extension (geometrical motif).

65.

F. J. PROKOP, 1934.

Draw.

A net of perpetual checks must be woven to stop Black's king moving about in the centre. There is no other chance of fighting the prospective queen. 1. R—Q4 ch would fail against 1. . . ., K×N 2. R—Q8, K—K2!

1. R—B6!   P—K8 (Q)

White threatened N—B4 (even after 1. . . ., K—K4) 1. . . ., N—R4 would have been met by 2. N—B7 ch and 3. R—K6.

2. N—B4 ch!   K—B5

2. . . ., K—B4 is forbidden on account of 3. N—Q3 ch and also the squares K4 and K5 are taboo because of 3. R—K6 ch. This restriction allows White to chase Black's king persistently along the sixth rank.

3. R—B6 ch   K—N4 (6)
4. R—N6 ch   and draws
through perpetual check, or—in case of a detour—through the loss of the queen.

★ ★ ★

The next study demonstrates how a knight makes possible a similar escape against Black's menacing pawns on both wings.

66.

A. A. TROITSKY, 1923.

Draw.

1. N—B2 ch   K—N6!
2. P—B7   P—R7
3. N—K4 ch!!   K—B6

3. ..., K—R6 (N5) 4. P—B8 (Q) ch!, or 3. ..., K—R5 4. P×N (Q) ch! Two diagonals are a danger zone to Black's king owing to White's passed pawn. This entails an interesting "merry-go-round":

4. N—Q2 ch   K—K6
5. N—B4 ch!   K—K5

There are not many choices left because the Q-file is "out of bounds" on account of P×N (Q) ch.

6. N—Q2 ch   K—K4
7. N—B4 (B3) ch   draws

by perpetual check.

★ ★ ★

Now let us watch a bishop giving the same performance:

67.

V. and M. PLATOV, 1905.

Draw.

1. P—B4!   B×P

Forced because of the mate threat B—K1, as ..., Q—K5 is no defence, for White then has another ace up his sleeve: 2. B—Q8 mate.

2. B—K1 ch!   K—N5
3. B×B ch   K×P

After ..., K—B6? 4. B—N2 ch would win the queen. Therefore the king is confined to the black squares.

4. B—Q2 ch   K—K4
5. B—B3 ch   K—Q3
6. B—N4 ch   K—B7
7. B—R5 ch   and draws,

because Black is compelled to walk back on the same route since after 7. ..., K—N1 8. B—N2 would "give mate" to the queen.

As was noted in our introduction, there are certain circumstances where not only the king but **any other piece may be exposed** to perpetual attack. The next study illustrates a transitional case.

68.

A. A. TROITSKY, 1895.

Draw.

1. N—Q7	B—Q3
2. P—B8 (Q)!	

Sacrifice with line interference intending to gain time for the next quiet move.

2. — —	B×Q
3. N—K5!!	

Threatening B—K2 ch followed by a knight check to king and queen. This can only be prevented by moving the queen.

3. — —	Q—N1
4. B—B4!	Q—R2
5. B—Q3!	

This is it! If the queen confines her movement to Black's N1 and R2 she will remain for ever within the bishop's reach. If again she deprives her consort, hard pressed as he is, of another square, the fire of perpetual attack will be turned on him.

5. — —	Q—R3
6. B—K2 ch	K—R5
7. N—B3 ch	K—R4
8. N—K5 ch	and draws,

since ..., K—N4 would be followed by N—B7 ch.

A pattern of "perpetual check to the queen" springs from the next position, very similar to the perpetual check to the king in Diagram No. 63.

69.

M. G. KLIATSKIN, 1925.

Draw.

Since the attempt 1. P—B7 would
lead to disaster after 1. . . ., Q—B3 ch,
2. K—Q7, Q—Q3 c- 3. K—K8, K—
Ke3! White sacrifices his vain hope in
the interests of driving the queen to
a less favourable place.

1. R—K8!!   Q×P ch

The capture is forced, otherwise
P—B7 would have become a serious
threat.

2. K—Q7 ch   K—B4

2. . . ., K—Q4?? 3. P—K4 ch mate!

3. P—K4 ch   K—B5

The chase of the king is over, but
now it is the queen's turn!

4. R—K6!   Q—B2 (N2) ch
5. R—K7   Q—N1
6. R—K8!   and draws,

because the rook keeps the queen in
perpetual check (K6, K7, K8).

* * *

Also the perpetual attack against the
queen—like that against the king—
may result from an indirect restriction
of movement, from the inaccessibility
of certain squares due to the threat of
some other damage. But it also may
result from another simultaneously
used threat at a time when the queen
under attack can move only to a square
from where she parries the threat. Let
us look at an example.

70.

A. S. GURVITCH, 1927.

Draw.

White loses a piece, therefore he
must do his best to scrape up some
kind of attack against Black's king.

1. N—K4   Q×B
2. R—N5 ch   K—B1

After 2. . . ., K—R2? 3. R×P ch!,
Q×R 4. N—B6 ch, the queen falls;
and also the continuation 2. . . ., K—
R1 would equalize the position (3.
N—B6 threatening R—N8 mate).

3. R—B5 ch   K—K1
4. R×P!

Attack and threat at the same time!
The rook can be captured only in
return for the queen (4. . . ., Q×R 5.
N—B6 ch), otherwise Black must
parry the mating threat R—R8. There
is only one way to do it:

4. — —   Q—QN7!
5. R—QN5!

The same image mirrored on the
other side! The rook is indirectly

protected because of the possibility: N—Q6 ch. The threat R—N8 forces the queen to return and the perpetual attacks rolls on.

| 5. — — | Q—KR7 |
| 6. R—KR5 | |

with a draw as a result.

* * *

It is possible—and worth our while —to keep even a protected piece under permanent attack because by doing so we can tie down the defending piece. If later also the defending piece gets into trouble, the opponent will find it twice as difficult to bring them both into safety. The forestalling or parrying of a double attack against the defending and the defended piece may often necessitate a compromise leading to the repetition of moves or even of whole variations.

71.

A. A. TROITSKY 1936.

Draw.

In this classical example, White's active king—always ready for launching a perpetual attack—holds both Black pieces at bay, standing his ground against an opponent a rook ahead.

1. B—N8	K—B1 (3)
2. P—R7!	K—N2
3. K—N5!	

Attacking only the protected knight but restricting the movement also of the defending rook. The "brutal" 3. K—N6? would not be good, because Black could extricate himself from its passive defensive position after 3. . . ., R—R1 4. P—R5, N—N6! (5. B×N, R—N1 ch! or 5. K—N7, R—R6 etc.) The repentant 4. K—N5 would activate the knight after 4. . . ., N—N2 5. K—B6, N—Q1 ch 6. K—Q7, N—B2!

3. — —	R—R1
4. P—R5	N—N2
5. P—R6 ch!	K—R1

With the king cut off, and thus the KB7 square under control, White can resume the chase of the knight.

| 6. K—B6! | N—Q1 ch |

The rook cannot defend the knight either from Black's QR2 or QN1 for fear of the double attack: 7. K—N6 or 7. K—B7.

7. K—Q7!

7. K—B7? fails against the possible reply . . ., N—B2!

| 7. — — | R—N1 |
| 8. K—B7 | R—R1 |

9. K—Q7!   N—N2
10. K—B6   N—R4 ch
11. K—N5!

11. K—N6? would be wrong again because of . . ., N—N6! And thus we have come back to an earlier position. Black cannot shake off his ties since after a knight move his rook or after a rook move his knight would come under attack.

11. . . ., R—R2 12. K—N6!, R—R1 13. K—N5! and draws.

* * *

The perpetual threat is equivalent in concept and in its forcing effect to perpetual attack. If one side renews his threats every move, the obligation to ward them off continuously prevents the opponent from realizing his own plans.

A familiar instance of a draw being forced by perpetual mate-threats—a motif known to have occurred also in several match games—is offered by the next study:

1. R—R1 ch!, K—N1 2. R—N1 ch, K—B1 3. R—QR1!, K—Q1 4. K—Q6!, K—K1 5. K—K6, K—B1 6. K—B6, K—N1 7. R—R8 ch!, K—R2 8. R—R7 ch, K—R3 9. R—R8!, K—R4 10. K—B5!, K—R5 11. K—B4—and draws because 11. . . ., K—R6?? is taboo!! (12. R—R8 mate.)

* * *

Besides the perpetually **repeated** threat there is also a perpetually **continuing** threat, the prevention of which compels the opponent to be in constant readiness. This obligation of readiness leads to a considerable restriction of mobility, which is why even a significant material advantage cannot often be realized.

The most suitable means of maintaining such a continuous positional threat is the well-advanced passed pawn.

For instance, the way leading to the perpetuation of the threat is, even in its simplicity, well concealed in the next study:

72.

J. MORAVEC, 1924.

Draw.

73.

R. RÉTI, 1928.

Draw.

White's obvious aim is to get his king to QB8 and win a piece for a pawn. It seems that the situation will clear up after a few moves: either White can promote his pawn or Black succeeds in preventing it.

At the first attempt the latter seems to be more probable, because after 1. K—Q8, B—Q3 2. K—B8, N—K2 ch 3. K—Q7 Black is able to regroup his forces effectively: ..., N—Q4! 4. K—B8, N—N3 ch and wins. The knight's intervention bids fair to win also after 1. K—Q7, B—Q3 2. P—N6, K—Q4 3. K—B8, N—K2 ch 4. K—Q7, N—B3!

Nevertheless these two attempts have revealed something: we have to prevent the intervention of the knight **either from Black's Q4 or B3!**— Let therefore White's NP stay on his N5 and Black's king be forced on his Q4!

1. K—Q8!   B—Q3
2. K—Q7!!

Though the threat K—B8 was on hand, there is no need to hurry! We can wait until the knight choses a worse place or te king bars its way to the good one.

2. — —   K—Q4

2. ..., N—B1 ch? or 2. ..., B—N1? 3. K—B8! costs a bishop; 2. ..., N—K2 3. P—N8 (Q)! costs a knight for the pawn.

3. K—B8!   N—K2 ch
4. K—Q7

P—N8 (Q) is again threatened and, therefore the knight must move on.

4. — —   N—B4 (N3)
5. K—B8   N—K2 ch

and draws.

Mutual threat or mutual Zugzwang may bring about a state of equilibrium even in positions where the material balance is upset. That is what we call **a draw by repetition of moves.** As we have seen, it is in fact nothing else than a logical extension of the concept of perpetual attack or perpetual threat.

II. FIGHT FOR VICTORY

ZUGZWANG

Most books on end-games begin with that very simple and readily understandable chapter from which the novice may learn how to give mate to an unsupported king with king and rook.

The process is indeed an easy one. The extra rook is sufficient in all variations to achieve an easy victory.

Through this simple example the beginner is given an idea of the concept of decisive material superiority and he also comes to realize that the right to move confers a certain advantage, since, even if a rook ahead, he must obviously move his pieces to arrive at the mating position. Few would think, however, that the advantage inherent in the right to move might in certain cases turn into a definite disadvantage.

If you were called upon to mate an opponent with a rook on condition that the opponent was allowed to exercise his right to move only at his own discretion unless forced to evade a check, you would find the task quite insoluble.

The opponent's lonely king falls victim to your king and rook for the very reason that he cannot help making a move, even when the move is not

to his advantage, but explicitly disastrous.

Apart from such simple cases, there are numerous more complicated situations in which the side to play cannot but weaken his position by any conceivable move. Often no immediate threat or danger is evident in a given position, yet the player to move finds himself unexpectedly at a disadvantage.

For a better understanding of the surprising tactical turns we have to get acquainted not only with the concept of the "harmful piece" but also with that of the **"damaging move,"** another decisive factor of tactical operations.

That moment in the course of play at which a situation arises when any move made by the side to play amounts to a definite weakening of his own forces, is termed **Zugzwang**.

The concept of Zugzwang must not be confused with the concept of the "forced move." The latter simply indicates that, in a given position, there is, for lack of a better, only one single move with which to parry some attack or threat, irrespective of whether it is satisfactory or not. In other words, it means that in a given position there is only one single move which is satisfactory or which can at least avert some graver trouble for the time being.

On the other hand, in a **Zugzwang position** it would be best **not to move at all,** to leave everything as it is.

We know, however, that according to the rules this is not possible. Therefore, our endeavour to achieve a Zugzwang position is a partial aim in a game, just as it is to bring about other kinds of theoretical winning positions.

Zugzwang may occur in every type of end-game. Its most frequent and best-known instance is the **opposition** in pawn endings. The opposition of the two kings is in essence nothing else than a Zugzwang position because the player with the move is in principle at a disadvantage; he is forced to give ground to the opponent's king. That is why the side on the offensive can in most cases force the win by "gaining the opposition," and that is why the weaker side can save the game if he is able not to "lose the opposition." We do not propose to deal with these familiar and simple cases, but later on in this book the reader will find examples in which the opposition has an essential part to play.

A classical demonstration of the concept of Zugzwang has been preserved from the pre-history of chess. The next pattern is a thousand years old and was taken from Arabian sources by the Arab author who lived two centuries ago.

74.

F. STAMMA, 1737.

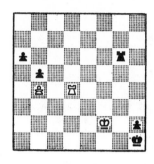

White wins.

White has an unexpectedly quick winning possibility because of the precarious position of Black's king.

1. R—Q1 ch   R—N8

There is nothing else left—a forced move.

2. R—KB1!!   R×R ch

But this is already Zugzwang—at least partially. Black might have moved his RP but the result would have been the same.

3. K×R   P—R4

Now we see the difference between the first rook move and this pawn move: in the first case Black was forced to defend himself by warding off the attack; now, however, he only had to play **something.** This "something" was the only possibility here.

4. P×P	P—N5
5. P—R6	P—N6
6. P—R7	P—N7
7. P—R8 (Q or B)	mate!

If, on the grounds of this example, somebody were inclined to think that such a Zugzwang was only possible when one side was bound hand and foot, in positions smelling of "stalemate," he would certainly be surprised at the finish of the next "airy" queen ending:

75.

A. A. TROITSKY, 1917.

White wins.

An extra minor piece can rarely make itself felt in queen end-games. The superior forces will be able to win only if they can drive the weaker side into a mating position or if they can bring him—as is the case here—into Zugzwang.

1. B—Q5 ch	K—B1
2. Q—Q8 ch	K—N2
3. Q—K7 ch	K—R3
4. Q—K5!!	

Now the enormous power of the queen makes its effect surprisingly felt in the centre. Two factors are worthy of special consideration. First: there is actually **no threat** on White's part; moreover, if he were to move and tried to chase the queen by B—K4, Black would immediately escape by ..., Q—N5 ch! stalemate. Second: though Black's queen has 22 squares (!) to go to, **all his 22 moves are disadvantageous!** (Of course, the only king move 4. ..., K—R2? is wrong because of the pinning 5. B—K4.)

Two moves of the queen would immediately be followed by mate. (4. ..., Q—N2?? 5. Q—KR5! or 4. ..., Q—R2??, 5. Q—KN5!), on fourteen other squares the queen could be captured right away. What other options are left for her?

4. ..., Q—KN8? 5. Q—R8 ch, K—N3 6. Q—N8 ch winning the queen.

4. ..., Q—QR3 (N3) 5. Q—R5 ch, K—N2 6. Q—B7 ch, K—R3 7. Q—B8 ch, K—R2 8. B—N8 ch, K—R1 (8. ..., K—N3 9. Q—B7 ch) 9. B—B7 ch and mate in two moves.

Black's relatively best choice is to stay on his KR2—QN8 diagonal, though even that will not help.

4. — —	Q—Q6
5. Q—N5 ch	K—R2
6. Q—N8 ch	K—R3
7. Q—B8 ch	K—R2

If 7. ..., K—N3 8. B—B7 ch and now 8. ..., K—B3 (B4) 9. B—B4 leads to the loss of the queen; otherwise 8. ..., K—R2 results in a mate in two.

| 8. B—N8 ch | K—N3 |
| 9. B—B7 ch | |

and White wins in the way indicated in the previous paragraph.

For all the options Black's queen had at her disposal, White's marked advantage of space was conspicuous in this example.

Another "airy" position follows in which White's advantage of space and the cramped position of Black's pieces lead to a Zugzwang.

76.

H. RINCK, 1926.

White wins.

| 1. R—B7 ch | R—Q2! |

1. ..., K—K3? results in a mate: 2. Q—B6 ch, K—K4 (2. ..., R—Q3? 3. Q—K4!) 3. R—K7 ch, K—Q5 4. R—K4 ch, etc. A quicker death is in store for Black in case of 1. ..., K—K (B)1? 2. Q—K (B)1 ch, etc.

| 2. Q—B5 ch! | K—Q1! |

2. ..., K—K1? or 2. ..., K—K3?

quickly loses on account of 3. Q—K (B)5 ch, etc. But what next?

| 3. K—R6!! | and White wins! |

It is hard to believe before you have convinced yourself by trying out Black's all possible moves.

* * *

All that is, however, dwarfed by Grandmaster Réti's study which embodies a move that is justly regarded as the "world record of surprise moves."

77.

R. RÉTI, 1922.

White wins.

A simple position. Of a kind that must have occurred in over-the-board play thousands of times. Yet it would hardly attract any particular attention if it did, for master and novice alike would most probably overlook the latent opportunity.

| 1. N—Q4 ch | K—B4! |

After any other move White would win by simple technical means. E. g.
1. ..., K—N2 2. K×P, K—R3 3. N—N3, B—B5 ch 4. K—R3, K—N4 5. K—N4, B—N1 6. P—B4, K—N5 7. P—B5!, K×N 8. P—B6, K—N5 9. P—B7, B—Q3 10. P—R6!, etc. But now, if we played 2. N—N3 ch, K—N4!, we should be short of the very tempo that secured the win in the former variation.

There is a single move that wins even now:

2. K—R1!!!

The reader should get over his astonishment and take a good look at the position. Black is in complete Zugzwang. His king cannot move, nor can he capture the knight lest White's RP should break loose. His bishop again cannot escape the scope of the knight wherever it might choose to go on the two diagonals at its disposal. (Except on White's K3, which is of course covered by the BP.)

2. ..., B—N2 (B1, N4, B5) 3. N—K6 ch

2. ..., B—Q7 (B8) 3. N—N3 ch—and wins.

It is quite simple that way, isn't it?

* * *

The question may arise, how such "wonder" moves can be hit upon.

There is no wizardry in that. We only have to **think over—before playing anything—what the opponent could do, were he on the move!** Then we shall overlook neither a **threat** nor a Zugzwang.

Let us examine some other example from that angle:

78.

F. J. PROKOP, 1935.

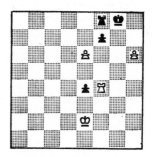

White wins.

White has no advantage that he could realize by aggressive means. He might, indeed, establish a passed pawn by 1. P—K7, but after 1. ..., R—K1 2. R×KP, K—R2 3. K—K3, K×P 4. K—Q4, K—N4! 5. K—Q5, P—B4 6. R—K1, P—B5 Black too would have a passed pawn able to secure a draw.

Black's difficulties lie in the shortage of available moves. His rook is tied down (1. ..., R—K1 2. P×P; any other move would be met by 2. R×P). A move with the KP makes no difference. Black has only ..., P—B3 or ..., P—B4! at his disposal. These moves must be prevented and the Zugzwang is achieved.

1. R—B6!   P—K6

1. ..., K—R1? 2. R×P, R—K1 3. P—K7, K—N1 4. R—B8 ch!, R×R 5. P—R7 ch!, etc. wins. But now it

"would be best" also for White not to move at all. After 2. K×P? Black can equalize the position by pinning White's KP (..., R—K1). Well, let us spare the pawn then and lose a tempo instead.

2. K—B1!   P—K7 ch

After 2. ..., P×P White would win with the same continuation: 3. P—R7 ch!, K—N2 4. R×R.

3. K—K1!   R—R1
4. R×P!   R—K1
5. R—B6!   and wins.

79.

L. I. KUBBEL, 1924.

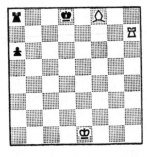

White wins.

As a material plus White's bishop is of no importance, but it is good enough to bring Black's forces—whose mobility is restricted as it is—into Zugzwang.

1. B—B5!   R—B1

Black had to ward off the threat 2. R—R8 ch.

The other possible defence is 1. ..., K—B1. It would be followed by 2. B—R7! and, after having exhausted his pawn moves, Black would lose in the same way as in the main variation. 1. ..., R—N1? would be a gross blunder owing to 2. R—R8 ch, K—B2 3. B—Q6 ch!

2. B—N6 ch   K—K1
3. B—B7   P—R4

Black can move neither with his rook nor with his king since as soon as they are more than one square apart the rook is lost after R—R8 ch (geometrical motif!).

4. K—Q1   P—R5
5. K—B1   P—R6
6. K—N1!   P—R7 ch
7. K—R1!   and wins,

because Black loses his rook on account of the Zugzwang. The last move was important, otherwise Black could have escaped after 2. K×P? by ..., R—R1 ch! (Rook and bishop against a rook is a theoretical draw.)

* * *

Not only can a rook get stuck on the edge of the board in Zugzwang but also a bishop moving along diagonals, if its king happens to bar its way. This possibility is demonstrated in the next end-game with a minimum amount of material:

80.

A. O. HERBSTMAN, 1927.

White wins.

1. B—N4!   B—N3 ch

1. . . ., B×N is wrong because of. 2. B—B2 ch, K—B8 3. B—R3 mate.

2. K—B4!   B×B
3. N—B3 ch   K—B8
4. B—R3 ch   K—B7

The time has come for White to "pass" since Black can make only bad moves.

5. K—N4!

and wins, because Black loses his bishop.

* * *

In the presence of a mobile pawn no Zugzwang position can be attained unless the advance of the pawn is disadvantageous.

But this occurs often enough:

81.

B. HORWITZ, 1879.

White wins.

In this simple, but very instructive, position White makes every effort to force through the advance of Black's RP.

1. K—N4   K—B1!

Black is ready all the time to counter White's aggressive K—R5 by . . ., K—N2, thus making a try for "triangulation" a futile effort. Of course 1. . . ., K—N2?? would be a gross blunder on account of 2. K—R5! resulting in an immediate Zugzwang.

2. K—B4   K—K1
3. K—K4   K—B1
4. K—Q5   K—K2!

Though only temporarily, it throws back the attack against the BP. White's king may stray as far as the QB6—Q6—K6 squares since he can always catch up with Black's RP.

5. K—B6!   K—K1

If 5. ..., P—R4? 6. K—Q5! and the king can retreat in time.

6. K—Q6   K—B1

The approach has been successful, but White cannot launch an immediate attack, for in case of 7. K—K6 Black can reply ..., K—N2 at the right moment, preventing 8. K—K7?? (8. ..., P—R4!)

How to continue now? Indeed, White has to make a "bold" move which, however, hides a plan calculated to a hair.

7. K—Q7!!   K—N1

Should not the RP take off now since White's king can no longer overtake it? Well, the joyful event of queening would be somewhat marred by the continuation 7. ..., P—R4 8. K—K6, P—R5 9. K×P, P—R6 10. P—N7 ch, K—N1 11. K—N6!, P—R7 12. P—B6, P—R8 (Q) and White mates just in time with 13. P—B7. So White can keep manoeuvring outside the "magic square!"

8. K—K7!!   K—N2

To give up the BP would lead to the former mating position. But now Black's king is in Zugzwang and his RP is forced to stick its head into the lion's den.

9. K—K6!   P—R4
10. K—Q5!

— and the rest is already a matter of routine. First of all White wins the

RP: 10. ..., K—R3 11. K—K4, K—N2 12. K—B4, K—R3 13. K—N3, K—N2 14. K—R3! (Triangle! Black can no longer do the same.) 14. ..., K—R3 15. K—R4!, K—N2 16. K×P—followed by a trip to K6 again and—owing to another Zugzwang—Black loses his BP too. **This is the way**—and there is none other—**for White to win.**

* * *

We have remarked above that in a Zugzwang position every move is damaging. We have intentionally avoided contrasting the Zugzwang position with what is called a "threat position," in the way that chess problemists will often have it emphasizing that **there is no threat** in a Zugzwang position. It is really so? Let us give this question a closer scrutiny.

What are the most "brutal" threats? The simultaneous attack against king and queen and the mate. How does such a threat arise? There are two ways: (a) The player on the offensive makes a threatening move. This is the direct threat. (b) The opponent blunders blindly into a mate or a double attack, i. e. he himself turns a non-existing threat into an effective attack.

In the first case the threat is of our own making, in the second it is "latent" in the position as a **possibility** and becomes effective only after a certain move of the opponent.

What happens if the opponent parries the direct threat? The threat will cease to be effective but it will be maintained as a more or less hidden, potential threat. It means that after the parrying move the defending piece will be **tied down** and any possible move with it will make the threat realizable again.

A sly player will resort to as many concealed threats as possible in the hope that his opponent will overlook one of them and blunder into a mate, double attack or the like. A really good player, on the other hand, endeavours to tie down and restrict the mobility of the greatest possible number of adverse pieces with threats, purposefully

pursuing his goal until the opponent will not merely blunder into defeat but accept it as an **inescapable** calamity.

Can such a thing be done? Why, of course! On the strength of the examples given in this chapter, we may safely risk the important statement that the **Zugzwang is a position in which the latent potential threats become effective because the player to move is compelled to stop trying to avert them (or one of them).**

The realization that the presence of certain pieces of one's own colour on the board is not always advantageous but may be expressly harmful, is one of considerable importance in a vast number of tactical operations.

The damaging effect of a piece will as a rule manifest itself in so far as it will, by its very presence, obstruct the movement of some other piece of the same colour. Accordingly, this disadvantage follows not from the strength and mobility of the piece in question but from its material existence.

Let us take a very simple example:

82.

C. SALVIOLI, 1888.

White wins.

It is obvious at the first glance that without Black's NP the situation

would be a draw, no matter which player has the move. But Black's pawn limits the manoeuvring freedom of its own king, and prevents it from reaching the critical square N4. White will win if he manages to thwart Black's efforts to get rid of his harmful pawn under favourable circumstances.

1. P—N5!	K—B2
2. K—Q7	K—B1
3. K—K6	K—N2
4. K—K7	K—N1
5. K—B6	K—R2
6. K—B7	

And now Black has to give up his harmful pawn at a time when he can no longer prevent White's queening his: 6. ...., K—R1 7. K×P, K—N1 8. K—R6! and White wins.

The fixing of the harmful piece is a very important factor in pursuing one's end. If White makes a king move, Black gains "breathing time," sacrifices his pawn under more favourable circumstances and draws. Thus:

| 1. K—K6 | P—N4! |
| 2. K—B5 | K—B2 |

Also ...., K—R2 (R1 or B1) is good; only ...., K—N2?? would be a gross blunder.

3. K×P   K—N2 draws.

Why has the presence of the "bad" pawn worked out to Black's disadvantage? Because he could not make a pawn move, nor could his king occupy a certain spot on the board.

* * *

In other cases again the very fact that some piece can move may prove to be a disadvantage. It is easy to guess that the possibility of moving is damaging when we are striving for total immobility, i. e. when we want to achieve a stalemate. E. g.:

83.

V. CHEKHOVER, 1936.

White wins.

With the BP on the seventh rank Black could draw if he had not another pawn on the square K4. As we know in such cases the idea is to move the king to R8 and to give up the BP. (After Q×P (B2) a stalemate is reached.) Here his own KP, which **can** move, queers the pitch for Black. All White has got to do is to prevent this pawn from advancing too far.

1. Q—B4 ch	K—K8
2. Q—K4 ch	K—Q7
3. Q—B3	K—K8
4. Q—K3 ch	K—B8
5. Q—K4!	

An important motif with a view to fixing the "harmful pawn" temporarily. White's immediate king move would not be satisfactory. E. g. 5. K—N3, P—K5! 6. K—B2, K—N7 7. Q—N5 ch, K—R7 8. Q—R4 ch, K—N7 9. Q—N4 ch, K—R7 and it is obvious now that White's queen cannot occupy the important square KB3 (to gain tempo), and the harmful piece has turned into a useful one.

5. — —	K—N8
6. Q—N4 ch	K—R7
7. Q—B3!	K—N8
8. Q—N3 ch	K—B8
9. K—N3	and wins,

because the time-gaining queen manoeuvre can be repeated.
(9. . . ., K—K7 10. Q—N2, K—K8 11. Q—K4 ch, K—Q7 12. Q—B3, K—K8 13. Q—K3 ch, K—B8 14. Q—K4!) and White's king has come nearer.

* * *

We shall not discuss here the cases in which the damaging effect of a piece is manifested in defeating a stalemate combination. Such examples are to be found in the chapters: "The Stalemate" and "Averting the Stalemate." Now we propose to examine some typical instances of the harmful piece as a factor limiting the mobility and sphere of action of its own side.

84.

B. HORWITZ, 1879.

Draw.

1. K—K4

1. K—N5 would lose because of ...
P—R5. This move of White aims not
at the continuation 1. ..., K×P 2.
K—B3, because after 2. ..., P—R5
3. K—B2, K—N5 Black would win.
White plans to carry out a counterplay
by winning Black's NP. It follows
that 1. K—K5 or 1. K—K6 would
lead to the same result.

1. — —	K×P
2. K—Q5!	K—N5
3. K—B6	P—R5
4. K×P	P—R6
5. K—R7	P—R7
6. P—N6	P—R8 queens
7. P—N7	

With a pawn on the seventh rank
one may as a rule only reckon on a
draw if the pawn stands on the R or
B file. Here is an exception to the rule;
the NP does the trick! How is this
possible? White's QRP has no active

part in enforcing the draw, but he is
"supported" by Black's QRP, whose
presence prevents Black's queen from
giving check on the QR file, so that she
cannot force White's king in front of
the NP. The continuation may readily
be understood:

7. — —	Q—R2
8. K—R8	Q—K5
9. K—R7	Q—Q5 ch
10. K—R8	Q—Q4
11. K—R7	Q—B4 ch
12. K—R8	draw.

The presence of a bad pawn can
alter the general theoretical theses surprisingly. It is a well-known fact, for
instance, that we cannot mate the
opponent's king with one knight, or
with two for that matter. If, however,
the weaker side also has 1 or 2 harmful
pieces, we may be able to enforce
victory. The earliest illustration of
this theme is the following study:

85.

A. SALVIO, 1634.

Winning position!

In this situation Black's king—
limited in its movements—cannot

escape mate with the knight, no matter which side has the move.

(A) 1. N—B6   P—N4
      2. N—N4 ch   K—R8
      3. K—B1!   P—R7
      4. N—B2 mate

(B) 1. . . .   K—R8

If, instead, 1. . . ., P—N4, then 2. N—B6, P—N5 3. N×P ch, K—R1 4. K—B1 leads to the same mate which we have seen in the first variation.

      2. N—B6   K—R7

Also 2. . . ., P—R7 gives no mercy because of 3. N—N4, PN4 4. N—K3, P—N5 5. N—B1, P—N6 ch 6. N×P (N6) mate.

The reduction of Black's movements to a total **Zugzwang** might be brought about even against four pawns, although according to the material evaluation four connected pawns are worth considerably more than a knight.

      1. N—N4   P—B6
      2. K—B2   P—K4
      3. N×KP   K—R7

3. . . ., P—R7 would be followed by 4. K—B1, P—N5 5. N×P, P—B7 6. N×BP mate, or 4. . . ., P—B7 5. N—Q3!, P—N5 6. N×P mate.

      4. N—N4 ch   K—R8
      5. K—B1   P—B7
      6. K×P   P—R7
      7. N—K3   P—N5
      8. N—B1   P—N6 ch
      9. N×P mate

* * *

We find ourselves confronted with a harder strategic task if we want to win with two knights against a freely moving king plus a harmful pawn. Naturally, there are also exceptional situations and possible quick decisions in positions of this type.

The following end-game strikingly demonstrates the value of two strong knights compared to the "valuelessness" or, indeed, harmfulness of those of the opponent.

86.

J. MENDHEIM, 1832.

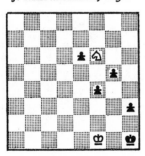

Mate in 9 moves.

87.

F. J. PROKOP, 1929.

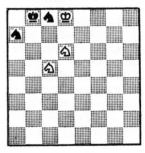

White wins.

1. N—Q7 ch	K—R1
2. K—B7!	N—B3

After 2...., N×N 3. N—N6 mate; while 2...., N—N5 ch is followed by N×N (4) and mate cannot be averted (N—N6).

3. N×N	N (anywhere)
4. N(7)—N6 mate	

* * *

The next example shows a marginal case in which the ill-famed "bad" bishop wins thanks to the opponent's harmful pawn.

88.

A. A. TROITSKY, 1896.

White wins.

In case of an outside passed pawn a bishop to the good is usually not enough for victory, unless the bishop can command the queening square which the opponent's king is able to reach in good time. At first glance we would hardly think that in this position it is the NP which prevents Black's king from reaching the square R1.

1. B—K6!	K—K2!

After 1. ..., K—B1 2. P—R6 would cut off Black's king from the square R1.

2. P—R6!	K—B3
3. B—B5!	K—B2

Here and in the previous move the bishop was of course "taboo" on account of the advanced position of White's pawn.

4. B—R7	K—B3

Now the harmfulness of Black's NP has become evident. Its absence would compel White to make a move with his bishop because of the threat ..., K—N4; in that case ..., K—B2 would follow. As it is, however, White gains time to bring the king nearer before Black can eliminate his own pawn.

5. K—N3	K—B2
6. K—N4	K—B3
7. K—R5!	P—N5
8. K×P	K—B2
9. K—N5	and wins.

* * *

89.

PAULSEN—METGER,
Nuremberg, 1888.

White wins.

White's main endeavour is to prevent the advance of Black's "bad" pawn giving check to White's king. E. g. 1. K—B5? would surprisingly lead only to a draw because of the reply 1. ..., P—N3 ch! 2. P×P ch, K—N2! (let us recall example No. 57!). Also 1. K—B4?, P—N4 ch! 2. P×P ch (if 2. K×P, 2. ..., K—N2 etc.) would lead to the same result. The correct continuation is to play:

| 1. K—Q4!! | K—B3 |

If instead 1. ..., P—N3 or 1. ..., P—N4 2. P—R6! wins. (E. g. 1. ..., P—N3 2. P—R6!, K—B3 3. K—B4, K—Q2 4. B×P!, K—B1 5. B—R7, etc., or 1. ..., P—N4 2. P—R6!, K—B3 3. K—B3!, K—Q3 4. K—N4, K—B3 5. K—R5 etc.) Also 1. ..., K—Q2 would lose after 2. K—B5!, K—B2 3. K—N5!, K—Q1 4. B—N8!, K—B1 5. B—K5 etc.

2. B—N6!	K—Q3
3. K—B4	K—B3
4. K—N4	K—Q3
5. K—N5	K—Q2
6. K—B5!	K—B1
7. B—R7!	K—B2
	(7. ..., P—N3 ch 8. K×P)
8. K—N5!	and wins.

* * *

Even a single bishop can mate a king forced to the edge of the board if the mobility of the latter is considerably limited by its own harmful pawns. In the following example we shall see that it would be an unfruitful attempt on White's part to strive for the elimination of Black's pawns at any price, on the other hand he will accomplish his aim by keeping them intentionally alive, i. e. by frustrating Black's efforts to sacrifice them.

90.

A. A. TROITSKY, 1897.

White wins.

| 1. N—Q4 ch | K—N8 |

After any other move 2. N—N5 and 3. B—B6 would make the pawns ineffective and untenable. Thereafter White would easily bring the issue to a decision.

| 2. N—N5 | P—R7 |
| 3. N—R3 ch | K—N7 |

Seemingly Black's pawn on R7 has become "useful" for it enforces the sacrifice on the part of White.

| 4. B—B ch!! | K×N |
| 5. B—R1!! | |

Now it is evident that the blockade of the "candidate for queen" becomes the cause of the king's fatal captivity. White threatens 6. K—B3 and 7. B—N2 mate!

5. — —	P—N4 ch
6. K—B3!	P—N5 ch
7. K—B4!	P—N6
8. K—B3	P—N7
9. B×P mate.	

* * *

The next diagram shows an "airy" picture with only a few pieces scattered over the board. It is like a wide meadow where the pieces may freely run about. It seems that the imprisoned knight might easily be freed by the king after a "pleasant stroll." There is only a single "lump of earth" in the king's way: the KP. And yet this small obstacle is enough to disrupt connection between Black's king and knight and at the same time to help White's pieces to co-operate smoothly.

91.

K. SARITCHEV, 1930.

White wins.

Before launching his attack against a distant target (Black's knight), White begins by fixing the "harmful pawn."

1. N—K5!	K—N2
2. B—Q8!	K—B1
3. K—B2	K—K1

| 4. B—R5! | K—K2 |
| 5. K—K3 | K—Q3 |

It seems that White cannot outsmart Black and will be late. But it is just an illusion!

6. K—Q4!

... and what happens now if Black moves at long last 6. ..., N—B2? A bolt from the blue: 7. B—N4 mate!

In order to reach this mating position it was necessary to fix the KP, and allow the useless knight to revive and thus cause the death of its own king.

Consequently, Black has to give up his plans for saving the knight, and after

6. — —	K—K2
7. K—B5 and	
8. K—B6 White wins the piece and the game.	

This clear illustration of the concept of the harmful piece also demonstrates in a delightful way the striking difference between a centralized and a trapped knight.

* * *

So far we have described the phenomenon of the harmfulness of a piece, which must be regarded as a negative factor in the appraisal of the balance of power. In the light of this we may accept as a rule that

the obtaining of material advantage is not always useful; therefore, we must be careful not to capture the harmful pieces of the opponent and, what is more, must prevent their elimination.

But what should we do if we have a harmful piece of our own which stands in the way of accomplishing our aim? **It goes without saying that the harmful pieces in our camp must be liquidated!**

Let us examine now the methods we might adopt for that purpose.

92.

P. FARAGÓ, 1937.

Draw.

Since he cannot prevent the queening of Black's pawn, White's only hope lies in advancing his KRP and QRP to the seventh rank.

This problem does not seem to be difficult, for the continuation 1. P—R5, P—N6 2. P—KR6, P—N7 3. P—R7, P—N8 (Q) 4. P—R6 would be a draw indeed. After Black's king move White can advance his pawn to QR7 and the capture would result in an immediate stalemate.

This plan is, however, rather superficial because after 1. P—R5? Black has time to fix the QRP (1. ..., K—R3!). Then White's fate would be sealed because there is no defence against defeat. (2. P—R6, P—N6 3.

P—R7, P—N7 4. K—N8, P—N8 (Q) ch 5. K—R8, Q—K6 6. K—N7, Q—N4 ch 7. K—B7, Q—R3 8. K—N8, Q—N3 ch 9. K—R1, K—N4 10. P—R6, Q—B2! 11. P—R7, Q—B1 mate.)

As soon as this danger has been realized the solution is quite simple:

1. P—R6!!	P—N6
2. P—R5	P—N7
3. P—R6	P—N8 (Q)
4. P—R7	

and Black cannot win because he lacks a tempo for reaching the above mating position.

* * *

In the following diagram we show a famous tactical motif which occurred during a simultaneous display involving world champion Lasker. (His opponent was Loman, who eventually won the game.)

93.

SCHEME.

White wins.

Black's RP has become very dangerous, it threatens P—R8 (Q) ch. White cannot approach it because of his own QNP. What is to be done?

| 1. R—R5 ch | K—N3! |

Another check with the rook would now lose because of . . ., K—R2 and Black's queening cannot be prevented. But the point is that the rook can help in liquidating the harmful pawn!

2. R—R5!!	K×P
3. P—N4 ch	K×P
4. K—N2	and wins.

This tactical motif (the sacrifice of the rook) will be thoroughly discussed in the chapter "Driving on." Nevertheless, let us also at this point look at an example which illustrates the rook as a harmful piece. This rook sacrifices itself so as to "reactive" a "shelved" bishop.

94.

L. I. KUBBEL, 1917.

White wins.

White could mate Black's king immediately did the presence of the rook not prevent it. White must act quickly because his king is also threatened by mate.

| 1. R—B2 ch | K—K4 |
| 2. R—B5 ch!! | |

And now 2. . . ., K×R would lead to the original position, less White's rook (3. P—Q4 mate!). But there are also other factors in this combination. The other—longer—variation reveals that there is a "useful" KP in Black's camp. If it leaves its place, the queen will get into a mess.

| 2. — — | P×R |
| 3. P—Q4 ch | K—Q4 |

The continuation . . ., K—K3 would not make any difference because of 4. B—R2 ch, P—Q4 5. P×P e. p. ch, etc.

4. B—R2 ch	K—K5
5. B×Q	K×P
6. P—Q5	and wins.

In the chapter on stalemate we have already stated that more often than not the weaker side is not bound to seek an exceptional stalemate position, achieved in a spectacular combinative way, but may as well strive to attain a simple book draw, one that is, in the last analysis, nothing more than a virtual stalemate. Stalemate hazards, often well concealed, are mostly a concomitant of positions arrived at after combinative manoeuvres when a hasty assessment of the situation would seem to indicate that the issue was already decided.

Let us take for instance this simple example:

95.

A. O. HERBSTMAN, 1934.

White wins.

One has the impression that this is in fact no ending but a middle-game position stripped of a couple of pawns and perhaps even of some minor pieces for the sake of simplicity, as they would have no active part to play in the winning combination that, so it seems, leaps to the eye.

True enough, the winning combination is based on a strikingly simple and familiar motif: Discovered attack with a bishop check and then capturing Black's queen. To make matters worse for Black, the loss of his rook too after an interpolated move appears imminent.

At first glance the win might well be conceived this way: 1. B—R7 ch! and to . . ., K—R1 or . . ., K—N2 we answer P×R (Q) ch and next we take the opponent's queen: 3. R×Q. The procedure consisting of 2 or 3 moves in all seems indeed to be too simple to be considered a combination. Nor is it less obvious that we can easily interpolate the capture of the rook even if the opponent accepts the sacrificed bishop, by simply resorting to the minor promotion P×R (N) ch.

If we think, however, that these primitive combinations do not call for care and circumspection in this "middle-game position stripped of

85

superfluous pieces," we shall be greatly mistaken. Let us look at the variations:

A. 1. B—R7 ch!, K—R1 (!) 2. P×R (Q) ch (?), K×B! 3. R×Q—stalemate!

B. 1. B—R7 ch!, K—N2 2. P×R (Q) ch (?), K×B! 3. R×Q—stalemate!

C. 1. B—R7 ch!, K×B 2. P×R (N) ch!, K—N1! 3. R×Q (?), K×N! 4. P—R6, K—N1! 5. P—R7 ch, K—R1! 6. R×B—stalemate!

How easy it is to fall into a trap even in this simple position, isn't it? Black has several hidden stalemate possibilities and we must by no means lose sight of them!

The simplest way of averting the stalemate is offered by variation C.

1. B—R7 ch	K×B
2. P×R (N) ch!	K—N1
3. N×Q!	and wins.

In the two other variations, however, we have to be careful with the promotion and adapt the general plan to Black's previous move.

A.

1. B—R7 ch	K—R1
2. P×R (R) ch!!	B—N1!
3. R×B ch!	K×B
4. R×Q ch	and wins.

B.

1. B—R7 ch	K—N2
2. P×R (B) ch!!	any move
3. R×Q	and wins.

In this example it is evidently the very absence of "superfluous pieces" that has made it possible for Black to try for a stalemate. Indeed, the stalemate hazard must never be left out of

account, particularly in positions where the opponent has but a few pieces left and our combination aimed at obtaining material advantage is likely to lead to a further dwindling of his forces.

Here follow the most frequently occurring tactical methods of averting the stalemate:

(I) To spare a harmful mobile piece in the opponent's camp;

(II) To abstain from over-increasing our forces, by way of resorting to underpromotion instead of queening our pawn;

(III) To remove the opponent's king from the stalemate nest by an interpolated sacrifice.

(IV) To prevent the achievement of the stalemate by time-gaining manoeuvres;

(V) To turn the combination aimed at obtaining some material advantage into a direct mating attack against the king seeking refuge in a stalemate nest.

* * *

Let us analyse these possibilities one by one through some illustrative examples:

96.

KLING and HORWITZ, 1851.

White wins.

1. K—Q7!!

1. B×P?, P—N6 2. B—K4, P—N7! and Black has already achieved a theoretical draw.

1. — —   P—N6!

1. ..., P—B5 2. B×P, P—B6 3. B—R3!!, P—B7 4. B—B1!, K—R1 5. B×P etc. wins.

2. B—Q5   P—B5
3. B—B3!   P—N7
4. B×KNP   P—B6
5. B—B1!   P—B7
6. K—Q8   K—R1
7. B×P!

Now we see the importance of sparing the BP in order to avert the stalemate! Black must not take the bishop, because 7...., P×B would be met by 8. K—B7! (no stalemate!), P—B8 (Q) 9. P—R7 ch, K—R2 10. P—N8 (Q) mate.

7. — —   K—N1
8. B—B1   K—R1
9. B—N2   K—N1
10. K—Q7   P—B8 (Q)

There is nothing else left since after 10. ..., K—R1 11. K—B7 the presence of the BP again foils the stalemate while its queening is no defence against the mate (B×NP).

11. B×Q   and wins,

because White can also sacrifice his bishop on QN7 and he will be two pawns ahead. Then he will be able to force his opponent into Zugzwang and exploit his positional advantage in a combinative way. E. g. 11. ..., K—R1 12. P—R6, K—N1 13. P—R7 ch, K—R1 14. B—R6!, P×B 15. K—B7, P—R4 16. P—N7 ch, K×P 17. P—N8 (Q) ch, K—R3 18. Q—N6 mate.

97.

B. HORWITZ, 1879.

White wins.

In this position Black's harmful pawns are too far advanced to be stopped and kept alive. Yet it is obvious that after the disappearance of Black's pawn triangle the end-game is a book draw.

How then should White tackle the job on hand? Simply by using the time Black requires for getting rid of his pawns to make his own king's necessary approach. Since Black's distant passed pawn will be promoted on White's KN1, White's first task is to relieve his king from guarding that square.

1. Q—N6!	P—B7 ch
2. K×P	P—B8 (Q) ch
3. K×Q	P—N7 ch
4. K—K2!	P—N8 (Q)
5. Q×Q ch	K—N7

So far Black has made nothing but forced moves while White has managed to bring his king somewhat nearer to his goal. In fact, the point from which the king would be able effectively to co-operate with the queen against Black's RP, or rather his new-born queen, is merely one square off. Therefore,

| 6. K—Q2! | P—R8 (Q) |
| 7. Q—N6 ch | K—R6 |

After 7...., K—R7 the quiet move 8. K—B2! will immediately follow and Black has no defence against the mate.

8. Q—R5 ch	K—N7
9. Q—N4 ch	K—R7
10. K—B2!	and wins.

★ ★ ★

Among the multitude of problem-like turns demonstrating the idea of averting the stalemate on the strength of the four available alternatives of promotion a familiar example, delightful in its simplicity, is the Saavedra position:

98.

F. SAAVEDRA, 1895.

White wins.

1. P—B7	R—Q3 ch
2. K—N5!	R—Q4 ch
3. K—N4!	R—Q5 ch
4. K—B3	R—Q8
5. K—B2	R—Q5!

With one eye on the stalemate after 6. P—B8 (Q)?, R—B5 ch! 7. Q×R. But White can avoid this pitfall.

| 6. P—B8 (R)!! | R—QR5 |

Forced, owing to the mate threat 7. R—R8.

| 7. K—N3! | and wins, |

because the rook is en prise and White threatens mate on B1.

If now you are inclined to say that we have an exceptional and unlikely case here, the win being made possible only by the extremely bad cornered position of Black's king, you should also remember that that same extremely bad position gave Black an opportunity to try for the stalemate; otherwise White could have won easily in a much less spectacular manner.

This simple, but impressive idea of the Saavedra position has been elaborated by many an excellent end-game composer in delightful studies which also give useful pointers to the detection of stalemate hazards. Let us take one of the best:

99.

M. S. LIBURKIN, 1931.

White wins.

The pattern shows an extra knight and pawn. Has the content too become any richer?

1. N—B1!   R—Q4 ch

1. ..., R×P is to be met by 2. P—B7, R—Q4 ch 3. **N—Q3!!** and this driving-on sacrifice helps White to achieve the former winning position without loss of time: 3. ..., R×N 4. K—B2! (4. ..., R—Q5 5. P—B8 (R)!, R—QR5 6. K—N3). We have already seen this. But how to proceed now?

2. K—B2!

2. K—K2? won't work on account of 3. P—B7, R—K4 ch and 4. ..., R—K1. Nor is the knight sacrifice any better for: 2. N—Q3?!, R×N 3. K—K2, R—QB6 and 4. ..., R—B4! or 3. K—B2, R—Q4! etc. There is only one solution left:

2. — —   R—B4 ch
3. K—Q3!!

This interpolation is much more cunning than one might first think. Doubtless it is not easy to notice that the natural 3. K—Q2 can be parried by 3. ..., R×P 4. P—B7, R—N7 ch 5. K—Q1, R—QB7!! and after 6. K×R Black is stalemated; otherwise the rook can capture the pawn. Therefore:

3. — —   R×NP

It is not much better to take the knight since after the continuation 3. ..., R×N 4. K—Q4!, K—R7 5. K—Q5, K—R6 6. P—N6 the united passed pawns would easily win against the rook.

4. P—B7   R—N1

The last stalemate attempt! Now the careless 5. P×R (Q) or 5. P×R (R) would lead to stalemate again, and after 5. P×R (N) the two knights would be powerless against the king. By good luck there is a fourth way of capturing the rook ...

5. P×R (B)!   and White wins.

We observe here underpromotion instead of queening in two variations, the choice between the two depending on the play of the weaker side.

In tactical turns one should often heed the saying, **Similia similibus curantur**, i. e. likes are cured by likes. Translated into the language of chess this means that if the side on the defensive adopts unusual, extraordinary methods, we must search for similar extraordinary ways and means to keep the attack going. Seekers will be finders!

* * *

A stalemate defence scheme prepared against an imminent queening can mostly be foiled by rook or bishop promotion. Of course the hidden trap should be detected in good time! An example of each:

100.

H. RINCK, 1920.

White wins.

Of the two passed pawns Black's seems to be the more dangerous. White forestalls the danger by a driving-on rook sacrifice first, and then brings about a geometrical position on the Q file.

1.	R—K4 ch	K—B6 (4)
2.	R—Q4!	K×R
3.	P—Q7	K—K6!

Either this continuation or the alternative 3. . . ., P—Q8 (Q) would seem to decide the issue in White's favour. Yet it would be a blunder in either case to play 4. P—Q8 (Q)? carelessly, because Black would be stalemated after . . ., P—Q8 (Q)! 5. Q×Q; and White would otherwise not be able to win against the surviving queen.

To **notice** this stalemate hazard might be difficult, but to avert it is easy enough:

4.	P—Q8 (R)!!	K—K7
5.	K—R3	

The immediate capture of the pawn would be a gross error because Black would win after 5. R×P ch?, K×R 6. K—R3, K—K7 7. K—N4, K—K6!. But 5. R—K8 ch, etc. would also meet the case.

5.	— —	P—Q8 (Q)
6.	R×Q	K×R
7.	K—N4	and wins.

101.

A. A. TROITSKY, 1929.

White wins.

White's pawn cannot be stopped, but by sacrificing the rook Black gains time to make his own promotion.

1. P—N7   R—B7 ch!

1. ..., R—N7, 2. K×R, P—N7 3. N—Q2 ch would simplify things for White because Black can reply only ..., K—K6 owing to the threat N—B3. (3. ..., K—B5? 4. P—N8 (Q) ch!) The continuation would result in a geometrical position on the diagonal and 4. P—N8 (Q), P—N8 (Q) 5. Q—R7 (N6) ch would easily win. "Won't the text continuation lead to the same position!" one might ask. As we shall see—not quite!

2. K×R   P—N7
3. N—Q2 ch   K—K6!

The knight is defended now—that makes the difference. And this fact allows Black to climb into a **stale-mate cage.** (4. P—N8 (Q)?, P—N8 (Q)! 5. Q—N6 ch, K—K7! 6. Q×Q.) What next? The queen-winning manoeuvre on the diagonal is practicable also with lesser strength so as not to restrict unduly the mobility of Black's king.

4. P—N8 (B)!!   P—N8 (Q)
5. B—R7 ch   and wins.

* * *

From a practical point of view the next end-game is very instructive, demonstrating as it does the fight against Black's passed pawns.

102.

Dr. M. LEWITT, 1917.

White wins.

White's most urgent task is to establish a passed pawn of his own. This aim is served by a **driving-off** bishop sacrifice.

1. B—K8!   P—R6
2. B×P!   P×B

Seemingly not the best, yet the trickiest defence. After 2. ...., P—R7 3. B—B7 ch, K—N7 4. B×P, K×B 5. P—N6! White will promote a pawn. If 2. ...., K—N7 3. B—B7, P—N6 4. P—N6, P×P 5. P—R7, P—R7 6. P—R8 (Q) ch, K—N8 7. B× QNP, P—R8 (Q) and White wins by the gradual approach of his queen: 8. B—B2 ch, K—R7 9. Q—N8 ch, K—N7 10. Q—N7 ch, K—R7 11. Q—B7 ch, etc.

3. P—R7   P—R7!

We must not overlook here that 4. P—R8 (Q)?, P—R8 (Q)! 5. Q×Q leads again to stalemate! Therefore:

4. P—R8 (B)!!   and wins.

* * *

The next study demonstrates through natural positions how effective a weapon the threefold possibility of underpromotion is in averting the stalemate.

103.

L. I. KUBBEL, 1928.

White wins.

1. P—Q7	R×R ch
2. B×R	R—Q8!

Since there is no other way of stopping the passed pawn Black tries to seek defence in stalemate.

3. B×R	N—N1
4. P—Q8 (B)!!	and wins.

For all the hidden subtlety, 4. P—Q8 (N)? would not be satisfactory on account of 4. ...., N—Q2 and 5. ...., N×P, one might say that the content of the study was not particularly striking.

One might, indeed, if there were not more to it. But of course Black may play his first two moves in reverse order, already offering the rook for sacrifice on his Q8 in the first move. Does that make any difference?

1. P—Q7	R—Q8!
2. B×R	R×R ch
3. B×R	N—N1 !

A queen or a rook promotion would of course lead to stalemate. What's more, the only winning move of the former variation 4. **P—Q8 (B)** would also work out to White's disadvantage, because Black might play 4. ...., N—B3! 5. B—B6, N—K4 ch! and White can't do better than choose between a stalemate (after his taking the knight) and a book draw (after the inevitable exchange on his KN4). Is the bishop really badly posted on KN4? In a way it is, but this disadvantage is more than offset by its being able to control the square Q7 and thereby thwarting Black's defensive manoeuvre: . . ., N—Q2 and . . ., N×P. In the light of this the winning move is the one that was wrong in the former variation:

4. P—Q8 (N)!!

. . . and the extra piece is enough for White's victory.

Now we can agree that the study is a veritable masterpiece.

An unusual picture of an extraordinary winning position arising after an averted stalemate is depicted in Troitsky's next study:

104.

A. A. TROITSKY, 1925.

White wins.

1. P—N7!

1. P×P?, R—QR5 2. B—B5, K—B5 3. P—Q6, K×B 4. P—Q7 would be a faulty plan because of 4. . . ., R—N5 ch! and 5. . . ., R—N1.

1. — —	R—N5 ch
2. K—B2	R—N1
3. P—Q6!	K—B5!
4. P—Q7	K—N4

Though Black's king cannot overtake the passed pawn, there is a "cosy" stalemate nest on his QR3 (the same one as we saw in the chapter "Stalemate.")

| 5. P—Q8 (Q) | R×Q |
| 6. B×R | K—R3! |

What now? 7. P—N8 (Q or R)? is stalemate; 7. P—N8 (N)?, K—N2 8. N—Q7, K—B1 a draw. But there is one solution left:

7. P—N8 (B)!!

Who would think of such a thing during a match game? The oddity of the position is that while **one bishop is not worth a straw, two bishops of the same colour secure an easy win!** This applies not only to the present case, but to the types of position defined by two vis-à-vis pawns on R6—R7. (The result is the same if Black has a pawn on his QR2, or any other harmless pawn for that matter.)

Why **two** bishops are needed is demonstrated by this simple finish. 7. . . ., K—N2 8. B—K5!, K—B1 9. B—R5, K—Q2 10. K—B3, K—K1 11. K—B4, K—B2 12. K—B5!, K—B1 13. K—B6, K—N1.

If White had only one bishop Black could mark time on the B1 and N1 squares and, in case of 14. B—Q6, sacrifice his superfluous pawn by . . ., P—R4—R5, etc. followed by . . ., K—R1. (K—B7 stalemate.) But now:

14. B—N4!, P—R4 15. B—K7, P—R5 16. B—R3!, K—R1 17. K—B7 mate! Hence two bishops can enforce **Zugzwang** and subsequently the **mate** with discovered check! This is worth remembering in the

same way as the fact that we can even win with two knights if the opponent has a fixable pawn.

* * *

We can draw the lesson from these examples: **The stalemate as a tactical weapon should not be underrated in the indirect prevention of queening.** This possibility must never be lost sight of and it is often wiser to promote to a piece of a lesser value because sometimes **less** means **more!**

* * *

Now we have to deal with the averting of stalemate by way of an interpolated sacrifice.

The theme is fairly clear and requires but little explanation. If we have an opportunity of obtaining a decisive advantage but the implementation of our plan is at a given moment prevented by the stalemate position of the opponent or his threat to achieve it, then we have to reduce the forces immobilizing the hostile camp in order to get the upper hand unhindered at a later stage. E. g.

105.

D. PRZEPIORKA, 1920.

White wins.

It is not easy to spot the necessity of an interpolated sacrifice, much less the looming danger of stalemate.

The natural opening move is

1. R—K2!   Q—N1

There is nothing better on account of the threat R—K8, for after 1. ..., P—R3 2. R—K8 ch, K—R2 3. N—B6 ch, K—N2 (3) 4. R—N8 ch, the queen is lost.

But now White would be rather surprised after the "natural" 2. N—B6!,; 2. ...,Q—N8! 3. R—K8 ch, K—N2 4. R—N8 ch, K—R3!—and the queen could only be taken at the cost of **stalemate!**

Realizing this White has to tackle the job from another angle, namely by a forcing sacrifice of the knight.

2. N—N7!!   P—R4

2. ..., K×N 3. R—N2 ch, or 2. ..., Q×N 3. R—K8 ch lead to the same result.

3. R—K8   K×4

3. ..., P—R5 4. R×Q ch, K×R 5. N—B5 wins. After 3. ..., Q×R, 4. N×Q, P—R5 5. N—B6, P—R6 6. N—N4 the pawn is overtaken.

4. R×Q ch   K×R
5. P—R5   and wins.

The next simple and instructive end-game also comes under this heading. It shows how hard it may prove to foil stalemate attempts even though the bishops are of the same colour and we are two pawns up.

106.

F. LAZARD, 1925.
Corrected by J. BÁN

White wins.

In the original form of Lazard's study, White's king was placed on KB4. To eliminate a difficult by-play, we have transferred it to KR4. In this form the idea contained in it finds a clearer expression.

1. P—R6	B—R7!
2. K—N5	B—N6!

If White's king were now on his KB4 he could frustrate Black's line of defence by 2. K—B5! (2. . . ., K×P 3. K—B6, K—R2 4. B—K8! —4. B—B2 ch?, K—N1 5. K—N6, B—N8!! —4. . . ., K—N1 5. K—N6! and 6. K—R6 followed by B—N6—R7 ch White's win.)

But now White's bishop is kept continually annoyed by its Black opposite number. We had better leave it to its fate then. But where? We must find the least favourable spot for Black's bishop to intervene in the further course of events.

3. B—Q7!	B—K3
4. K—B6!	B×B
5. K—B7!	and wins

because White threatens to promote his pawn with check, and the diverting sacrifice (5. . . ., B—K3 ch) is useless since the victorious pawn is supported by its comrade on R6.

* * *

As the fourth method of averting stalemate we have mentioned **time-gaining manoeuvres** which can mostly be resorted to in queen endgames.

In the next study, for instance, the possibility of winning the queen is offered on a plate, but it would be ill-advised to swallow the bait at once on account of Black's good stalemate chances.

107.

R. RÉTI, 1925.

White wins.

1. N—B3 ch	K—R8!

2. Q×Q?: Stalemate position No. 1.

2. Q—R4 ch!   K—N7
3. Q—R2 ch   K—B8!

4. Q×Q?: Stalemate position No. 2.

4. Q—N1 ch!   K—Q7
5. Q—N2 ch   K—K8!

6. Q×Q?: Stalemate position No. 3.

6. Q—B1 ch!   K—B7
7. N—Q1 ch   K—B6

The last rank is a danger zone because of 8. N—K3 ch. 7. ..., K—K7 8. Q—N2 ch leads to the main variation.

8. Q—B3 ch   K—K7

After 8. ..., K—B5 9. Q—B6 ch, K—K5 10. Q—B6 ch?, K—Q6! 11. Q×Q **stalemate position No. 4.** would arise, but White can do better with 10. Q—Q4 ch!, K—B6 11. Q—Q5 ch—winning the queen safely at last.

9. Q—N2 ch   K—Q6!!

Black's queen is still taboo.

10. Q—N3 ch!   K—K7
11. Q—R2 ch!   K—Q6

The **fifth** chance, and there is still no occasion to rejoice; but now the knight intervenes again ...

12. N—N2 ch   K—K7

If 12. ..., K—B6, 13. N—R4 ch; otherwise the next move decides Black's fate.

13. N—B4 ch   K—B6

In case of 13. ..., K—B8 14. N—K3 ch, K—K8 15. N×Q wins. (Not 15. Q×Q??, bringing about **stalemate position No. 6.**)

14. N—K5 ch   K—K6
15. Q×Q   and wins.

After a troublesome redeployment of his forces White has at last managed to find a gap for Black's hard-pressed king ... Not as easy as one might have thought it would be!

* * *

Under the barrage of a centralized queen and knight, a king may get into trouble not only at the edge of the board but even in the middle. Of course, it is a bad break for the attacker if the shots miss the target by a hair and during a momentary ceasefire only the monarch's own square remains intact. But the concerted action of two strong pieces can, as a rule, eliminate the re-emerging stalemate hazards.

108.

O. DEHLER, 1908.

White wins.

1. N—B6 ch!

Taking four squares of refuge from Black's king. The sixth rank is marked with a "No entry!" sign. (2. N—Q8 ch.) If 1. . . ., K—Q4 2. Q—N3 ch. The latter does not mean an immediate winning of the queen . . . well, let us see why:

1. — —   K—B4
2. Q—B2 ch   K—K5!

After 2. . . ., K—K3? 3. N—Q8 ch would follow. In case of 2. . . ., K—N3 3. N—K5 ch wins the queen. But now the queen is taboo—owing to the stalemate!

3. Q—K3 ch   K—Q4

3. . . ., K—B4 is a speedier defeat. Sooner or later Black's king will be forced to go there.

4. Q—N3 ch   K—K5!

Black's queen survives (5. Q×Q? stalemate), but only for a short time.

5. Q—Q3 ch!   K—B5
6. Q—K3 ch   K—B4

There is nothing else. 6. . . ., K—N5? 7. N—K5 ch.

7. Q—B3 ch and wins

because any defending move would be met by a check from the knight. (Fork!)

* * *

Among the tactical means of averting stalemate we have also mentioned the possibility of **changing our plan as we go along**, i. e. of launching an **unexpected mating attack** against a king escaping into a stalemate nest. There are positions in which there is no trace of any short-term mating possibility, no prospect of any mating combination, but the stalemate line of defence taken by the opponent so much worsens the situation of his king that all of a sudden a chance arises of enforcing mate in a combinative way. In most cases the mate is of course one of the alternatives of the combination, but it is exactly that variation that prevents the successful defence and makes it possible to obtain a decisive material advantage.

Let us look at some of the most characteristic examples.

109.

A. S. GURVITCH, 1928.

White wins.

White has good prospects of securing an easy win once his pawn is in safety. The introductory moves are accordingly aimed at defending the pawn.

1. N—Q7	B—B2!
2. N—B8	B—K4
3. K—N4	B—N7!

Now the purpose of the bishop manoeuvre becomes clear as well as the obstacle in the way of a seemingly easy win. Black's bishop can menacingly face up its counterpart on the diagonal because its loss would result in a stalemate.

White has to resort to some kind of sacrifice to lift the stalemate position. If after B—B1 ch Black had only ..., K—N2 to reply we could strive for blockading White's KN7 square with a driving-on sacrifice. 4. P—N7!? would be a good idea if Black captured the pawn with his bishop; but the king too might take it attacking the knight at the same time. Consequently, the sacrifice must be prepared in a way that White should, and Black should not, have time to come to the rescue of their respective attacked pieces. Therefore:

4. B—B5!	B—Q5
5. P—N7!	K×P

In case of 5. ..., B×P an unexpected turn: 6. B—K3 mate!

6. N—K6 ch	K—B3
7. N×B	and wins.

The mate can only be averted at the cost of decisive material loss. In the

98

next example we shall see its opposite as the main variation.

110.

R. RÉTI, 1928.

Corrected by H. RINCK.

White wins.

In order to annihilate the dangerous pawns White must bring his rook onto the K file without loss of time. Therefore he has to decide between the preparatory moves 1. B—B6 ch and 1. B—B5 ch. In either case Black tries to find defence in stalemate against White's superior forces.

E. g. 1. B—B6 ch, K—Q3 2. R—Q4 ch, K—K4 3. R—K4 ch, K—Q3! and at the last moment White is confronted with an unsurmountable obstacle, because after 4. R×P, P—K8 (Q)! 5. R×Q—Black is stalemated. With the bishop on B6 this cannot be avoided, nor is there any possibility of tricking Black's king into a mate trap. Let us try then the second alternative.

| 1. B—B5 ch | K—Q3 |
| 2. R—Q4 ch | K—K2! |

If 2. . . ., K—K4? 3. R—K4 ch, etc. easily wins.

| 3. R—K4 ch | K—Q1 |

The other stalemate nest! The pawn must not be touched. (4. R×P, P—K8 (Q)! 5. R×Q stalemate.)

But now Black's king is on his Q1 and to mate him in not so remote a possibility. Once we have realized this, a sacrifice intending to lift the stalemate suggests itself.

| 4. B—Q7!! | P—K8 (Q) |

After 4. . . ., K×B Black loses his pawns and White remains strong enough to win. Now—after Black's queening—we cannot speak about White's material superiority, yet the positional advantage decides the issue in his favour.

| 5. B—N5! | and wins, |

because Black can only delay the unparriable mating threat (R—K8) by giving up his queen. Note the harmful presence of Black's K6 pawn in the final situation.

In the next diagram too the contingency of stalemate renders the realization of White's great material superiority more difficult. Here the stalemate is no hidden threat but rather too obvious a reality; our concern is just how to get round it.

111.

F. AMELUNG, 1883.

White wins.

If the solution is not difficult, it is simply because White has only one self-interfering move, allowing Black's king to leave the corner.

| 1. K—N4! | K—N7 |
| 2. R—KB8! | |

The pawn cannot be won but the new-born queen will perish in the tightening noose . . .

2. — —	P—R8 (Q)
3. R—B2 ch	K—N8
4. K—N3!	Q—B3
5. R—B5 ch!	

with the alternative of mate or the queen's loss.

* * *

By and large, we have gone through the most typical technical methods of averting stalemate. There is also the **preventive** method the essence of which may, for practical purposes, be summed up as follows: If our immediate objective is to obtain material superiority rather than to launch a direct mating attack, one is well advised to allow the opponent's king some breathing-space and not to subject him to the concerted attack of too many of our pieces. Plain common sense, you will say. So it is, but how often has it been lost sight of even in important match games to the bitter disappointment of the side that neglected to take the most elementary precautions! ...

Wise and useful as the warning is, "Look out for every single check for it may turn out to be a mate!", just as important is another that applies to end-games, **"Look out for the stalemate!"**

In support of this truth we could quote innumerable instances of "masterly" blunders. But we propose rather to stick to examples which are worthy models for our play.

This warning is interpreted by Grandmaster Réti in the development of his brilliant study:

Two pieces—against two pawns. This is the balance. Surely, it is no problem to make such a superiority prevail? White's knight can stop Black's NP in two moves from QB3, and his king can prevent the Black ruler from intervening.

112.

R. RÉTI, 1922.

White wins.

This simple-looking plan can be realized in two ways:

1. N—K4, P—N6 2. N—B3, P—N7 3. K—B4 or

1. K—B4, P—N6 2. N—Q5, P—N7 3. N—B3

but now White's forces are too close to Black's king placed at the edge of the board. And we have not long to wait for the surprise move frustrating the win:

3. ..., P—N8 (Q)! 4. N×Q, K—R5! (A rare situation! The immobilized king on the offensive!)—and **draws** because after the bishop's move Black is stalemated.

Let us heed the warning then, and play:

1. K—K4!	P—N6
2. N—Q5	P—N7
3. N—B3	K—N6
4. K—Q3	and wins.

If we put a piece in the middle of an empty board and examine its powers there, our attention is first drawn to the squares that can be occupied by the piece in one move. These squares constitute the **range** of the piece, and are within the scope of its "control effect."

But what about the square on which the piece is posted, which is occupied by its own "body"? That square differs from the rest in that it is not vacant and therefore the file, the rank and the two diagonals running through it, are not entirely open. This means that on the square it occupies the piece causes **line interference**. This effect has nothing to do with the strength, value and kind of the piece but is derived solely from its material presence, and might, as distinct from the "control effect," be termed "corporal effect" for want of a better translation of Voellmy's **Körperwirkung.*** Now, let us move the piece. What happens? The "control effect" is shifted to another group of squares and also the "corporal effect" of line interference is transposed to another square. But this coincides with the **opening** of the lines (rank, file, diagonals) that run through the **vacated** square.

The **opening** of a **line** is a **natural result of every single move.** More precisely, it is the result of the first phase of the move when the square occupied is just being **vacated.**

The moving of a single piece on an otherwise empty board does not reveal the importance of line opening. But as soon as we examine the problem in connection with the position and "control effect" of another piece, it will leap to the eye that the opening of lines can extraordinarily increase the effectiveness of one single move and often extend the range of several unmoved pieces as well.

To get an idea of how "devastating" a single move can be, let us turn to the following curious diagram:

---

* Other definitions of this term have been given in various books on chess problems. For instance, Jacobs-White calls it a "dummy effect" in his work *Variation Play*. He also suggests the term "movebound" for "Zugzwang". (J. B.)

113.

G. R. REICHHELM, 1882.

White wins.

The "devastating" offensive move!
A printer's error? No, Black really
has **ten** kings on the board and you
will note that none of them is in
check.

And now White plays a single move:
1. N—K5!

114.

White wins.

And a good look at the diagram will
convince you that **all the ten of them
are mate!**

We have no intention of taking the
reader into the wonderland of fairy
chess and away from the realistic

appraisal of endings that can arise in
everyday practice. Nevertheless, this
playful product of fancy translated into terms of sober prose only teaches
that a multiple opening of lines **allows
ten different pieces to be attacked
at the same time with a single
move!** Of course, that is the limit.

In practice there is no need for such
peak achievements, it being quite
enough to exploit an occasional line
opening for a **double attack**.

DISCOVERY

A double attack made by way of
line opening involves the motif of
discovery whose best-known instance
is the discovered check.

Discovery is a situation in which
one of two pieces of the same camp
standing on the same line (file, rank,
or diagonal) moves away and by doing
so brings a third—hostile—piece within the scope of the one that stood behind it. In problem literature this formation is called a "battery" and discovery itself the "firing" of the "battery." The piece that actually carries
out the discovery is the "opening
piece," while the one behind it might
be referred to as the "piece in ambush."

A discovery turns into a double attack if both the "piece in ambush"
and the "opening piece" attack a hostile piece each.

* * *

In the next queen end-game—with
a perfect material equilibrium—
White's more active king, as an "opening piece," assures the victory.

115.

A. NEUMANN, 1887.

White wins.

White's extra pawn cannot be capitalized by technical means because of the perpetual checks threatening his king from all directions. Only an exchange of queens or a direct mating attack against Black's cornered king offers a winning chance. Both ends are served by the first move which threatens discovery.

   1. Q—Q5!!   Q×P ch

Black has not many alternatives for if 1. ..., Q—N6 (against K—B3) 2. K—B5 ch!, K—N8 (R7) 3. Q—Q1 (2) ch the exchange can be forced in two moves. After 1. ..., Q—N3 ch 2. K—B4 ch, K—R7! 3. Q—K5!, Q—Q6 4. P—N5, etc., White wins owing to the possible discovery. A similar motif appears also in the text continuation.

   2. K—B3!!   and wins,

because the direct (3. Q—Q1 or 3. Q—KR5) or indirect (3. K—B2 or 3. K—N3) intervention of the queen makes any defence impossible.

It is worth noting that, even in this two-move end-game the **threat** had to be **maintained** up to the moment when by "firing the battery" we were sure to hit the target. In the first move a side-stepping of the king with a counter-check would have been useless, but in the second it was already effective, for the mating threat could no longer parried.

* * *

From a practical point of view, it is always as well to think twice before putting a threat into effect, and to see whether we can intensify the existing threat or add something to it. In short, the threat should be maintained as long as its realization is likely to bring some measurable advantage. Soberness and patience are the signal virtues of the chess player!

It is very seldom that we cannot obtain some advantage from the possibility of discovered check; therefore we must not exhaust our ammunition too early and to no purpose. This is the moral we can draw from the next artistic example:

116.

V. BRON, 1947.

White wins.

It would be a good thing to win the queen by moving the rook with discovered check, but the queen is "sheltered" by the knight which closes the rook's rank.

Let us open this line and uncover the queen. But where should we move the knight? Black will obviously try to escape from the line of fire, therefore White has to prevent the possible ..., K—B3 or ..., K—Q4.

1. N—N6!!   Q—Q4 ch!

Let us observe that after any other move of the queen or after ..., K—Q3 or ..., P—K4 the rook would win Her Majesty with discovered check. ..., K—B3 or ..., K—Q4 are also wrong because of N—K7 ch.

2. K—R1!   P—K4!

On account of the threat neither the king nor the queen could move. The queen is relatively safely posted, therefore she must be chased off!

3. N—K7   Q—K3!

Making the best of a bad bargain! By **opening** his KN1—QR7 diagonal Black found a refuge for his queen. Therefore it would still be purposeless to "fire the battery."

4. K—N1!!

This "finesse" is absolutely essential not only on account of the escape line 4. K—N2?, P—N4! 5. K—B3?,

Q—R6 ch, but also because of the more hidden continuation: 4. K—N2?, P—N4! 5. K—N1!?, P—N5 6. K—N2, Q—KR3!!. In this latter variation Black has a double profit from his PN4—N5 move: he **closes** the rook's rank (towards the KR file) and **opens** his KR3—QB8 diagonal for the queen with the possible threat ..., Q—K6 ch after 7. K—B3.

4. — —   P—N3!

Black also tries to resort to trickery: he wants to delay his P—N4 till after White's K—N2, so as to achieve the former variation.

We have now reached the point at which level-headed deliberation is the better part of valour. Before charging head first to strike the decisive blow there is need for some circumspection.

5. K—R1!!   P—N4
6. K—N2!   P—N5
7. K—B3!   Q—R7

Any other move would be followed by mate or the loss of the queen. Thus Black's queen does not fall victim to direct attack but is forced to sacrifice herself so as to delay the mate.

8. R—N3 ch!   Q×B
9. R×Q   and wins.

* * *

A possibility of discovered check—with some advantage in space—can give special content to otherwise barren endings with bishops of **opposite colours.** A bishop hiding in the shadow of its king can take aim at a hostile king that is cramped for space and threaten him with a double attack or indeed with mate.

Examples:

117.

L. I. KUBBEL, 1937.

White wins.

It is more efficient to "camouflage" the battery temporarily than to fire it at once.

1. P—B6!	P—R8 (Q)!

Necessary opening of Black's KR7 for the bishop because if 1. . . ., K×P 2. P—B7, K—N2 3. K—Q6 ch!, K—B1 4. B—N4 ch White wins.

2. B×Q	B—R7

After 2. . . ., K×P the win is assured by 3. P—B7, K—N2 4. K—Q6 ch, K—B1 5. B—N7 ch!, K×B 6. K—Q7. As we see, the discovery assists the pawn in two variations. In the third, however, it makes possible the winning of Black's bishop.

3. P—B7!	B×P
4. K—B6!	B—R4 (Q1)

The bishop may not leave the diagonal under penalty of 5. K—N6 mate (!).

5. K—N5 (Q7) ch	and wins.

Perhaps more eventful but essentially similar is the next end-game.

118.

J. HASEK, 1923.

White wins.

To set up a battery it seems most expedient to play 1. K—B6. But in that case 1. . . ., B—N1! 2. P—B6, B—Q4 3. P—B7, N2 would solve B—Q4 3. P—B7, B—N2 would solve Black's problems. Nor is the other attempt 1. B—B1 more promising since after 1. . . ., P—B5! (opening the diagonal), 2. P—B6, B—Q6! 3. P—B7, B—R3 would take the sting out of the pawn. A third attractive possibility: 1. K—Q6, P—R7! 2. P—B6 (2. B—K5 ch?, K—N1 3. P—B6, P—B5!) 2. . . ., P—R8 (Q) 3. B—K5 ch would meet the case if Black captured the bishop: but unfortunately there is no win after

3. ..., K—N1!! since 4. B×Q would again be met by ..., P—B5 and ..., B—B4.

By a process of elimination we sooner or later arrive at the sound opening move:

| 1. P—B6! | P—R7 |
| 2. K—B6!! | B—N1! |

If 2. ..., P—R8 (Q) White can set up his battery with 3. B—K5! and the victory is assured. (3. ..., Q—R7! 4. P—B7, Q—N1 5. K—K7 ch!) After the text continuation 3. B—K5? is wrong owing to ..., B—Q4, but White may bravely face up to the seeming dangers of Black's queening.

| 3. P—B7! | P—R8 (Q) ch |
| 4. B—K5! | Q—KN8 |

White threatened 5. K—N6 discovered mate, therefore Black's reply was a forced one.

| 5. P—B8 (Q) | Q—N5 |

Otherwise 6. Q×P or—in case of 5. ..., Q—N2 ch?—6. K×P wins.

| 6. Q—R8! | Q—R4 |

Black must defend both his KN3 and KR8. If 6. ..., Q—N8 7. Q—B3 wins. (The threat is Q—R5 and Q—R3 since Black must not play ..., B—R2 because of the reply K—B7!)

7. Q—N2!	Q—R3 ch
8. Q—N6!	Q×Q ch
9. K×Q ch	and mate!

* * *

Very similar in its features to the discovered check is the **check with discovery** (Voellmy's **Schachabzug**). In this case not the "piece in ambush" but the "opening piece" gives check to the opponent's king. This action extends the range of the piece lying in ambush, offering a possibility of attack on the open line.

In end-games this motif draws our attention most of all to the perils incident to opening a line with a **pawn**.

119.

H. RINCK, 1920.

White wins.

Though tucked away behind two pawns in the initial position, White's bishop manages in a few moves to capture the hostile queen which is conveniently standing on the same diagonal. All one has to do is to force Black's king to such squares as can be attacked by the line-vacating pawns with check.

| 1. R—R6 ch | K—K4 |

The seventh rank is a danger zone for fear of 2. R—R7 ch. 1. ..., K—B4 would be followed by 2. P—K4 ch and in case of 2. ..., K×P or 2. ..., K—N5, 3. P—B3 ch wins; after 2. ..., K—K4 or 2. ..., K—N4 3. P—B4 ch leads to the same result. Finally if Black chooses the continuation 1. ..., K—B4 2. P—K4 ch, K—B5! 3. R—B6 ch! will force the king into the range of White's KBP.

The same fate awaits Black after 1. ..., K—Q4 2. P—K4 ch!, K—B5 3. R—B6 ch!

| 2. P—B4 ch! | K—K5 |

If 2. ..., K—B4 or 2. ..., K—Q4, 3. P—K4 ch.

| 3. R—K6 ch | K—Q4 (B4) |
| 4. P—K4 ch! | and wins. |

* * *

White's one and only pawn is the hero of the next queen end-game:

120.

L. I. KUBBEL, 1927.

White wins.

| 1. Q—B3 ch | K—K4! |

If 1. ..., K—N4, then 2. Q—N2 ch!, K—R4 (3) 3. Q—N6 mate or 2. ..., K—B4 (5) 3. P—K4 (3) ch wins the queen owing to the opening of the second rank.

| 2. Q—K3 ch | K—B4 |

2. ..., K—Q4?? 3. Q×KP ch wins.

| 3. Q—B2 ch! | K—K4! |
| 4. Q—R2 ch! | and wins, |

because any of the four possible moves would be followed by the opening of the second rank with check: 4. ..., K—Q4 (B4) 5. P—K4 ch! or 4. ..., K—Q5 5. P—K3 ch! or 4. ..., K—K5 5. P×P ch! and Black loses his queen and the game.

* * *

If subtle manoeuvres get us nowhere we may often find it expedient to resort to line opening in order to help an insignificant pawn to promotion. We cannot expect our opponent to hand us the advantage accruing from opening a line on a plate—it is much more likely that we shall have to work hard to reach a winning position. Discovery with check, the motif we have seen in the former example, is enforced by energetic means in the next study:

121.

V. and M. PLATOV, 1911.

White wins.

White has a strong passed pawn, but the position of his king is rather shaky. These two factors determine the line of attack and counter-attack.

1. P—B7!	Q—K4!

A strong reply against the menacing 2. R—R8 ch. Black plans to play 2. ..., K—N6 threatening ..., Q—N7 mate. The queen also prevents the annoying 3. R—N8 ch.

But Black's move has a drawback to it, one that is not easily spotted at this stage ...

2. R—R8 ch	K—N6
3. R—R3 ch!!	K×R

This is the right moment for White to queen and gain time. But his troubles are not over yet.

4. P—B8 (Q) ch	K—N6!

After 4. ..., K—R7 5. Q—R8 ch White's queen would appear on the scene; but now reserves too must be mobilized to decide the issue.

5. Q—N4 ch!!	K×Q
6. P—Q4 ch!	

This possibility of opening the diagonal was the drawback to Black's first move. It was of course "present" in the initial position, our job has merely been to spot it and find a way to exploit it to White's benefit.

White wins, although the annihilation of Black's pawns with the bishop still calls for accurate and careful play.

PRELIMINARY OPENING OF A LINE

If by moving a piece we open a line which will be occupied by the offensive "line-piece" (queen, rook or bishop) only on the next move, we speak of **preliminary line opening.** The attribute "preliminary" applies not to the motif of the line opening itself but to the fact that the open line will not be immediately utilized for some tactical operation, but at a later stage.

122.

H. RINCK, 1917.

White wins.

In this situation, for instance, the piece for which we have to open a line **now** in order to secure its successful intervention, is not even on the board yet.

1. B—Q4!!   P×B
2. P—R8 (Q)   P—R8 (Q)

And now we can see why it was necessary to vacate the QR file: White's queen goes into action with checks and defeats her cornered counterpart.

3. Q—R8 ch   K—N7
4. Q—N7 ch   K—R7!
5. Q—R6 ch   K—N8!

In this way Black can at least hamper the queen's advance, though the achievement of the winning position—the capture of the QP by tempo included—is only a matter of time. The instructive technique of liquidation:

6. Q—Q3 ch!, K—R7! 7. Q—B4 ch!, K—R6! (7. ..., K—N8?? 8. Q—B2 mate!) 8. Q—R6 ch!, K—N7 9. Q—N5 ch, K—R6 10. Q—R5 ch, K—N7 11. Q—N4 ch, K—R7 12. Q—R4 ch!, K—N7 (..., K—N8? is wrong again because of mate!) 13. Q×P ch, K—N8 14. Q—K4 ch, K—R7 15. Q—R4 ch!, K—N7 16. Q—N4 ch, K—R7—and now the coup de grâce: 17. K—B2!, White wins.

* * *

In the next—somewhat more complicated—example White has first to open the way for his bishop so that his minor pieces can co-operate smoothly in their fight against Black's queen.

123.

L. I. KUBBEL, 1925.

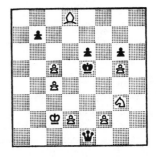

White wins.

1. P—B6!!   P×P

Though the sense of this line-opening pawn sacrifice is not obvious at once, Black cannot help accepting it, otherwise the pawn can no longer be stopped. (After 1. ..., Q—QR8? 2. B—B6 ch wins.)

2. B—B7 ch   K—Q5
3. B—R5!!

This "quiet" threatening move demonstrates the queen's plight. It is difficult to find how 4. B—B3 ch and 5. P—Q4 ch (with discovery) can be averted, for after 3. ..., Q—N8 4. N—K2 ch wins. In case of 3. ..., Q—QR8 or 3. ..., Q—K4 4. B—B3 ch decides the issue. If the king moves, White immediately wins by giving check with the QP.

There **would** be only one possibility...

3. — —   Q×BP

...if we had not vacated the QR7—KN1 diagonal before, just for the purpose!

4. B—N6 ch   P—B4
5. B×P ch!   K×B
6. N—K4 ch   and wins.

* * *

Nor can the third line-piece, the rook, display its full powers unless it has open files and ranks at its disposal. The rook's freedom of action is hampered much more by the presence of pawns than is the bishop's; rook manoeuvres are, therefore, very often preceded by some line-opening pawn sacrifice.

124.

L. I. KUBBEL, 1916.

White wins.

Here the most promising plan is to rush the rook to the KN file. Therefore:

1. P—K6!   P×P

The pawn must be taken, to take the sting out of the mate threat on the KN file. This could not be parried even by Black's closing his fourth rank, for after 1. . . ., P—Q4 2. R—B2, P×N 3. R—KN2 the mate would be inevitable.

2. R—KN5!   Q—B3!

If 2. . . ., Q—N2 White wins by the forced opening of the seventh rank: 3. R—N8 ch, K—B2 4. N—Q6 ch! P×N 5. R—N7 ch. We shall come back to this motif later.

3. R—N8 ch   K—B2
4. N—N5 ch   K—B3
5. N—B3!!

Not only closes the queen's diagonal against the threat of . . ., Q—R8 ch, but also threatens mate (R—KB8). If Black tries to parry the threat by way of 5. . . ., K—B2 or 5. . . ., Q×N he would lose his queen owing to the extended scope of the knight or the rook. (5. N—K5 ch or 5. R—B8 ch.)

5. — —   P—K4

Only this "square vacating" is possible, yet it has the drawback that the sixth rank is also opened for White's rook.

6. R—N6 ch   K—B4
7. R×Q   and wins.

* * *

125.

A. A. TROITSKY, 1897.
(Amended by A. Kotsis, 1970.)

White wins.

White's active pieces decide the course of events by way of line opening. This possibility is offered in several variations.

| 1. Q—B8 ch | K—K3! |

1. ..., K—N3 would result in 2. Q—B7 ch, K—R3 3. N—B5 mate. But we shouldn't overlook that in case of 1. ..., K—K4? 2. **N—B4 ch!** would bring about the desired line opening because after the removal of the obstacle on the Q file (2. ..., P× N) 3. Q—B5 ch would win the queen.

| 2. N—N7! | Q—Q7 |

After any other queen move (2. ..., Q—N3 or —B2 or —B6) 3. N—B5 ch would follow and Black's queen would soon fall victim to a double attack. The result is also the same after 2. ..., Q—R2 3. N—Q8 ch! etc.

Besides the text move Black's K8 also seems to offer a safe refuge to the queen; after 2. ..., Q—K8, however, 3. N—B5 ch, K—K4 4. N—Q3 ch!! would force the opening of the K file with the continuation 4. ..., P×N 5. Q—K8 ch and 6. Q×Q. This pattern appears also for the third time in the text continuation.

3. N—B5 ch	K—K4
4. Q—R8 ch!	K—Q3
5. N×P ch!!	P×N
6. Q—Q8 ch	and wins.

Note. This end-game study, as originally published by Troitsky in his **500 Endspielstudien**-without Black's QRP—proved incorrect. That is why, in the first edition of this book, we published an "amended position" from the Sutherland—Lommer collection (1234 **Modern End-Game Studies**, No. 1010), with the Knight placed from KN1 to QR1 and no QRP added. A young Hungarian chessplayer, A. Kotsis, pointed out, however, that this replacement does not eliminate the error, in fact it gives rise to another one. If the Knight is posted on KN1, White can also win with 1. Q—B8 ch, K—K3 2. N—B5! (2. ..., Q—B2 3. N—N7 ch, K—Q2 4. Q—K8 ch, K—Q3 5. Q—N6 ch, K—K2 6. Q—K6 ch, K—B1 7. Q—B6 ch, K—N1 8. N—B5!, K—R2 9. N—K7, Q—Q2 ch 10. K—N5!).

If we eliminate the QRP, a "by-solution" will emerge: 1. Q—B8 ch, K—K3 2. N—B5, K—Q2 3. Q—Q6 ch, K—B1 4. N—K7 ch, K—N2 5. Q—B6 ch, K—R2 6. N—B8 ch,

K—N1 7. N—Q6!, Q—B2 8. Q—K8 ch, K—R2 9. N—N5 ch, etc. and White wins. (A detailed analysis is given in the *Magyar Sakkélet*, No. 9, 1970.)

CLEARING THE PATH, CLEARING A SQUARE

There are also instances of line opening in which the piece moving away does not open a line completely, but only in part, leaving room for the movement of another piece. Sometimes the stress is only laid on the square that has been vacated by the "opening" piece. This is what we call **clearing a square**. If again the opening move lengthens a line for another piece to pass along it, we speak of **clearing the path**. The two concepts need not be sharply separated from each other or from the concept of line opening for that matter, since the underlying motif is the same in all. The difference in form will be illustrated by some examples.

126.

L. I. KUBBEL, 1935.

White wins.

1. P—K5!

This opening move all of a sudden increases the activity of White's pieces. Black is threatened by 2. P—N4 mate.

| 1. — — | P×P |
| 2. N—K4 ch | |

The knight move closes the recently opened fourth rank. It will be seen that the first move not only opened the fourth rank for the rook but also vacated a square for the knight. Both the "square" and the "line" are important here. The former because it enables the knight to take up an offensive position near the queen, the latter because on account of the discovery threat Black's king is shut off from the QN, QB and Q squares of the fourth rank. (2. ...., K—N5(B5 or Q5) 3. N—B6 ch!

| 2. — — | K—N4! |
| 3. P—N4!! | K—R5 |

Forced, since White threatened 4. N—B3 mate! Now White renews his threat and forces the win of Black's queen with a discovered check.

| 4. K—N2! | K×P |
| 5. N—B6 ch | and wins. |

127.

A. P. GULYAEV, 1930.

White wins.

White's rook is unable to leave the eighth rank, yet it is obvious that it must **vacate** the QR8 square for the pawn, since Black too is ready to queen. To vacate the square is in itself not enough, however. We must also reckon with the possibility that after queening (P—R8 (Q) ch) Black can interpose his bishop (..., B—R6), therefore some other opportunity of further intervention must be sought. Accordingly:

1. R—R8!

vacates the square for the pawn and **opens the way** for the prospective queen in advance!

1. — —	P—N8 (Q)
2. P—R8 (Q) ch	B—R6
3. Q—N8 ch!	K—R8

The activity achieved by line vacating slackens now, but the rook can still render good services by driving off Black's queen from guarding her KN2 pawn.

4. R—R1!	Q×R
5. Q×P ch	and wins,

because the queen can gradually approach the king, by continuous checks (Q—B7—B6—K6—K5—Q5—Q4—B4—B3—N3), and mates by Q×B. (The finish is a typical example of time-gaining manoeuvres.)

* * *

A fine example of preliminary line opening is shown by the next study:

128.

L. I. KUBBEL, 1914.

White wins.

Even those well versed in queen-trapping combinations realizable by the concerted action of rook and knight and who "see" a few things at first glance (e. g. that there is no risk in playing 1. R—R1 !; or even in 2. R—KN1 after Black's ..., Q—N7) will find it hard to hit upon the first move:

1. P—N6!!

Strange as it may be, this opening move paves the way for the intervention of the rook on QR8 (!) with a view to winning the queen!

The pawn must be taken lest it be promoted after 1. ..., Q—N7 2. P×P, Q—N5 ch 3. N—B3 ch.

1.— —   P×P
2. R—R1!   Q—N7!

2. ..., Q×R or ..., Q×RP would be followed by a knight fork to king and queen. The same fate would await Black after 2. ..., Q×QP 3. R—R4 ch, K—K4 4. R—R5!, Q×R 5. N—B4 ch.

But White can force Black to capture the QP—though from the other side.

3. R—KN1!   Q×QP

3. ...,Q×R? 4. N—B3 ch, etc.

4. R—N4 ch   K—B4!
5. R—N5!

We can also ensnare the queen on this wing, but only because we have previously taken care to vacate the KN file to the fifth rank.

5. — —   Q×R
6. N—K4 ch   and wins.

We devote a special chapter to the examination of knight forks and other extraordinary feats of the knight. (See: The Range of the Knight, pp. 190—193.)

* * *

It is enough to remember—on the basis of the examples in this chapter—that **in order to increase the mobility and activity of our pieces, we have to secure paths, space, open lines for them.** We should watchfully explore the chances of increasing the range of our pieces; and remove obstacles as quickly as possible.

Nimzovitch once said: "Do well by your pieces—and they will be grateful for it!"

You can't do better by them than to give them ample elbow-room . . .

In the previous chapter we have pointed out that the pieces display, besides their "control effect," a certain "corporal effect" which is worthy of particular attention during tactical operations.

The "corporal effect" is manifested in that the piece, irrespective of its kind, closes, by its very presence, the file, rank and diagonals running through the square occupied by it.

If we regard line opening as a natural consequence of each move (line interference), we may say the same about line closing. **Every single move leads to the opening of certain lines** and, **at the same time, to the closing of others.** The opening is the consequence of vacating a square, the closing is the result of *occupying* another with the same piece.

If we examine the closing of lines not as a general phenomenon, but as an intended operation, we should begin with weighing its pros and cons, that is its **useful** and **harmful** sides.

While the opening of lines tends to increase the mobility and extend the range of the pieces, line closing evidently has the reverse effect; it restricts both the mobility of the pieces and their scope.

We may accordingly benefit from a line-closing manoeuvre if it eventually **restricts the mobility of the opponent's pieces** without interfering with the freedom of movement in our own camp.

In principle, line interference can be effected, like line opening, in two different ways.

One is to play a piece so that it **obstructs** a mobile piece of the opponent, the other to **force** the opponent to make a move by which he **closes the line of his own piece.** Besides these methods we can also make use of line interference by sparing a hostile piece that is closing a line and is thus harmful to its own camp— and, if necessary, by blocking it on its square. In short, by preventing the opponent from opening a line or by avoiding a disadvantageous line opening we can make capital of some existing line interference as well.

In case of line interference it is always the "corporal effect" and not the "control effect" of the "closing" piece that restricts the freedom of movement.

129.

A. A. TROITSKY, 1924.

White wins.

White's task is to shut off Black's rook from the Q file and, by controlling the eighth rank, keep it away from the Q8 square. This task cannot be solved by 1. K—Q2 owing to the continuation 1. ..., R—K5! 2. K—Q3, R—QN5! and 3. ..., R—N1. It will be clear already at this stage that there is no point in chasing the rook to another rank where it can roam freely, for it is exactly on the third rank that it enjoys the least freedom of movement, being impeded by its own king.

1. B—N6!

This move does not "close" the Q file to the rook, yet it takes the Q3 square from it through the **control effect** of the bishop. The same control effect extends directly to the K4 and K8 squares, and indirectly to K5 and K6. (In case of 1. ..., R—K3 White can pin the rook by 2. B—B7; and if Black chooses to play 1. ..., R—K4

then follows 2. B—B7 ch and White's Q5 square is forbidden to the rook, leaving no defence against 3. P—Q7 and 4. P—Q8 (Q).

That is why Q3 must be guarded from KN6 and not from K2. After 1. B—K2 Black can secure a draw by 1. ..., R—K3! 2. P—Q7, R—Q3 ch, etc.

1. — —   R—R6

Only in this way or by 1. ..., R—KB6 can Black manage to play his rook to his first rank. There is no essential difference. ..., R—R6 is only preferable because Black can prolong his agony by several "spite checks."

2. P—Q7   R—R1
3. B—K8   and wins,

because there are no more checks for Black after 3. ..., R—R8 ch 4. K—K2, R—R7 ch 5. K—K3!, R—R6 ch 6. K—K4!, R—R5 ch 7. K—K5; nor can he approach White's Q8 either from the eighth rank or the Q file.

The winning move (3. B—K8) has demonstrated a typical case of line interference by the simple interposition of a White piece.

* * *

As mentioned before, line interference may also arise through one side obstructing the path of its **own** piece by another. This is termed self-interference. Being in principle harmful, self-interference is mostly a situation one of the players is forced into, rather than chosen by him voluntarily.

130.

H. WEENINK, 1917.

White wins.

The diagram is rather reminiscent of the preceding one, and in fact the solution hinges again on the prudent exploitation of the motif of line interference.

If the natural opening move 1. P—R7 is met by 1. ..., R—N1, the line-interference manoeuvre introduced by 2. B—N3 ch! and completed by 3. B—N8! leaps to the eye. This would be of the very same type we have seen in the previous study. Black, however, can put up a more stubborn resistance.

1. P—R7	R—N7 ch!

This intermediate check puts a spoke in White's wheel which seemed to roll so smoothly towards victory, for now his king must stay shy of the third rank, otherwise Black could

safely accept the bishop to be offered on KN3, capturing it with check. Nor may the king give up his watch over QR1 and QR2 for fear of ..., R—QR8 (7) with the capture of the pawn.

The bishop should therefore intervene by another kind of line interference.

2. K—N1!	R—N8 ch
3. B—K1!!	

Line interference again. The only thing out of the common is that the bishop is undefended, and thus easily removed by Black.

What has then been the purpose of this sacrifice? To force Black into **self-interference.** We can see that the presence of the king on the K file is disadvantageous to Black on account of his barring the rook's way towards his K1.

Though Black is not compelled to accept the sacrifice, after the possible 3. ..., R—N1 White wins again with 4. B—N3 ch! etc.

3. — —	R×B ch
4. K—N2	R—K7 ch
5. K—N3	R—K6 ch
6. K—N4!	

Naturally not 6. K—R4? because of 6. ..., R—K8! and 7. ..., R—QR8.

6. — —	R—K5 ch
7. K—N5!	and wins,

since the promotion can no longer be prevented.

* * *

131.

J. BEHTING, 1893.

White wins.

This end-game is a fine example of preliminary line interference by pawn sacrifice.

1. P—B6!   P×P

1. ..., P—R8 (Q)? 2. R—R1 ch, K—N7 3. R×Q, K×R 4. P—B7 wins. Also 1. ..., P—B7 offers no help, since after 2. R—R1 ch, P—B8 (Q) 3. R×Q, K×R 4. P—B7, P—R8 (Q) 5. P—B8 (Q) ch, K—N7 White forces the king to play ..., K—R7 and then he wins with K—B2. (See the text variation of Diagram No. 122.)

2. K×P   P—R8 (N)!

2. ..., P—R8 (Q) ch 3. K—N3 and the mate or the queen's loss is inevitable. The cornered knight is of course no match for the rook, but in view of the extra BP. White has to play very accurately.

3. R—N2   P—B4
4. R—K2!   P—B5

White's third move was only a tempo move, but the fourth was very essential and deeply calculated. It is very important that the rook be now placed on K2 in order to prevent the escape of the knight via K3 (..., N—K6) after K×P.

5. K×P   N—B7
6. K—B3!   N—R8
7. R—KR2   and wins.

★ ★ ★

In order to force through the closing of a line even major sacrifices may prove expedient if the returns are expected to be in proportion to the "investment." The aim in view is mostly to restrict the range of a queen or a rook. In Diagram No. 130 White's queening cost a bishop; in the next end-game a knight is sacrificed to curtail the radius of Black's queen.

132.

L. I. KUBBEL, 1924.

White wins.

Menaced by Black's far-advanced passed pawn, White seeks his chances in a mating attack.

| 1. P—N6 ch | K—N1 |

White's pawn move—opening the fifth rank—would have led to mate if Black had played 1. ..., K—R3?. (2. R—R5 ch)

| 2. R×P | K—B1 |

The danger of mate is over and Black's queen is in the making. How to counteract this? We must contrive to intensify the attack by bringing White's king to help and that without permitting Black to interfere.

| 3. N—Q5!! | KP×N |

The sacrifice must be accepted on account of the mate threat. 3. ..., K—K1 would be met by 4. N—K(B) 3. Now, with the Q file closed, White's king can safely set out his Q6 to seal Black's fate.

| 4. K—B5! | P—Q8 (Q) |
| 5. K—Q6! | Q—K8 |

The mate can only be avoided by interposing the queen (that is why Black has taken the knight with his KP), but after the liquidation the ensuing pawn end-game is favourable for White.

6. R—N8 ch	Q—K1
7. R×Q ch	K×R
8. P—B3!	and wins,

because White will promote his BP after 8. ..., K—Q1 9. K×P, K—K2 10. K×P, K—B3 11. P—B4, K×P

12. K—K6. 8. K×P would also win, though White must be very careful. After 8. ..., P—Q5! 9. K—Q5, K—K2 White has to force Black's king to retreat: 10. K—K5!!. 10. K×P? would be premature since after 10. ..., K—B3 11. K—Q5, K×P 12. K—K6, K—R2!! 13. P—B4, P—N4! 14. K—B5, P—N5! 15. K×P, K—N3! the position is a dead draw.

* * *

Here again we have a model example of the "harmful piece" to illustrate that sometimes line interference may also be brought about in a "passive" way. All we have to do is to curb our greed and spare the opponent's line-closing piece, no matter how alluring its capture may seem.

133.

J. MORAVEC, 1913.

White wins.

It would not do to stop Black's RP by 1. R—R4, because after 1. ..., P—N4 2. R—R5 Black can secure a draw even with a single pawn. It is far better to rush after the pawn with the king, though not with the purpose of overtaking it, but rather with the same mating threat in mind that we have seen in Diagram No. 131. We also remember the trouble we took there to close the long diagonal! Therefore:

1. K—R7!!	P—R5
2. K—N6	P—R6
3. K—N5	P—R7
4. K—N4!	P—R8 (Q)
5. K—N3!	and wins,

because Black cannot parry the mate threat with . . ., Q—KR1 owing to the NP closing the diagonal. White also wins after 4. . . ., P—R8 (N): 5. K—B3!, P—N3 6. R—N2, P—N4 7. R—Q2!, P—N5 ch 8. K×P, N—B7 ch 9. K—B3! etc. (A familiar pattern!)

It is also worth our while to examine the alternative which demonstrates the expediency of sparing the harmful pawn: 1. K—R7, P—N4 2. K—R6. P—N5 and now 3. K—N5!! wins. 3. K×P?, P—N6 4. K—R4, P—N7 5. K—R (N)3, K—R8! 6. R×P would be **stalemate!**

* * *

After having outlined the concept, the importance and the technique of line interference, let us get acquainted with types of end-games in which the line-closing manoeuvre is of very frequent and indeed a characteristic occurrence.

In the great majority of end-games the capitalization of a **passed pawn** is of decisive importance. An advancing pawn can be stopped by a knight from certain points of the board and also by a queen from several directions. Line interference is no weapon against a knight which simply jumps over the head of any obstacle and of little avail against a queen. If on the other hand the duty of stopping a pawn devolves on a hostile rook or bishop, its radius of action will mostly be restricted to a single line (diagonal) whose closing may and should be thought of.

That is why **line-interference manoeuvres accomplished with a view to promoting a passed pawn are mostly encountered in bishop and rook end-games.** The most frequently applied tactical means of curtailing the scope of a bishop is self-interference with pawn (or possibly piece) sacrifice. **The intervention of a rook** can usually be prevented by the interposition of a knight or a bishop. We have to point out that the **materially weaker side can achieve surprising successes with line-interference combinations especially in positions where he is an exchange to the bad.**

Let us look at some examples of closing a **diagonal**:

134.

H. MATTISON, 1914.

White wins.

1. P—B6!

After 1. N—Q6 ch, K—Q1 or
1. N—K5, B—K7 Black can stop
White's RP. Even 1. K—B2? gets us
no further because of 1. ..., B×N!
2. P—B6, P×P 3. P—R6, B—Q4
4. P—R7, P—B4.

1. — —	P×P
2. P—R6	B—B6
3. N—N5!	B—Q4

3. ..., K—Q1? 4. P—R7! wins.

4. N—K6!	P—B4

White threatened to "lock up" the
diagonal permanently with N—B5,
even in case of 4. ..., K—Q2. Now
Black opens the diagonal, only he has
no bishop to control it.

5. N—B7 ch	K—Q2
6. N×B	K—B1

6. ..., K—B3 is a Zugzwang position (see Diagram No. 77). White's
king simply walks up to take the BP
and wins. The same happens also
after the text continuation only the
RP must be secured first against ...,
K—N1—R2.

7. N—B3	K—N1

7. ..., K—B2 8. N—R4! etc.

8. N—N5!	P—B5
9. K—B2	and wins.

★ ★ ★

In the fight of a knight and pawn
against a bishop, line interference is
part and parcel of the elementary
technique of achieving victory. A
pawn may be advanced to a square
controlled by the bishop if we previously close the bishop's diagonal by
interposing the knight.

Of course, we cannot think of effectively restricting the bishop's scope by
the short-range knight unless our
pawn is rather close to the promotion
square. Often it is also necessary to
make use of the many-sided indirect
threats of the knight.

135.

KLING and HORWITZ, 1851.

White wins.

1. K—K7!	K—R2

1. ..., B—R6 ch 2. K—K8, B—B1
(2. ..., B—B4 3. N—N6 and 4. N—
K7!) 3. P—B7 ch, K—N2 4. N—
N6!, B—Q3 5. N—K7 and White
wins.

2. P—B7	B—R6 ch
3. K—K8	K—N2

Threatening ..., K—B3, therefore
White's line interference must be
accomplished with a gain of tempo.

| 4. N—B4! | B—N5 (B1) |

4. ..., B—B4 5. N—N6!, B—Q3 6. N—Q5, etc., leads to the main variation.

| 5. N—K3! | B—B4 |

Of course 5. ..., K—B3 was wrong on account of 6. N—Q5 ch.

| 6. N—Q5 | B—Q3 |
| 7. N—K7! | and wins. |

The piquancy of the finish lies in the fact that after 6. ..., B—B1 too the winning move is 7. N—K7! From this we can see that Black was in Zugzwang. It is worth noting, however, that the Zugzwang is the result of White's knight (and also the king) blocking the way. Thus the line interference makes its effect in another sense as well.

★ ★ ★

Finally a very colourful and lively bishop-ending demonstrates line-interference motifs on diagonals.

136.

HERBSTMAN and GORGIEV, 1929.

White wins.

| 1. P—B6! |

A motif we have seen before. But it is followed by a new one.

| 1. — — | B—K5 ch! |
| 2. P—B3!! |

This rather "ephemeral" line interference soon proves to be a valuable gain of tempo, resulting in a quicker mobilization of the king (!). It is worth remembering that while the king is an important protagonist in most end-games his intervention is of **particular** significance in the presence of bishops of opposite colours.

2. — —	B×P ch
3. K—R2!	P×P
4. P—R6!	P—B4!

Now Black would be relieved of his troubles after 5. P—R7?, P—Q5!. Therefore some other threat must be interpolated by which we can eventually frustrate Black's plan of opening the diagonal with ..., P—Q5.

| 5. K—N3! | B—R8 |
| 6. K—R4! | K—N2 |

White has threatened Black with no less than 7. B—B8! mate. The forced flight of Black's king, however, makes possible the blockade of the QP with the bishop.

| 7. B—K5 ch | K—B2 |
| 8. B—Q4!! | and wins, |

since neither the capture nor its refusal can prevent queening.

In end-games without pawns a knight or a bishop is equivalent to a rook, hence the exchange has no particular importance. If we have one or two pawns besides the minor piece, they may often suffice to tip the scales.

Line interference is also a handy weapon in the struggle between rook and knight, or rook and bishop.

137.

F. LAZARD, 1911.

White wins.

In face of the threat . . ., R—K1 and . . ., K—N3 (or R3) the knight has to perform a miracle, indeed, in order to secure the promotion of one of the pawns.

1. N—B4 ch!	K—R3
2. N—K6!	R—K1!

White threatened to close the rank with 3. N—Q8. He does the same now with a pawn sacrifice from the other side.

3. P—N8 (Q)!	R×Q
4. N—B8!	

In Black's place most players would resign now, but the game is not finished yet; Black can still prevent an immediate queening.

4. — —	R—N4

In case of the unsuspecting 5. P—K8 (Q)? Black would play . . ., R—K4 ch! to be stalemated after 6. Q×R. To avert this threat a move must be found that prevents both . . ., R—K4 and the defensive . . ., R—N1 with one stroke.

5. N—N6!!	and wins.

The crowning line interference is one of fascinating efficiency.

138.

L. I. KUBBEL, 1909.

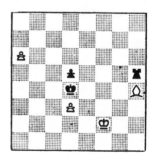

White wins.

1. P—R7	R—B4 ch

1. . . ., R—R1? 2. B—B6 ch wins.

2. K—K2	R—K4 ch

2. ..., R—B1 fails against 3. B—B6 ch!, K—B4 4. B—K7 ch! etc.

3. K—Q2	R—K1
4. B—B2 ch	K—K4
5. B—N3 ch	K—K3
6. B—N8!	and wins.

★ ★ ★

The problem of parrying the rook's harassing checks is also posed in the next end-game. The hero is, however, not the king but the bishop.

139.

J. VANCURA, 1916.

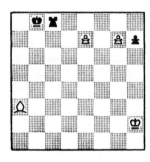

White wins.

1. P—K8 (Q)!	R×Q
2. B—B8	R—K7 ch
3. K—R3	

3. K—N3?, R—K3 and 4. ..., R—KN3.

3. — —	R—K6 ch
4. K—R4	R—K5 ch

3. — —	R—K6 ch
4. K—R4	R—K5 ch

If 4. ..., R—K8, then 5. B—Q6 ch, K—N2 6. P—N8 (Q), R—R8 ch 7. K—N4, R—N8 ch 8. B—N3 etc., wins.

5. K—R5	R—K4 ch
6. K—R6	R—K8!

The strongest! In case of 6. ..., R—K3 ch?, 7. K×P and 8. P—N8 (Q) easily wins. In the present situation, however, 7. B—Q6 ch? would be a blunder, since after 7. ..., K—N2 Black can threaten either..., R—K1 or ..., R—KR8—N8 ch.

7. B—B5!!	R—K1
8. K×P	R—Q1

Black threatens to pin the pawn with ..., R—Q2. White parries it by way of another preliminary line interference.

9. B—K7!!	R—QB1

If 9. ..., R—K1 10. B—B8 wins—as well as in the text variation—because..., R—K2 cannot be played.

10. B—B8	R—B2
11. B—Q6	and wins.

★ ★ ★

In this example the vigorous bishop parries the intervention of the rook, by making full use of its line-closing corporal effect and its control effect.

140.

F. SACKMANN, 1912.

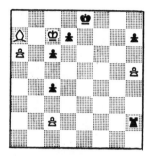

White wins.

1. B—B2!!

Time-gaining line interference that opens another line. In the next chapter we shall enter into a more detailed analysis of such motifs. Now White needs two moves to promote his pawn, therefore the task is to prevent the rook from seizing the QR file in two moves.

| 1. — — | R×P |

After 1. ..., R—R8 2. B—Q4 would control White's QR1; and after 1. ..., R—R6 2. B—B5 White's QR3. As will be seen, every rook move is appropriately met by White and eventually the QR file is completely closed.

| 2. B—N6! | R—R6 |
| 3. B—B5 | R—R8 |

There would have been no sense in ..., R—R4, for the bishop barred the way.

4. B—Q4!	R—R6
5. B—N2!	R—R4
6. B—B3!	and wins,

since there is not a single rank left by which the rook can reach the QR file.

* * *

In similar positions line interference may serve the purpose of shutting out the defence as well as intensifying the attack, e. g. the side having a rook also possesses a pawn. In this case the only conceivable way to win the protected pawn is to close the line of the defending rook.

141.

W. von HOLZHAUSEN, 1903.

Draw.

Obviously, White cannot afford to let Black's king rush to the aid of his pawn. When trying to prevent this we shall find that the natural-seeming plan of line interference (1. B—B6 and 2. B—N2) cannot be implemented, for after 1. B—B6 Black can reply 1. ..., R—Q3 and 2. ..., R—R3 with an easy win.

Though White's only defence admittedly lies in his closing the line by B—N2, he must find another approach, one that would foil Black's every attempt at a counter-attack.

1. B—B7!!	K×P

1. ..., R—Q2 would have been met by the simple 2. B—B4 ch and 3. K×P. The potential bishop check also frustrated the defensive 1. ..., R—K7.

2. B—K6!	R—Q3 (or any other move)
3. B—R3!	R—Q7
4. B—N2	and draws.

FOCAL POINT

An interesting and very effective instance of line interference is if, on a certain square, we succeed in closing the lines of two hostile pieces operating in two different directions. The point (square) at which the control effects of two pieces meet is the **focal point** (focal square). Usually a focal point can be closed by a negative sacrifice, by placing a piece en prise. This is, however, a forcing action, since it shuts out two defensive pieces. The acceptance of the sacrifice has the result that the capturing piece closes the line of its companion behind it.

142.

T. B. GORGIEV, 1936.

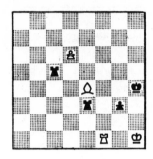

White wins.

1. P—Q7	P—N7 ch!

The only chance to hold up the pawn. In case of 1. ..., R—Q6 2. B×R, R—Q4 White wins after 3. R—B4 ch, K—N4 4. R—B5 ch. The pawn sacrifice aims at diverting the bishop since after B×P? Black secures a draw by 2. ..., R—Q6.

2. K×P!	R—K7 ch

2. ..., R—N4 ch? fails against 3. K—B2!, and 2. ..., R—N6 ch against 3. K—B2, R—N1 4. R—R1 ch and 5. R—N1 ch.

3. K—B3!	R—Q7

Thus Black has parried White's original threat. But it is to his disadvantage that he has been compelled to make such defensive moves as give White an opportunity to hammer out new threats. Such a transition of threats is very frequent in chess play.

4. K—B4!   R—B6

This seems to be the only satisfactory move against the mate threat R—R1.

But now we have to notice that both Black rooks have separate and rather serious responsibilities. One of them must always have its line open on the Q file so as to prevent queening, the other must be ready to occupy its KR6 square. Therefore, neither of them must stand in the other's way.

Realizing this, all we have to do is to find a move to close the lines of both rooks for a moment, forcing them somehow in each other's way.

5. B—Q3!!   and wins,

because 5. ..., R (B6)×B would be followed by 6. P—Q8 (Q) ch, R×Q 7. R—R1 ch. In case of 5. ..., R(Q7)×B White wins by an inversion of the moves: 6. R—R1 ch, R—R6 7. P—Q8 (Q) ch etc.

The problem of closing focal squares also arises when the control effects of two pieces of different laws of movement (e. g. bishop and a rook) cross each other on a certain square. It is utilized—as in the former example—mostly in the struggle for the promotion of pawns with a view to the partial liquidation of the obstructive forces.

143.

A. A. TROITSKY, 1926.

White wins.

1. P—Q7   P—B6

Some way must be opened urgently for the rook to its Q5, because the danger—as soon appears—is very serious!

2. P—Q8 (Q)!   N×Q
3. P—K7   R—Q5

Directly guards its Q1 and indirectly—threatening discovered check with B—N3—its K1.

4. K—B1!   B—N4

The troubles are apparently over, since both queening squares are under direct control. But at a certain point the paths of the rook and the bishop cross each other and there—an accident lies ahead . . .

5. N—Q7!!   and wins,

because . . ., B×N would bar the way of the rook and . . ., R×N of the bishop. (5. . . ., B×N 6. P×N (Q) ch or 5. . . ., R×N 6. P—K8 (Q) ch, K—R (N)2 7. Q—R (K) 5 ch, and 8. Q×B is a sure win.)

SQUARE BLOCKING AND BLOCKADE

In the chapter on the opening of lines we have also mentioned the closely related cases of clearing a path and clearing a square. Now, when dealing with the closing of lines, it is necessary to speak about fixing and blockade. We have considered clearing a path and clearing a square as useful motifs that can be brought about in one move. If we now examine the move which effects, on the contrary, the closing of a square or of a line, we must regard it as a motif harmful to the side with the move. Therefore, our active tactical operations are to be based not explicitly on the occurrence of line interference or square blocking, but rather on the methods to be applied to force such a closing.

This forcing manoeuvre—which is disadvantageous to the opponent—may be called the establishment of a blockade. The operation consists of one pair of moves, the first of which is line interference by way of placing a piece en prise and the second—presuming that the line interference has a forcing effect—is self-interference resulting from the capture. This will disadvantageously restrict the mobility of the pieces of the side accepting the sacrifice.

In order to understand what advantages might be expected from the establishment of a blockade, let us examine the following illustrative study:

144.

E. HOLM, 1932.

White wins.

A surprisingly simple win results from the fact that the movement of Black's bishop is hampered by the presence of the QP and—as we shall see—of the BP.

| 1. K—N7 | B—Q1 |
| 2. K—B8 | B—K2 |

2. . . ., B—R4? or 2. . . ., B—N3? fails against 3. N—B4 ch.

| 3. K—Q7 | B—B1 |
| 4. K—K8 | B—N2 |

4. . . ., B—R3 is wrong again owing to the knight check.

| 5. K—B7 | B—R1 |
| 6. K—N8 | and wins. |

Square closing is of special importance in close proximity to the opponent's king; often it may lead to mate patterns similar to the well-known "smothered mate."

145.

A. A. TROITSKY, 1897.

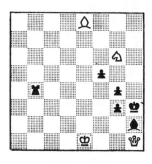

White wins.

In this position White has a certain material superiority which, however, cannot be realized, owing to the threatened ..., P—N7. But he can, by giving up his material plus, obtain such a positional advantage as will eventually work out to a forced smothered mate with the knight thanks to the self-restricting effect of Black's forces.

1. B—B6!!　　　R—N8 ch

1. ..., R—N7 2. B—N2 ch, R×B 3. N—B4 ch etc. and White wins. Therefore the negative queen sacrifice must be accepted.

2. K—K2　　　　R×Q
3. B—N2 ch!!　　K×B
4. N—B4 ch　　　K—N8

The self-blockade of Black's pieces is nearly complete. Only one waiting move is needed and Black's KN7 square will be closed owing to Zugzwang.

5. K—K1!　　　　P—N7
6. N—K2 ch　　　mate!

* * *

A knight fleeing from the attack and compelled to block a square gives rise to an interesting mating position in the next end-game:

146.

G. N. ZAKHODJAKIN, 1931.

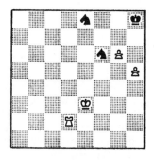

White wins.

1. P—R6!　　　　N—N5 ch
2. K—B4　　　　N×P
3. K—N5!　　　　N—N1

If 3. ..., K—N2, 4. R—Q7 ch etc. wins.

4. R—R2 ch	K—N2
5. R—R7 ch	K—B1
6. R—B7 ch	mate!

The next example also demonstrates a wonderful and startling "self-block-ade mate" resulting from closing a square with a knight:

147.

T. B. GORGIEV, 1929.

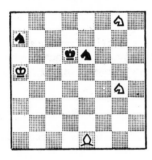

White wins.

1. K—N6	N—B1 ch
2. K—N7!	M—K2

2. . . ., K—Q2? is ill-advised, for after 3. N (8)—B6 ch, K—Q1 4. B—R5 ch Black loses a knight and White wins with his three pieces. White could win a piece even now by playing 3. B—N4 ch, N—B4 ch! 4. B×N ch, K×B 5. N×N, but with his remaining two knights no mate is possible. Though the text continuation soon refutes this assertion, it elucidates the very fact that the presence of a square-blocking harmful piece might also increase the value of small material.

3. B—N3 ch!	K—Q2
4. N(8)—B6 ch	K—Q1
5. B—B7 ch!!	N×B
6. N—K5	and mate

next move on KB7 or QB6.

* * *

We would not deny the highly problematic nature of the foregoing example. To gain an advantage by square blocking is, however, frequent; it occurs at every turn in more practical end-games also. In rook endings it is quite typical to launch a mating attack against a king squeezed to the edge of the board when the restriction of movement of the hostile rook often raises the alternative of "mate or loss of the rook."

148.

J. HASEK, 1929.

White wins.

As White's extra bishop alone is worthless, it seems a sound idea to try and create a mate threat by advancing the king (K—B5—Q6). But this attempt fails against Black's possible ..., P—B4! shaking off the shackles. White's intervening king would be then repelled by ..., R—B3 ch at the crucial moment.

Though it is easy to discover that Black's ..., P—B4 must be prevented, few would think of the surprise move achieving this.

1. B—B5!!   P×B

No other move can extricate Black from his plight; e. g. White wins after 1. ..., P—B3? 2. B—K6 or 2. B×P ch, K—Q1 3. B—B7!

2. K—B5   P—B3
3. K—Q6   R—N1

3. ..., R—B2?? 4. R—R8 mate.

4. K—K6   K—B1
5. K×P (6)   and wins.

* * *

Square blocking is also very important in the struggle to promote a passed pawn; or—conversely—to prevent such a promotion. By closing a certain square an obstacle can be put in the way of the hostile king as he rushes to hold up our passed pawn. But a blockade in front of the pawn may yet allow time to overtake and stop it.

An example of stopping a pawn by square blocking.

149.

E. HOLM, 1932.

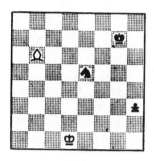

Draw.

1. B—N1   N—B6
2. B—R2!!

The temporary fixing of the pawn is enough to secure a "book draw." On the other hand, 2. K—K2, N×B ch 3. K—B2 would lose because Black could prevent White's king—by way of ..., N—K7!! (a remarkable point!)—from getting any closer.

2. — —   N×B
3. K—K2   N—N5
4. K—B3!

In order to force Black to advance his pawn sooner or later.

4. — —   K—N3
5. K—N3!   P—R7
6. K—N2   drawn.

The next end-game demonstrates a multiple barring of the way to the passed pawn:

150.

A. A. TROITSKY, 1913.

White wins.

With 1. P—R4! White could obtain an unstoppable passed pawn but Black would be able to launch a decisive mating attack after 1. . . ., P×P e. p. 2. P×P, K—N6! Should White lose time by first capturing the NP, Black would hit the road towards his QN2 via K—N4—B3—K2—Q1—B1.

Since White cannot afford to spare Black's KN7 pawn, he must first take steps against the blocking of his prospective distant passed pawn.

1. P—KB6	P×P
2. K×P!	K—N5 (N4)
3. P—R4	P×P e. p.
4. P×P	K—B4
5. P—R4	K—K4

Now Black's king is inside "the magic square" i. e. he would catch up with White's advancing RP by way of . . ., K×P and . . ., K—B3 etc. Therefore the crossing points (White's Q5 and Q6) must be closed.

6. P—Q6!	P×P
7. P—B6!	P×P
8. P—R5	and wins.

151.

A. O. HERBSTMAN, 1927.

White wins.

In this position the fight is for White's Q6 and K5 squares. In case of the immediate capture (P×P) Black would be able to stop White's passed pawn by . . ., B—B1 ch and . . ., B—Q3, and the result would be an obvious draw owing to the bishops of opposite colour. Therefore White's task is either to prevent Black's parrying move or to find some way of profiting from its harmful points.

1. P—Q4 ch	K—K5

If 1. . . ., K—K3, then 2. B—N4 ch, P—B4 3. B×P ch!, K×B 4. P×P, B—B1 ch 5. K×P wins.

2. B—B3 ch	K—Q6
3. B—K2 ch	

3. P×P?, B×P ch! 4. K—Q6, P—B3! is drawn on account of the threat . . ., B—K4 ch.

3. — —	K—K5

Only this move can prevent queening, yet the square blocking at once has very serious consequences:

3. ..., K×B	4. P×P wins.
4. P×P	B×P ch
5. K—B4	B—K4

6. B—Q3 ch	and mate!

Being now acquainted with the advantageous and disadvantageous points of line opening on the one hand and line interference on the other, let us remember once again that **both motifs** are, in fact, the result of a **single move**.

On each move a certain piece leaves a certain square and occupies another. The **leaving** of the square is in itself **a line opening** and the **occupation** of another is, at the same time, a **line interference**. From this it follows that in the course of tactical operations —even if they are relatively short-timed—the motifs of line opening and line interference may be applied and utilized alternatingly or, for that matter, simultaneously. In the majority of unexpected and startling combinations some moves appear to be particularly striking on account of the very fact that the normal control effect of the pieces manifests itself side by side with their corporal effect as a result of line-opening and line-closing manoeuvres.

The alternating or simultaneous utilization of line opening and line interference in various combinative operations will be illustrated by numerous examples in the next chapter. Here we propose to restrict ourselves to the examination of some basic ideas.

Line opening extends the range of the pieces; line interference restricts it. In certain cases it may be necessary to restrict the scope of a piece temporarily even if we aim at an eventual extension of it. Such a case presents itself if we are up against a temporary stalemate hazard. E. g.:

152.

B. HORWITZ, 1851.

White wins.

White cannot win unless he annihilates Black's R7 pawn without stalemating the hostile king. To this end he has to active the bishop, i. e. extend its control effect, and at the same time restrict the rook's power temporarily.

1. S—B8!　　　　K—N7
2. R—N8 ch　　　K—R8
3. B—N7!!　　　　K—N7

Line interference has lifted the stalemate position and now line opening makes it possible to intervene in good time.

4. B—K5 ch!　　　K—R8
5. B×P　　　　　K×B
6. K—B3　　　　　and wins,

because after 6. ..., K—R8 7. R—KR8! mate in two will follow (7. ..., P—R7 8. R—R8! or 7. ..., K—N8 8. R×P or 7. ..., K—R7 8. K—B2 etc.).

A pleasing time-gaining manoeuvre through alternating line interference and line opening is developed in the next end-game:

153.

A. A. TROITSKY 1909.

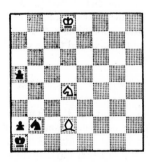

White wins.

1. N—B2 ch　　　K—N8
2. N—R3 ch　　　K—R8
3. B—R6!　　　　P—R5

Pinning by B—N7 would now result in stalemate. Only the "timely" intervention of White's king can eliminate this danger and intensify the attack. Black cannot escape his fate. 3. ..., N—B5?! or any other knight move would lead by inversion of moves to the text variation after 4. B—N7 ch, N—N7 5. K—K7.

4. K—K7!　　　　N—Q6 (B5)
5. B—N7 ch　　　N—N7
6. K—B6!

By closing the diagonal White's king is able to go into action. He can gradually approach his goal, since it is obvious that Black's knight must retreat after each move to its base on N7, being forced to do so by repeated discovered checks. The finish:
6. ..., N—Q6 7. K—B5 ch, N—N7 8. K—K5!, N—Q6 ch 9. K—K4 ch, N—N7 10. K—Q4!, N—Q8 11. K—Q3 ch, N—N7 ch 12. K—B3!, N—Q8 ch 13. K—B2 ch, N—N7 14. B×N ch—and mate!

* * *

We have seen numerous examples demonstrating how the bishop's range depends on the arrangement of the pawns. We should always bear in mind that each pawn move opens a diagonal and closes another of the opposite colour (unless of course the pawn moves from the second to the fourth rank). The strength of two bishops is based partly on the fact that the more the hostile pawns restrict the mobility of one bishop, the less they hinder the other.

If there is only one bishop on the board, it can either be very "good" or very "bad" depending on the restricting effect of the pawns. Certainly the "value" of a bishop is apt to change with each pawn move.

154.

V. LOMOV, 1934.

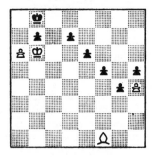

White wins.

The first move is at hand:

1. P—R7 ch   K—R1

Now White's bishop has to single out for attack the opponent's QNP before it succumbs to Black's four united passed pawns.

This is, however, not as simple as it seems, since e. g. 1. B—N2? would be met by ..., P—Q4 and then ..., P—B5—B6. Therefore the first task is to deprive Black of his base on his KB 6, i. e. to force him to advance his KNP.

2. B—N5!   P—N6

White threatened to play 3. B×P 4. B—B8 and 5. B×NP mate. Black had only a Hobson's choice (the text move) yet now he threatens to promote his pawn with check.

3. B—B1   P—K4!

Black's defence is getting more and more cramped by Zugzwang. He must always be prepared to close the long diagonal in reply to White's B—N2, but he must not be overhasty, because the useful moves would be exhausted after the immediate 3. ..., P—Q4? 4. B—N2!, P—B5 5. B—B3. Subsequently he would be compelled either to reopen the diagonal or—at least—to leave the blocking pawn undefended.

4. B—R3!   P—K5
5. B—N2!   P—Q3!

5. ..., P—Q4 6. B—R3 etc. would bring White closer to victory.

6. B—B1   P—Q4

Forced, because after 6. ..., P—K6? 7. B—N2!, P—Q4 8. B×P White mates Black's king. 6. ..., P—B5? would completely open White's KR3—QB8 diagonal to the dangerous bishop.

7. B—R3!   P—Q5

This opening of the long diagonal would be no major trouble in itself, for Black still has his KP at his disposal. But the text move is disadvantageous to Black because it closes his

QR2—KN8 diagonal, i. e. White gains a tempo for his own line opening, as Black **does not now threaten** to promote his KNP with **check** (!).

8. B×P!	P—N7
9. B—B8	P—N8 (Q)
10. B×P ch	and mate.

* * *

The utilization of opening-shutting motifs is especially important in the struggle to realize a passed pawn. If we get an opportunity to open the way in one move for our dangereous passed pawn and keep off the opponent's obstructive piece from the squares leading to the queening point, then this double effect will in most cases work out to a decisive gain of time.

155.

Dr. H. NEUSTADTL, 1897.

White wins.

It is a long-established theoretical fact that two unsupported passed pawns advanced to the sixth rank win against a rook. In this end-game

White attempts to mobilize his blockaded pawn by sacrificing the bishop.

1. B—R5!!	K—N6!

It is always a drawback of a "negative" sacrifice that the opponent is not obliged to accept it. White would easily win after 1. . . ., P×B? 2. P—R7, R—B1 3. P—N6, etc., but now Black threatens to attack White's NP.

2. B×P!	K—B5
3. P—R7	R—B1

How is the NP to be saved now? It is not sufficient to follow the "book pattern" of line interference (4. B—B7, K×P 5. B—N8!?) because Black can give check from his QB6 and overtake the pawn from KR6. The idea of closing the eighth rank must be carried out more energetically, in order to gain time to advance the NP towards its goal.

4. B—K8!!	R×B
5. P—N6	and wins.

We can also enjoy this beautiful opening-shutting bishop manoeuvre on the KR file if Black tries to prevent queening by way of 3. . . ., R—B6 ch 4. K—N4, R—KR6! Then 5. B—R5!! leads to the same result. (It should be noted in parentheses that the second "beauty" variation is not obligatory for White, because after 1. B—R5!, K—N6 he can also proceed with the more "brutal" 2. P—R7 forcing Black into the next variation.)

In the chapters on line opening and line interference we have grown acquainted with the corporal effect of the pieces and with the restricting or expanding effect of certain moves on the range of the rest of the pieces. In judging the real **active value** of a piece, i. e. its power to attack or capture certain hostile pieces, we must never fail to take all these effects into consideration.

The powers of a piece are determined in the first place by the number and importance of the lines and squares it has under direct control from its own square. This is the **static power** of a piece. In the second place its powers are defined by its ability to attack or threaten other groups of squares in one or two moves. This is its **dynamic power.**

Generally speaking, the static power is a strategic factor and the dynamic power a tactical one. In end-games characterized by the presence of only a few pieces and by the active participation of both kings the dynamic powers of the line pieces are clearly in evidence. This is of course due to the fact that the lines are open in nearly all directions and afford a greater freedom of movement, while the possibility of intermediate checks is a handy means of occupying or threatening fresh groups of squares without any loss of time.

The simplest and at the same time the most "brutally" forcing tactical operations are based on the direct utilization of dynamic power, i. e. ruthless attacks executed without any finesse.

The operation by which we make a direct attack on a hostile piece with a view to forcing it to move away we call a **chase.**

A **chase** may serve various **aims,** viz.:

(a) to trap and capture the piece under attack,

(b) to create a situation suitable for launching a double attack by driving the opponent's piece to a less convenient square,

(c) to gain space and time for other profitable operations.

A purposeful utilization of the dynamic powers of our pieces may decide many an end-game for us in which we have no appreciable superiority either in material or, at least seemingly, in position.

To illustrate this concept of chase we have chosen a very simple example:

156.

I. EROCHIN, 1928.

White wins.

Black has the material superiority, and White's only hope lies in a direct attack against the opponent's king.

1. N—B2 ch   K—R5
2. Q—N4 ch!

We shall soon see that this is the only sound continuation.

2. — —   K—N4

Otherwise 3. Q—N4 mate!

3. N—Q4 ch!   K—N3!

Any other move would be followed by 4. N—K6 ch winning the queen (or 3. . . ., K—R4 4. N—B6 ch).

4. Q—N6 ch!   K—N2!
5. Q—K4 ch!   K—B1

After 5. . . ., K—N3 6. Q—N1 ch Black cannot avoid being forked.

6. Q—R8 ch   K—Q2

Saves the queen but precipitates his own death.

7. Q—B6 ch   K—K2
8. Q—K6 ch   and mate!

Winning this end-game was a straightforward job because victory was already there, offered up on a plate; White had only to give, one by one, the checks leading to mate or loss of the queen.

None the less we have learned something from this example. We have learned that we must always **reckon with every possible check,** for the check is the most forcing motif in chess play; **but we should actually give check only if it brings us nearer to our goal.**

* * *

From the point of view of dynamic power the mightiest piece is the queen —especially on a vacant board, in positions with few pieces. In the struggle between queens the chase by checks is of great importance. In positions without pawns an extra piece makes no difference as a strategic factor, but with an advantage of tempo the stronger side can often launch such harassing attacks as will lead to mate or to the loss of the opponent's queen.

157.

B. HORWITZ, 1851.

White wins.

Here again victory results from drastic forcing—provided we always happen to give the **right** checks to Black's king.

1. Q—K3 ch   K—B4

1. ..., K—Q4? 2. Q—N3 ch would mean immediate defeat.

2. Q—B3 ch!

This check is already a fruit of due deliberation. To make the right choice between Q—B3 ch and Q—B4 ch we must see in advance from which point the queen is more likely to intervene with success. It will appear that the route via KB4—QB4—QB8 is not equivalent with that via KB3—QN3—QN8.

2. ——   K—K3
3. Q—N3 ch   K—K2!

3. ..., K—B3? 4. B—N5 ch etc.

4. B—N5 ch!   K—B1!

4. ..., K—K1? 5. Q—N8 ch, K—Q2 6. Q—N7 ch! and White wins because after 6. ..., K—K1 7. Q—B8 Black is mate; and after 6. ..., K—K3 7. Q—N3 ch the queen is lost.

5. Q—N8 ch   Q—K1

If White's queen at this point were posted on QB8 she could not forcibly increase the attack. (If you don't believe it, try it for yourself!) But now Black's king will be strangled in a mating net.

6. Q—Q6 ch   K—N1
7. B—K7!   and wins.

The last "quiet" move is worthy of special notice; any further checks would have missed the target.

The next study is surprising on two accounts. The lesser surprise is that, in the interests of victory, we have to allow Black to promote his pawn; the greater that we have to chase the hostile king from his worst possible place, the corner, to the very centre of the board. Naturally both are at once understandable if we can foresee the final developments . . .

158.

A. A. TROITSKY, 1924.

White wins.

1. N—B5!!

Prevents ..., N—K2 and also controls the KN7 square.

1. — —	P—Q7
2. P—B7	N—K2!

Black has to decoy the dangerous knight away since White threatened mate after 2. ..., P—Q8 (Q)? 3. P—B8 (Q) ch, K—R2 4. Q—B7 ch even in case of a forced sacrifice. E. g. 4. ..., N—K2 5. Q×N ch, K—N3 6. N—R4 ch, K—R3 7. Q—B6 ch, K—R2 8. Q—B7 ch, K—R1 9. N—N6 ch —mate.

3. N×N	P—Q8 (Q)
4. P—B8 (Q) ch	K—N2

Now Black's king can escape mate, but in a few moves he will be forced onto the file of his idle queen.

5. Q—N8 ch	K—B3
6. N—Q5 ch!	K—K4

If 6. ..., K—B4?, 7. N—K3 ch wins the queen.

7. Q—N7 ch!	K—Q3

Now we can see in what a plight Black's king finds himself even in the middle of the board due to the lethal danger to his new-born royal consort. If 7. ..., K—K5?, then 8. N—B3 ch would follow; 7. ..., K×N would allow 8. Q—Q7 ch.

8. Q—B7 ch!	K—K3
9. Q—K7 ch!	and wins,

because either of the king's possible moves leads to the queen's loss.

* * *

In positions with few pieces a rook's dynamic power—like that of the queen—can also considerably increase. True enough, this extra power is not altogether conspicuous against a minor piece because the struggle of king and rook versus king and bishop or knight is a theoretical draw; a win can be imagined only in exceptional positions. It is enough, however, to add a minor piece to each camp to give the side which is the exchange up good winning prospects.

159.

F. J. PROKOP, 1924.

White wins.

Here the rook and the knight can give a relentless chase to the opponent's light forces, but White must play very accurately to exploit his chances.

1. N—Q4!	B—Q6

Against the threatening R—K8 and R—K6 ch Black may also take 1. . . ., B—R2 into consideration. This is a trickier move than it seems because after the obvious 2. R—KN1 Black would not watch the threat R—N7, N—B3; R—KB7 with folded arms and meekly try to seek defence in 2. . . ., N—B3? because of 3. R—KR1! and 4. R—R6!, but would launch an unexpected counter-attack: 2. . . ., N—K2! 3. R—N7, N—B4! and the storm would be weathered.

In case of 1. . . ., B—R2 White wins by playing 2. R—K8!, K—N3 3. N—B3!!, K—B2 4. N—N5!, and Black loses a piece.

2. R—K8	B—B5

Of course the knight could not move for fear of 3. R—K6 ch.

3. K—N4!	B—B2
4. R—KB8!	N—R3

. . ., B—R7 would be as wrong now as it would have been earlier because of R—R8 ch. . . ., B—Q4? would have been followed by K—B5! with gain of tempo.

5. K—B5!	K—N2

Forced move because the bishop is tied down owing to the potential threat R—B6 ch.

6. N—B5!	and wins,

since after the removal of the defending piece White is a whole rook to the good.

* * *

A knight and a bishop—both beyond a safe distance from their king—are so ill suited for mutual defence that often they are no match for a single freely moving rook of great dynamic power. A characteristic motif in the course of a chase is the **attack against the defending piece.**

160.

L. I. KUBBEL, 1923.

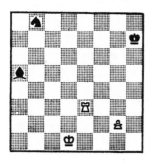

White wins.

1. R—QN3!   N—B3!

After 1. ..., N—Q2?? White immediately wins by pinning the knight (2. R—N7). On 1. ..., B—B2? follows 2. R—N7, N—R3 3. R—R7! with successful intervention.

2. R—N5!   B—Q1

White was threatening to play 3. R—B5 or—in case of ..., B—N5— 3. R—N6!
Now White makes another offensive and threatening move, and the powerful centralized rook soon captures the bishop though the latter can move freely on two diagonals.

3. R—Q5!!   B—K2

There is no salvation. If 3. ..., B—B2? then 4. R—Q7 ch, wins. 3. ..., B—R5? 4. R—R5 ch etc.; otherwise 4. R—Q6 would have ensued.

4. R—Q7   K—N3
5. R—B7!   and wins.

In these illustrative examples the chase has actually consisted in a sequence of forcing moves made by strong offensive pieces and involving a series of constantly renewed direct attacks and threats.

The basic motif of chase is, accordingly, such a single offensive move as will force some hostile piece to leave the square it occupies and go to a less convenient square.

In tactical operations it is very often necessary to resort to that basic, one-move form of chase. A common instance of this is the **intermediate** check, a typical time-gaining manoeuvre.

161.

L. VLK, 1917.

White wins.

The motif in question is based on the chase and "fall" of the rook which gets stuck between its pawns.

1. K—N8   R—B3
2. R—B6!

It would clearly be unwise for Black to exchange off rooks as White's pawn would be promoted first.

2. — —   P—B5!

Now White in turn would not profit by the exchange because Black's BP would also reach the queening square. But he can quicken the pace of his own pawn!

3. R—R6 ch!!   K—N7

After 3. . . ., R×R 4. P×R White's pawn would be promoted with check (!), and Black's BP would only reach its seventh rank. The text move leads to the same result and thus White has gained the necessary tempo by the intermediate check.

4. R×R   P×R
5. P—N6   P—B6
6. P—N7   P—B7
7. P—N8 (Q) ch (!)   and wins.

In the interest of promotion with gain of time, it is often important to know well in advance whether there is a chance during the process to chase the opponent's king to a less favourable place, incidentally as it were, by an interpolated move.

This truth is borne out by another example:

144

162.

L. I. KUBBEL, 1909.

White wins.

White must give up his rook for Black's far advanced QP, therefore he pins his hopes on his pawns. What is our first impression of the situation and how far is it modified upon some reflection?

We may be tempted to say off-hand that 1. R—Q4, P—Q8 (Q) 2. R×Q, B×R 3. P—N7 — wins. On second thoughts we are likely to amend that statement, seeing that we cannot win because Black can play 3. . . ., B—N5! 4. P—N8 (Q), B—K3 ch! and the queen is lost.

All of a sudden another uncertain question presents itself: isn't the game still won for White? After 5. Q×B, P×Q 6. P—N4 we start to examine the ensuing pawn end-game again with steadily ebbing optimism. It soon turns out that after 6. . . ., P—K4 White hasn't the slightest chance to win.—Let us start afresh from the very beginning!

Eureka!—a new thought flashes through our mind: 1. R—R4 ch!,

K×P (or . . ., K—N6) 2. R—Q4, P—Q8 (Q) 3. R×Q, B×R 4. P—N7!—and wins because the pawn will be promoted with check—or, in case of 4. . . ., B—N5, queening results in pinning the bishop. Simple, isn't it? Or it would be, if it were not for Black's rather unexpected reply 1. . . ., K—N8! to the rook check.

Never mind! Let us at any rate start with a check to the king and see what happens later.

And, indeed, it works:

1. R—R4 ch, K—N8! 2. R—Q4, P—Q8 (Q) 3. R×Q, B×R 4. P—N7, B—N5! 5. P—N8 (Q)!, B—K3 ch 6. Q×B, P×Q 7. P—N4!, P—K4 8. P—N5, P—K5 9. P—N6, P—K6 10. P—N7, P—K7 11. P—N8 (Q) ch—and White wins because the second NP is also promoted with check!

True, enough it was not necessary to calculate the whole variation over before giving check with the rook. But we had to see definitely that the only possibility of creating winning chances was to interpolate a check before doing anything else. So little is often sufficient to start with—even in the case of intricate combinations.

* * *

We have not yet reached the end of our topic. In the next chapter we shall examine whether there are, besides the chase or simple direct attack, any other means of forcing hostile pieces to inconvenient squares.

In the previous chapter we dealt with the simplest form of forcing moves and operations: the direct attack or chase. We saw how great an advantage it is to keep the initiative and chase the opponent's pieces to inconvenient squares. But we do not always have pieces at our disposal so powerful as to leave the opponent no other option but unconditional retreat. How then can we expect to deprive the opponent of his freedom of action and at the same time harness his pieces to the furthering of our aims?

What cannot be done by sheer force may be achieved by guile. The weapon most commonly used for the purpose in chess tactics is the **sacrifice.** In the examples dealt with so far we have seen an abundant variety of sacrifices, so that the concept needs but little explanation. In essence, a sacrifice is the putting or leaving en prise of a piece, or its exchange for a hostile piece of lesser value; in short, a voluntary and intentional offer of some material advantage.

What is the use of a sacrifice? Many would say that that depends on its purpose, but on that basis we could easily miss the wood for the trees. We'd rather watch what happens on the board when a sacrifice is accepted.

If the opponent captures the piece offered for sacrifice, the situation changes on two counts: (1) a piece has disappeared from the board; (2) a hostile piece has left its original square and occupies the place of the sacrificed piece.

The first change may in itself be the purpose of the sacrifice in the light of what we already know about the harmful piece and the importance of liquidating it. But this is seldom the case. The purpose of the sacrifice is generally the second change, since it amounts to nothing less than **directing** the movements of the opponent's piece, because the position of the sacrifice exactly determines the **square** a certain hostile piece **is to occupy.**

Consequently, we can **direct the movement of the opponent's pieces by a sacrifice** (if it is an active and forcing one, of course) **in the same way as we can by the process of chase.**

The two types of directing manoeuvres bear more or less the same relation to each other as the physical phenomena of repulsion and attraction. The invulnerable offensive piece chases away, or repels as it were, the defenceless enemy; the piece offered for sacrifice and openly exposed to enemy fire attracts the hostile piece, decoys it to its own square. Of course a sacrifice can be as forcing as the chase; indeed it may turn into chase if the opponent refuses to capture and chooses to retreat instead.

The tactical operation by which we force a hostile piece to move to a definite square by sacrificing one of ours is called driving on.

Driving on is an essential element of most combinations; as a tactical factor it can be utilized in many ways. The idea is illustrated both in its simplicity and in its profundity by this enjoyable study:

163.

N. D. GRIGORIEV, 1930.

White wins.

White could advance his RP to its queening square without any hindrance, but then Black's QP would also be promoted, and with check at that; White's king is unable to overtake it, because Black is better posted to support his pawn.

Perhaps the BP might give some hope? It would certainly be promoted with check, but there is the rub that Black's king could easily catch it! But the BP has another good point; with its help we can drive Black's king in the desired direction . . .

| 1. P—B4! | K—N5 |
| 2. P—R4! | P—Q4 |

The only countermove, for after 2. . . ., P—R4? 3. P—R5, etc., would follow, and White's queen would be able to command Black's QR8 from the promotion square. It is not yet possible to advance White's king towards Black's QP because Black can reach his QB7 in two moves. Therefore, we must continue to drive Black's king on.

| 3. P—B5! | K—B4 |
| 4. P—R5! | P—Q5 |

Now we might think of overtaking the QP, but it is no longer necessary. The shoulder-to-shoulder advance of the two white pawns brings a "straight win" in sight, making further calculations superfluous.

5. P—B6	K—Q3
6. P—R6!	P—Q6
7. P—B7!	K—K2

The BP will fall victim to Black, but it paves the way for a quicker intervention by the RP.

| 8. P—R7! | P—Q7 |
| 9. P—B8 (Q) ch |

The driving-on sacrifice! Its purpose is to force Black's king to a "bad" place; the RP will be promoted with check!

| 9. — — | K×Q |
| 10. P—R8 (Q) ch | and wins. |

You will have noted that the self-sacrificing BP has pulled Black's king on a "string," as it were, on its journey from QR3 to KB8.*

The **driving-on manoeuvre** has a double purpose: (a) to bring about a **favourable situation** and (b) **to gain time** for the realization of certain **beneficial operations**. In the preceding chapters we have seen that a piece driven to an inconvenient place is apt to "stymie" its companion, close lines and block squares, and bar the way of its own king so much as to expose him to immediate mating attacks. Now let us see what are the tactical possibilities of **gaining a material advantage** by the judicious use of the driving-on motif.

* * *

* We hate to mar the good impression made by the harmonious main variation, yet for the sake of accuracy we have to point out that from the fifth move there is also a "by-play" that leads to victory: 5. K—N2, K—B5 (otherwise White's king would manage to reach his Q1 square). 6. P—B6!, P—Q6 7. P—B7, P—Q7 8. P—B8 (Q), P—Q8 (Q) 9. Q—B1 ch, etc. As for our analysis, this "by-play" reveals that K—N2 also contained a sufficient threat to drive Black's king forcingly. In this sub-variation Black's QB5 was the ominous square because of the possible exchange of queens.

By tactical means we can generally obtain a material advantage if we launch a **double attack.** In order to be able to attack two hostile pieces simultaneously we have to force the opponent's pieces to squares answering our purpose. An effective means of forcing is the **driving-on sacrifice.**

164.

J. SEHWERS, 1916.

White wins.

| 1. R—B4 ch | K—N4 |
| 2. R—B7! | |

First by chase, then by offering itself for sacrifice, the rook tries to create favourable conditions for the knight's intervention. The acceptance of the sacrifice would be answered by a double attack. (2. ..., Q×R 3. N×P ch)

| 2. — — | Q—B4 |

With 2. ..., Q—R3? or 2. ..., Q—R1? the queen would voluntarily put her head in the noose. (3. N—B7

ch!) After 2. ..., Q—N3 or 2. ...,
Q—N1 another driving-on sacrifice
would force the loss of the queen: 3.
R—QN7!, Q×R 4. N×P ch.

In the text continuation also Black's
fate is sealed after a simple combination preceded by a driving-on sacrifice.

3. R—B5!   P—Q4

Or 3. ..., Q×R 4. N×P ch etc.

4. R×P!   Q×P
5. N—B7 ch   and wins,

because after the liquidation White's
king can walk up to Black's RP, while
his own pawns mutually defend each
other.

* * *

The driving-on sacrifice is genuine-
ly forcing if the piece offered is itself
attacking or threatening. Now we present an end-game exemplifying a
driving-on manoeuvre forced through
by a threat:

165.

H. RINCK, 1908.

White wins.

In an open position a queen and a
bishop have very great dynamic powers; hence even a brutal chase holds
out good prospects.

1. B—B2 ch   K—K4!

1. ..., K—B5? 2. Q—QN7!
(threatening Q—N3 mate) 2. ..., P—
Q5 3. Q×P ch, K—N5 4. B—K1 ch,
K—R6 5. Q—R6 ch wins.

2. B—N3 ch   K—Q5!

..., K—B3?? would again comply
with White's most ardent wish. (4.
B—R4 ch wins the queen.)

But now more checks wouldn't
help. There are no mating chances,
nor is Black's queen posted unfavour-
ably enough to be captured. Therefore she must be driven on to a still
less favourable square.

3. B—Q6!!

The bishop has no hostile piece
under attack, but it controls the B5
and K5 squares, weaving a mating net
round Black's king. 4. Q—Q3 mate
can only be averted by capturing the
bishop. It turns out that the sacrifice
has aimed at driving the queen to Q6!

3. — —   Q×B
4. Q—Q3 ch   K—B4

Black's fate would also be the same
after 4. ..., K—K4 5. Q—N3 ch! ...

5. Q—R3 ch   and wins,

149

since the king, with the harmful pawns in his way, cannot help leaving the queen to her fate.

* * *

The driving-on manoeuvre can also be resorted to in operations when the aim is not to capture a hostile piece but to increase our own forces by **promoting a pawn.**

In order to force a passed pawn through we usually have to drive the hostile piece which threatens our pawn or guards the queening square on to a **closed line** from an open one, or drive a line-blocking piece in its way. Typical examples of this idea are mostly to be found in **rook endgames.**

166.

A. A. TROITSKY, 1910.

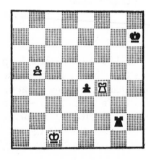

White wins.

1. P—N6	R—N3

The rook could as well go to its N4 or N2, the continuation being the same. Black has no other satisfactory counterplay. The attempt by . . ., P—

K6 to entrap White after 2. P—N7, P—K7 3. R—R4 ch, K—N2 4. K—Q2?, P—K8 (Q) ch! 5. K×Q, R—QN7! catching his pawn, is simply countered with 4. R—K4! instead of 4. K—Q2? and wins.

2. R—R4 ch	K—N2
3. R—4!	

Driving Black's rook to its fifth rank from where—on account of its harmful KP—it cannot reach the QN file in one move. Now we see the double meaning of the preliminary chase (2. R—R4 ch); it has resulted in a forcing driving-on sacrifice and also in closing the KN file.

3. — —	R×R
4. P—N7	R—N8 ch
5. K—B2	R—N7 ch
6. K—B3	R—N6 ch
7. K—B4	and wins.

167.

H. RINCK, 1911.

White wins.

It is obviously urgent for us to open the way for the RP, yet it is not unimportant how we do it. We cannot gain time by giving check since Black's intention is to play ..., K—B7 opening the eighth rank for his rook to its QR8. Incidentally, Black also threatens to carry out the manoeuvre ..., R—K8—K1.

1. R—KN7!!   K—B7

The reason for White's R—KN7 move was to knock out the other line of defence. In case of 1. ..., R—K8 (B8) White by 2. R—N1!! would drive the hostile rook to a file from which it could not reach its first rank. (2. ..., R×R 3. P—R7.)

2. R—N2 ch   K—N6

If 2. ..., K×P 3. R—QR2! etc. wins. Now White must render Black's threat (..., R—QR8) harmless. It can be done by a driving-on sacrifice which also forces Black into self-interference:

3. R—QR2!!   K×R
4. P—R7   and wins.

* * *

In **knight end-games**—as in the example shown in the chapter elucidating the fundamental concepts—it is a characteristic form of driving on which poses an alternative of advancing or promoting a pawn.

168.

L. I. KUBBEL, 1915.

White wins.

In this situation both the "obvious" 1. P—B7 and 1. N—K8!? would be followed by 1. ..., N—K3 not only meeting White's threats but even giving winning chances to Black owing to the presence of the pawns on the queen's wing. Therefore, we must "ask" Black's king where he will go after a pawn check and our action should depend on the "answer".

1. P—N3 ch   K—N5

If 1. ..., K—R6?, then 2. N—K4 would follow threatening N—B2 mate. After Black's loss of tempo (2. ..., K—N5) White would gain time to play 3. N—B5! and deprive the opponent of his K3. Then White would easily win by P—B7—B8 (Q).

After 1. ..., K—R4?, however, the driving on by 2. N—K8! would be decisive since the defensive 2. ..., N—K3 would be followed by the double attack. 3. N—N7 ch! The same conditions would arise also after 1. ..., K—R4? 2. N—K8!, P—QN5 3. P—B7!, N—K3 4. N—N7 ch!

2. N—K8!   N—K3

2. ..., N×N? P—B7! would demonstrate the purpose of the driving-on manoeuvre: the threatened promotion—on K8 or KB8—cannot be prevented. After 2. ..., K—B4 3. N×N, K×P4. N×RP White's extra piece would win.

3. N—N7!   N—B1

3. ..., N×N?? would lose at once because of 4. P×N and 5. P—N8 (Q). Any other knight move would also be followed by queening. Black's only counter-chance seems to lie in: 3. ..., P—QN5!, but after 4. N×N, P—N6 5. K—N2 White would gain a decisive tempo since after 5. ..., P—N7 6. N—N7! there is no defence against 7. P—R3 mate. In case of the parrying 5. ..., K—B4 6. N—Q4 ch wins Black's dangerous passed pawn and the extra knight decides the issue.

4. K—N2!   and wins,

because there is no escape from 5. P—R3 ch and mate!

* * *

Both the corner square and the neighbouring squares are very unfavourable to a knight. Therefore it is often worth our while to drive the knight to such a square and then capture it with small forces.

169.

M. B. NEWMAN, 1926.

White wins.

In this end-game even two knights are no match for White's passed pawns. It is evident that one of them must be given up for the RP, yet it is hardly conceivable that the other one cannot hold the two NP's. Therefore the final situation after White's eighth move is also very instructive from a practical point of view.

1. K—N6!   N—K4 ch
2. K—B6

2. K—N7 would not be successful on account of 2. ..., K—N4! 3. P—R7, N—B4 ch 4. K—N8, N—N3 etc.

2. ——   N(4)—N5 ch

2. ..., N(6)—N5 ch 3. K—K6! and White wins more quickly.

3. K—K6!	N×P
4. P—N6	N—B2!

White's seemingly unstoppable NP will be not only overtaken by this driving-on sacrifice, but also captured in return for a knight. This active defence is beautiful but—unlucky, because the knight winning the pawn lands on a "bad" square.

5. K×N!	N—B5!
6. P—N7!	N—Q3 ch
7. K—7!	N×P

This is where Black's combination ends. It is White's turn now: or rather, at this point we realize that White has been planning for this driving-on sacrifice all along, and Black has had to play ball for want of a better alternative.

8. P—N4!	and wins (!),

because Black's knight cannot escape capture by K—Q7—B7. 8. ..., K—N4 9. K—Q7, K—B4 10. K—B7, N—Q1! 11. K×N, K—K4 12. K—B7!, K—Q4 13. P—N5 etc.)

* * *

It may happen that a pawn can win against a knight, but it is very seldom that it can hold its own against a bishop. Yet if we are able to drive the bishop onto a diagonal where it is restricted in its movement, then, in exceptional cases, a pawn posted even behind the "demarcation line" may triumph.

170.

H. OTTEN, 1892.

Draw.

1. P—R5	B—B1!
2. K—Q5!	B—R3!

Black tries to occupy his QR2—KN8 diagonal via his QB4 or K6. But now White deprives him of the possibility of this "pendulum manoeuvre," by way of a driving-on sacrifice.

3. P—N5 ch!	B×P

If 3. ..., K×P? then 4. P—R6! wins immediately since Black's king closes the bishop's way to his K6. Now, however, Black is prevented from playing ..., B—K2—B4; therefore the only task White's king has to solve is to guard his K3 and KB2 squares.

4. K—K4!	B—R5
5. K—B3!	and wins,

since the advancing pawn cannot be held up.

An accurately elaborated study by Grandmaster Réti illustrates how the scope of a bishop can be decreased when its own king is driven on to its diagonal.

171.

R. RÉTI, 1929.

White wins.

It is easy to win the bishop in exchange for the BP, yet it would be not only a bad, but also a sad bargain because the ensuing pawn end-game would be lost for White. E. g. 1. K—N8, K—K4 2. P—B8 (Q), B×Q 3. K×B, K×P 4. K—Q7, K—K4 5. K—K7, K—B5, etc. Even worse is: 1. K—R7?, since after 1. . . ., B—B1 2. K—N8, B×P 3. P—B8 (Q), B×Q 4. K×B, K—K4! the QP is lost and Black's RP will be promoted.

There is no other choice but to try the third alternative.

1. P—Q6!　　　　K—K3!

1. . . ., B—B1?? 2. K—N8, B×P 3. P—B8(Q), B×Q 4. K×B and White's QP has become a big shot.

But now White must not insist on winning the bishop because 2. K—N8?, K×P would lead to a losing end-game. After 2. K—R7!?, B—B1 3. K—N8, K—Q2 White would be in Zugzwang.

2. P—Q7!!　　　　K×P

The purpose of the sacrifice is to force through the driving-on manoeuvre at the **proper time.** The tempo thus won makes it possible for White to force Black into Zugzwang, leading to a draw by a repetition of moves.

3. K—R7!　　　　B—B8
4. K—N8!　　　　B—R3
5. K—R7　　　　　B—B1
6. K—N8!　　　　and draws,

since Black must reply again . . ., B—R3. Even an attempt at liquidation —unlike the variation mentioned at the beginning—would not yield much because. Black could not win after 7. K—R7, K×P 8. K×B, K—Q3, 9. K—N5, K—K4 10. K—B4, K—B5 11. K—Q3, K×P 12. K—K2!!, K—N6 13. K—B1!

The finish of this study is a suitably logical link in bringing us to the discussion of driving-on manoeuvres in pure **pawn endings.**

It is well known that rook pawns cannot be realized so easily as their companions on the inner files. There is many a position in which a NP wins, but a RP only draws. For the defence it is therefore generally desirable to drive the opponent's NP on to the rook's file.

172.

Dr. F. CASSIDY, 1884.

Draw.

If this position emerged in a game you were watching you would probably be inclined to say that the matter was as good as settled, for after 1. K—B3 and K—N4 White would take Black's RP and then easily promote his NP.

Unfortunately, 1. K—B3?? would give up the win at once, because Black's reply 1...., P—R6! would considerably "devalue" White's queening prospects. But if we are familiar with the concept of driving on, we shall be aware of the danger in good time to do something against it.

The RP must be captured, yet not on White's R4 but on his R3! Well, it doesn't always pay to take the short cut.

| 1. K—N1!! | P—R6! |

Still the strongest.

2. P—N3!

2. P—N4?, K—K3 3. K—R2, K—Q3 4. K×P, K—B3 5. K—R4, K—N3 and Black has occupied the square so badly needed by White.

2. — —	K—K3
3. K—R2	K—Q3
4. K×P	K—B3(!)

From a practical point of view this is "better" than 4...., K—B4 which would not "offer an opportunity" to White to commit a mistake. But now White still may spoil everything by 5. K—N4??

| 5. K—R4! | K—N3 |
| 6. K—N4! | and wins. |

* * *

Besides driving a pawn on the R file there is another method of driving on in pawn endings, which we may call **the shifting of the critical square.**

It is known that a single king cannot put up a successful fight against a pawn (other than a RP) supported by its king unless he manages to get in front of the pawn or, at least, prevent the advance of the hostile king by taking up the **opposition.** In this case the struggle is fought for the square in front of the pawn and for those neighbouring it. The squares in question are called critical squares.

To clarify this concept we shall revert to the previous example. In relation to White's NP the critical area is marked out by the QR4—

QR6—QB6—QB4 squares. Black would have been able to secure a draw if he had occupied either QN4 or QN5, or at least secured the opposition on his third rank against White's king on the fifth. Therefore, K—R4 ought to have been countered with . . ., K—R3!, K—N4 with . . ., K—N3! and K—B4 with . . ., K—B3! in order to avoid defeat. Black had no opportunity to do so, because after the fourth move White decided for the sound continuation 5. K—R4! instead of playing 5. K—N4? and thus giving Black a chance to oppose by 5. . . ., K—N3!

It goes without saying that even the moves K—N4?, K—N3! would have been of no account if White's pawn had been posted on its QN2 instead of on QN3. In that case Black's every attempt at achieving the opposition would have been thwarted by a potential **reserve move** that might have compelled him at any time to give up the opposition.

From this it follows that the side on the defensive is hopelessly lost if the hostile king can occupy the **second** square in front of his advancing pawn.

By tactical means that "second" square can sometimes be turned into a "first" square, by simply **driving** the pawn behind the offensive king **a square ahead.** If we manage to do so, we shall have achieved the same result as though the hostile king had been thrown one rank back.

The manoeuvre under review is peculiar to positions in which the weaker side too has a pawn, though a doomed one. A classical example:

173.

H. MATTISON, 1918.*

White wins.

White's two pawns are as good as lost. Should Black be able to capture the pawns where they now stand, the game would be lost as well, no matter where White's king was posted, for Black would still have the necessary reserve move at his disposal.

Thus the only way to secure a draw is to drive Black's pawn not one but two squares forward, and then take up the opposition:

1. P—N6!!   P×P

1. . . ., K×P leaves White sufficient time to defend his BP.

* The original position: White: king on KR1, pawns on KB4 and KR4; Black: king on KR3, pawns on KB2 and KN4. Instead of that rather artificial basic position we present the one derived after the moves 1. RP×P ch!, K—R4, which we believe is for practical purposes of higher instructive value.

2. P—B5!!

The second sacrifice was as indispensable as the first, since after 2. K—N1 (2), K—N5 3. K—B1?!, K×P 3. K—B2, P—N4! White would lose the opposition. Nor could it be delayed even a single move as proved by the following variants: 2. K—N2, K—N5 3. P—B5, P×P! or 2. K—N1, K—N5 3. P—B5, K×P! 4. K—B2, K—B5, etc.

| 2. — — | P×P |
| 3. K—N1! | K—N4! |

Both sides are waiting for the other to advance. 3. K—R2?? or 3. K—N2?? would be a gross blunder on account of Black's oppositional reply 3. ..., K—R5! or 3. ..., K—N5! assuring the victory. That is the reason why White's king must not go to the second rank.

| 4. K—B1! | K—B5 (N5) |
| 5. K—B2 (N2)! | and draws. |

* * *

We now present an instance of a prolonged struggle between king and rook. This is a typical case illustrating the impotence of a rook driven on to a bad line against an advanced passed pawn. On the other hand, it also demonstrates how stubbornly the rook can prolong its life by fighting back.

174.

A. A. TROITSKY, 1912.

White wins.

In such positions an extra knight is no asset, therefore White has to seek victory in the realization of his pawn.

| 1. P×P! | R—B8 ch! |

Stronger than it first seems, because after the exchange of the rooks White cannot safely protect his pawn with the knight. For instance: 2. K—N2, R×R! 3. K×R, K—B2! and after 4. N×P Black immediately wins the pawn (..., K—Q3). If 4. N—B8, then Black plays again 4. ..., K—Q3! (4. ..., K—Q1?? 5. N—N6!) and 5. ..., K—K2!

The lesson is that the rook must not be **exchanged off,** but it can be **sacrificed** in the interest of the pawn.

| 2. K—B2!! | R×R |

The best, otherwise White's material superiority assures the win.

3. P—K7.

And now the real battle begins. Black cannot directly prevent the promotion, therefore he endeavours to chase White's king onto the K file, then to eliminate the new-born queen by way of . . ., R—KR8 and . . ., R—K8 ch or . . ., R—RK4 and . . ., R—K4 ch. For this reason White must temporarily keep off the K file, but he must not stray too far away lest Black's rook should seize control over it.

Consequently, the next moves are made under mutual duress.

3. . . ., R—R7 ch 4. K—B3, R—R6 ch 5. K—B4, R—R5 ch 6. K—B5, R—R4 ch 7. K×P!

The first obstacle has been removed and also the potential danger of . . ., R—R4—K4 ch is over. But the K file may be "crossed" only at the K2 point; the end is still a long way off.

7. . . ., R—R3 ch! 8. K—B5! (8. K—K5?, R—R8!) 8. . . ., R—R4 ch 9. K—B4! (9. N—N5?, R—R1!) 9. . . ., R—R5 ch 10. K—B3, R—R6 ch 11. K—K2!

The Jordan has been crossed. But we still don't see why.

11. . . ., R—R7 ch 12. K—Q3!, R—R6 ch 13. K—Q4, R—R5 ch 14. K—Q5, R—R4 ch 15. K—Q6!

The time has come for the knight to burst in. Should Black, for instance, continue with 15. . . ., R—R8 (in hope of . . ., R—Q8 ch and . . ., R—K8 ch), then 16. N—B6! would follow and after 16. . . ., R—Q8 ch 17. N—Q5 ch would close the file with gain of tempo. If 16. . . ., R—K8, then the line interference ensuing after 17. N—Q7 ch and 18. N—K5 would decide the issue.

15. — —   R—R3 ch
16. N—B6!!

Now the intervention of the knight assumes the form of a typical driving-on sacrifice. After 16. . . ., R—R1 the knight would display its many-sided line-closing powers in a third variation. (17. N—Q7 ch and 18. N—B8!) Following the acceptance of the sacrifice the fourth phase of the king's wanderings marks the end of the fight:

16. . . ., R×N ch 17. K—Q5!, R—B4 ch 18. K—Q4, R—B5 ch 19. K—Q3, R—B6 ch 20. K—K2!—and (at long last!) wins.

A tactical weapon no less important than the one described in the preceding chapter is the motif of **driving off** or diversion. In discussing the fundamental concepts we have already hinted (see Diagrams Nos. 13–17) that the driving-off manoeuvre is one of the ways of directing the movement of hostile forces efficiently. The only difference between driving off and driving on is that in the former case we force a hostile piece to **leave** a certain square instead of to occupy one. In other words, it is in practice unimportant to which square the piece in question goes; the main point is that it vacates its original square and as a result it **ceases to exercise its control effect over certain squares.**

In form the driving-off manoeuvre reveals a **sacrifice** of the same type as in the previous chapter. Its field of application is, however, rather different, unless it can be combined with a driving-on manoeuvre.

In most positions arising after a driving-on sacrifice the directed piece itself is the one that gets into the limelight, either as an excellent target or as an obstacle hampering the activity of its own camp. After a driving-off manoeuvre the directed piece disappears as it were from the battlefield,

becoming an idle onlooker of no practical use. Accordingly, by means of a driving-off sacrifice we can increase the potential radius of action of our pieces, but their increased powers are directed not against the piece driven away but rather against the area left undefended by it.

It follows that the driving-off manoeuvre as a tactical weapon is mostly resorted to in **mating combinations** or when **a passed pawn is to be realized.** In positions with few pieces the latter motif is of far greater practical importance. Therefore, we propose to examine various forms of driving-off sacrifice **intended to pave the way for pawn promotions.**

175.

SCHEME.

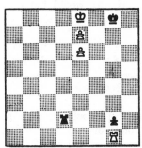

White wins.

Black's plan is to keep White's king imprisoned in front of his pawns, by the endless repetition of the moves ..., K—N2—N1. If White refuses to acquiesce in what would be something like a positional draw, he must try to drive off the rook governing the Q file.

1. R×P ch!!   R×R

The driving off has been accomplished. It is of little import that the rook is now posted exactly on White's KN2. (He might just as well stand anywhere on the second, third, fourth or fifth rank of the QB, K, KB or KR file.) The point is that the Q file is cleared and the king can get out of his pawn's way.

2. K—Q7   R—Q7 ch
3. K—B6   R—B7 ch
4. K—Q6!

It is important not to stray far from the eighth rank, lest the rook should be reactivated, e. g. in case of 5. K—Q5? Black could secure a draw by 4. ..., R—B1 5. K—Q6, K—N2! 6. K—Q7, K—B3! Now, however, 4. ..., R—B1 would fail owing to 5. K—Q7! and 6. P—K8 (Q) ch, etc.

4. — —   R—Q7 ch
5. K—K5   R—K7 ch
6. K—B5   R—B7 ch
7. K—N5

7. K—N4? would again be an error on account of 7. ..., R—B1!. Yet this sacrifice is not satisfactory now because the king is sufficiently close to

the pawns. Also 7. ..., R—N7 ch would serve no purpose since there would be no more checks for Black after 8. K—R4, R—R7 ch 9. K—N3.

7. — —   R—B1
8. P×R (Q) ch   K×Q
9. K—B6!   K—K1
10. P—K7   and wins.

176.

F. J. PROKOP, 1925.

White wins.

White must clear the way for his NP, but how? 1. K—B5, Black counters with 1. ..., K—K2 with an eye on the queening square. On 1. K—B7, 1. ..., N—B5! follows (threatening White's Q5) and the knight catches up with the pawn after 2. K—Q6, N—Q6, 3. P—N6, N—N5 4. P—N7, N—R3. It seems best to take the middle course:

1. K—B6!   K—K2!

Clears the knight's path, since the promotion square can only be reached via Black's KB3 and Q2.

2. P—N6   N—B3
3. P—N7   N—Q2

The worries caused by the NP are just about over, but now the innocent-looking BP intervenes as a vigorous driving-off piece.

4. P—B6 ch!   K—K3
5. P—B7!   K—K2
5. ..., N—N1 ch 6. K—B7, N—R3 ch 7. K—N6 wins.
6. P—B8 ch!   and wins,

since either the king or the knight will be forcibly driven off.

On the strength of these simple examples it may already be stated that the purpose of the driving-off manoeuvre is **to scatter the opponent's defensive forces** and to secure for our own pieces free access to certain squares. With a passed pawn on the board, our primary objective is, of course, to assume absolute control of the **queening square.** The method employed varies with the type of end-game.

In **rook end-games** a realizable pawn may decide the issue in two ways, namely **(a)** it is escorted to the queening square under adequate support so that the opponent cannot help giving up his rook for it, or **(b)** we **drive off** the adverse rook, if need be by sacrificing our own, from its post commanding the queening square. In this way we may not only promote our pawn but also retain the new-born queen against the hostile rook. The former method is a general, strategic way of winding up a game, the latter is a widely applied tactical possibility.

177.

A. A. TROITSKY, 1909.

White wins.

1. P—R7!   R—N4 ch

1. ..., R—N1? would be wrong because of 2. R—R1 ch and 3. R—N1 ch.

2. K—B6!   R—QR4

The driving-on manoeuvre enforced with threats is the first link in White's combination. Now comes its reverse: the driving off of the rook from the R file with new threats.

In case of 2. ..., R—N3 ch 3. K—B5, R—QR3 4. R×P ch, K—R3 the rook would be driven off by 5. R—B6 ch!! If Black had tried to deviate with 4. ..., K—N1, White would have triumphed after 5. R—B8 ch, K—N2 6. P—R8 (Q).

3. K—B7!   K—R3

There was no other defence against the mating threat. Now we see why we had to spare Black's harmful BP: it

prevents Black from escaping by ...,
R×P ch.

| 4. R—B6 ch | K—R2 |

After 4. ..., K—N4 the same driving-off sacrifice would follow.

| 5. R—B5!! | R×R |

Forced because White threatens
mate after R—R3 or R—R5.

| 6. P—R8 (Q) | R—KN4 |
| 7. Q×P | and wins. |

White has a simple win also if Black
chooses to play 4. ..., K—N4. (5. R—
B5 ch!, R×R 6. P—R8 (Q), R—B6
7. Q—Q5! etc.)

* * *

The following very instructive end-
game demonstrates White's elaborate
strategy being crowned with a fine
tactical point.

178.

M. EISENSTADT, 1932.

White wins.

1. R—N7 ch!

This driving-off manoeuvre paves
the way for the realization of further
plans with an important gain of tempo; it chases the king a step farther
from the main theatre of operations.
The immediate 1. P—N7 is not
enough, since after 1. ..., R—KN8
2. R×P, R—N4! 3. R—K7, K—B8!
4. R—K1 ch, K—Q7 White cannot
create the strategic conditions for
victory by bringing his rook to the
KN file. Even the continuation 1.
P—N7?, R—KN8 2. R—N7 ch is of
no avail, because then Black's king
may proceed without penalty to the
QB file and White has no promising
play after 2. ..., K—B6 3. R×P ch,
K—Q5 4. R—QR7, K—K4.

1. — —	K—R6!
2. P—N7	R—KN8
3. R×P	K—N5!

The sooner Black can leave his seventh, sixth and fifth ranks, the better.
Only in this way can he hope to
prevent White from carrying out a
strategic redeployment: 4. R—K7!
and R—K2 (3, 4) ch followed by
R—KN2 (3, 4) threatening a forced
exchange of rooks.

4. K—R4!

Since after 4. R—K7 Black's reply,
4. ..., K—B4! would thwart White's
plan, the offensive side strives for a
simple technical realization of his

pawn by bringing his king to its support. Black must obstruct the king's route (K—R5—R6 etc.) to avoid the inevitable defeat after 4. . . ., P—B4 5. K—R5, P—B5 6. K—R6, P—B6 7. R—KB7, R—N6 8. K—R7, R—R6 ch 9. K—N8, K—B5 10. K—B8!.

| 4. — — | R—N4! |
| 5. R—K7! | K—B4! |

Is everything all right? By no means. The seemingly strong main bastion of defence can be blown up by means of a splendid driving-off sacrifice!

| 6. R—K5 ch!! | and wins, |

since 6. . . ., P×R leaves Black's rook undefended, and after 6. . . ., R×R the newly obtained queen will seal the fate of the BP.

★ ★ ★

In **bishop endings,** as in knight endings, the driving-off motif is of especial importance because the material advantage obtained by capturing the hostile bishop for a pawn is not in itself enough for victory.

The general ideas underlying such an ending are condensed in the following textbook example:

179.

H. COHN, 1929.*

White wins.

1. B—K3!

White's bishop tries to reach his QN8 via QR7. White has to act without any loss of time to forestall the advance of Black's pawn after a possible . . ., B—Q3.

1. — — P—R5

The circumstances, as will soon be seen, are not altogether favourable for the pawn to advance, but any alternative waiting move would only bring White nearer to his original plan, e. g. 1. . . ., B—Q3 2. B—R7!, P—R5 3. B—N8!, B×B 4. K×B, P—R6 5. K—B8, P—R7 6. P—N8 (Q), P—R8 (Q) 7. Q—N7 ch—and Black has lost

* This theme was originally elaborated by L. Centurini, in 1856, in an analysis of the realization of White's NP posted on QN7. In Centurini's example White's bishop stood on Q8, Black's on its KR7, and there was no Black RP.

the new queen. The result is also the same after 3. ..., B—B4 4. B—R2, B—R2 5. B—N1!, P—R6 6. B×B, P—R7 7. P—N8 (Q).

2. B—B2!

The first driving-off manoeuvre. Though it does not solve White's problem, it at least wins the RP.

2. — —	B—Q3!
3. B×P	K—N3!

Black must seek defence against the threat 4. B—B2, 5. B—R7 and 6. B—N8.

4. B—B2 ch	K—R3!

It is difficult now to find a sound continuation. Having no access to his QR7, White ought perhaps to wriggle his bishop to QB7 via Q8. But after 5. B—R4, K—N3! 6. B—Q8 ch, Black can play ..., K—B3, renewing his control over White's QB7 in good time. White may attempt now to divert the hostile bishop by 7. B—K7, but Black will be wise enough to keep it on the diagonal and, as before, the KN1—QR7 diagonal cannot be occupied in **one move.**

Why not? Because it is on its K7 that the bishop has come face to face with its counterpart, from where it could proceed only to QB5, a square controlled by Black's king. What if we tried to drive off Black's bishop with ours on KB6 or KN5 or KR4? Then we could in fact attack the opponent's bishop with a gain of tempo, for after its removal we could immediately

seize control over the route leading to QR7!

Let us wait a little then for Black's bishop to leave its cosy Q3 ...

5. B—K3 (Q4)	B—R7!

The only move that still delays the implementation of our plan, because we cannot grapple with Black's slippery bishop from our Q1—KR4 diagonal. This goes to show that the bishop has two convenient squares to go to: its Q3 and KR7. Our task is obvious. **We must force Black's bishop to leave its QR7 without its being able to go to Q3!**

6. B—B5!!	B—K4

Black could as well play 6. ..., B—B5 or 6. ..., B—N6, the point is that his bishop can now be engaged in the open field.

7. B—K7!	K—N3

Necessary on account of the threat B—Q8—B7.

8. B—Q8 ch!	K—B3
9. B—B6!	

The second driving-off manoeuvre brings us closer to victory.

9. — —	B—Q3
10. B—Q4	B—R7

From now on the moves of Black's bishop are indifferent. It will soon have to leave the long diagonal for the shortest, and lose the game.

11. B—R7!	B—Q3
12. B—N8!	B—B4
13. B—R2	B—R2
14. B—N1!	

The third, unconditionally forcing diversion. Black's bishop cannot escape it because the diagonal is too short.

14. — —	B×B
15. P—N8 (Q)	and wins.

180.

R. RÉTI, 1925.

White wins.

The foregoing lesson might lead us to believe that a similar end-game could be enforced here by exchanging the RP for Black's BP.

But after 1. K—K2?, K—N5! 2. B—K7!, K×P 3. B×P, K—N4 4. B—R3, K—B3 5. K—K3, K—Q2 6. K—B4, K—K1 7. K—B5, K—Q2! it turns out that White's king cannot worm his way into black's position and no advantageous exchange of the bishops can be forced through. Nor is it much better to secure the RP by

1. P—R5, for after 1. ..., K—N4 2. K—K2, P—B5! 3. K—K3, P—B6! Black's pawn too becomes a permanent menace.

The solution is as short as it is poignant.

1. B—R5!	K—N6

1. ..., K—Q6 White counters with the text, any other move with 2. K—K2 etc. and wins.

2. B—B3!!	

A surprisingly strong driving-off sacrifice based on the fact that momentarily Black's king is outside the "magic square" of the RP, and the bishop is unable to stop both pawns.

2. — —	B×B

2. ..., K×B or 2. ..., B—R3 would be answered by the same move:

3. P—R5!	and wins,

because one of the pawns can be realized by giving up the other as a driving-off sacrifice.

In **knight endings** too, the driving-off manoeuvre is a frequently applied tactical weapon for realizing an extra pawn. In this respect the knight is more vulnerable than the bishop, for on account of its shorter range it cannot escape attack and still maintain its control over certain squares. Yet it is a good end-game fighter, mostly thanks to its extensive secondary range, its ability to threaten a number of squares **indirectly.**

A simple but substantial textbook example of a "knightly" driving-off manoeuvre:

181.

R. RÉTI, 1929.

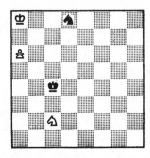

White wins.

1. K—R7!   K—N4

White threatens K—N6 and P—R7 etc. In case of 1. ..., N—B3 ch 2. K—N6, K—Q4 the simplest driving off: 3. N—N4 ch! would follow. 1. ..., K—B4 would be countered by 2. N—Q4!! forcing Black into a Zugzwang position or into defeat after 2. ..., K×N.

2. N—N4!

This is no active driving-off sacrifice, since Black is not forced to take the knight, but remaining alive the knight does a good job by defending the pawn.

2. — —   K—R4

There is no salvation after 2. ..., K—B4 3. K—N8!, because White's knight commands also the QB6 square.

3. K—N8   N—B3 ch!

A driving-off attempt, now on Black's part, with a view to depriving the pawn of its support. It is easily repelled though, for after the next continuation neither the king nor the knight may capture White's undefended piece.

4. K—N7!

In case of 4. K—B7? Black would be free to play 4. ..., N×N! 5. P—R7, N—Q4 ch 6. K—B6, N—N3!

4. — —	N—Q1 ch
5. K—B7	N—K3 ch
6. K—N8!	K—N3
7. P—R7	N—B2

And now a forcing diversion:

8. N—Q5 ch!   and wins.

* * *

We have so far examined driving-off operations carried out against various pieces, but our analysis should also cover the **king** whose intervention in end-games is very often of the utmost importance for both attack and defence.

If the opponent's king obstructs our pawn and prevents its promotion, which is often the case, we shall concentrate our efforts on driving him off. Let us look at an illustrative example:

182.

O. DURAS, 1923.

White wins.

Since he has only an outside pawn and a "bad" bishop which does not cover the queening square, nothing but energetic driving-off manoeuvres can assure the win.

1. B—N2!

Clears the way for the pawn with a gain of tempo. As a driving-off attempt it has little weight, because Black's king is already as uncomfortably placed on his KB7 as he would be on KN7.

1. — —	K—K6!
2. P—R4	K×P
3. B—B3!	

But this is a more significant move, since it denies the KN4 square to Black's king and forces him to make a detour. Black must not accept the invitation, for in case of 3. . . ., K×B 4. P—R5, K—N7 5. P—R6, P—B5 6. P—R7, P—B6 7. P—R8 (Q), P—B7 the queen will reach her KN3 after several checks and Black's forced . . ., K—B8 is a prelude to mate in two moves (Q—R2 and Q—R1).

3. — —	K—K4
4. P—R5	K—K3
5. B—Q5 ch	

Sometimes even a bad bishop has its good points. The third driving-off sacrifice is decisive because it prevents the king from getting in front of the pawn, though it does not force him to turn his back on it.

5. — —	K—K2
6. P—R6	K—B1
7. K—Q2	and wins,

because Black's monarch must stay put, while his pawns will fall one by one, resulting in a total Zugzwang for Black.

* * *

In more complicated and longer combinations the driving-off manoeuvre often occurs in a more complex, two-stage form. Let us remember that the control effect of a certain piece can also be decreased by way of line interference. Diversion and line interference sometimes make a happy combination.

In the cases examined so far, the piece driven off had to leave its original place; consequently it ceased to exercise its control effect over certain squares. In the examples on line interference the piece preventing the realization of some plan remained on its place, but it was blocked by another piece and its control effect nullified in certain directions. The combination of these two factors is sometimes so powerful as to work wonders or, at least, achieve what could not be done by resorting to one or the other motif alone.

Let us presume that in order to reach some goal it would be desirable to eliminate the control effect of a hostile piece, but we cannot drive it off from its original line nor can this line be closed. In such a case it must be considered whether there is a possibility of decoying that piece farther from the critical point. Then the line in question may be lengthened sufficiently to allow of creating an interference on some square in between.

Such a preliminary driving-off manoeuvre carried out in the interest of line interference may be termed **driving over**. Its essence is that the piece driven out, though remaining on its original line, will be transposed to such a section of that line that it can be cut off by means of line interference. Of course, only "line pieces" (mostly the bishop and the rook) can be driven over to a certain square. (Driving-off and driving-over manoeuvres against the highly mobile queen are very rarely effective; therefore in this chapter we shall not deal with examples of this kind.)

Respective examples of the successful driving over of rook and bishop:

183.

H. RINCK, 1911.

White wins.

1. P—K7!

1. B—B5 ch?, K—R5 2. P—K7, R—R1 or 2. P×P, K—N4 ch, 3. K—N2, R—Q3! leads only to a draw.

1. — —   K—N5 ch!

A necessary interpolation, because the immediate 1. . . ., R—K3?? fails against 2. B—B5 ch.

2. K—N2   R—K3

It would be a good thing now to cut off the control effect of the rook towards its K2—K1. This cannot be done **either** by driving off **or** by line interference **alone**. But should the rook, for instance, be posted on its K8, we could slam the door behind it by way of P—B3 ch and B—K4. Therefore the rook must be **driven over** the K4 square towards K1.

3. R—K2!!   R×R
4. B—K4!!   R×B
5. P—B3 ch   and wins.

DRIVING OFF (DIVERSION) BY PINNING

The control effect of pieces can also be eliminated or decreased by **pinning**. The piece under pin cannot leave its place, lest a more precious piece standing on the same line should be exposed to danger. In this respect the pinning is only effective if the laws of movement of the pinned piece differ from those of the piece pinning it. For example a rook can pin a bishop or *vice versa*, and a line-piece can pin a knight or a pawn.

If, however, the pinning piece and the pinned one are of the same kind, the pin is not complete, being confined not to a given square but a given line. (Line pinning.)

By way of line pinning a piece can be forced to exchange off or capture the pinning piece. The latter option is a typical form of driving off, not differing, in principle, from the motifs dealt with thus far.

1. B—B8!

Threatening a discovered attack (2. P—K7!) against the bishop even after 1. . . ., K—Q3. It is not sufficient for Black to capture the KP at the price of exchanging off the bishops, because after 1. . . ., B×P 2. B×B ch, K×B 3. K—K4!, K—Q3 4. K—Q4, K—B3 5. K—B4!—White would win with his remaining pawn. Black's bishop must, therefore seek safety in flight, and be ready to control his K1 at the same time.

1. — —   B—B8
2. P—K7   B—N4
3. P—B4 ch!

A powerful directing move! Either the bishop is driven **off** the QR4—K8 diagonal (followed by the immediate queening of White's pawn) or the king is driven **on** the QR6—KB1 diagonal and the stage is set for a driving off by pinning.

3. — —   K×P
4. B—R6!   and wins.

184.

F. SACKMANN, 1909.

White wins.

185.

A. O. HERBSTMAN, 1926.

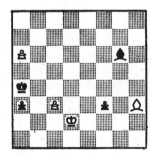

White wins.

Here White's king prepares the ground for a driving off by a pin of Black's bishop, in order to realize his RP.

1. K—K3!	B—B2
2. K—Q4!	B—K1

It is a matter of life and death for Black to occupy the long diagonal. 2. ..., P—R7? would fail on account of 3. P—R7, P—R8 (Q) 4. P—R8 (Q) ch and 5. Q×Q.

3. P—R7	B—B3

Black has reached his goal but on this particular square the defensive powers of the bishop can be paralysed by pinning.

4. B—Q7!	and wins,

because after 4. ..., P—B7 5. B×B ch, K—N6 6. B—N5 (N2) the outside pawn is safely promoted.

★ ★ ★

In the next end-game White in realizing his passed pawn wields an array of tactical weapons, including threats, a driving-on manoeuvre forcing Black into line interference, chase and finally the motif of driving off by pinning. This goes to show how efficaciously the several motifs described so far can be interlinked to build up a successful combination.

186.

H. RINC, 1907.

White wins.

1. P—N7	B—Q4
2. P—B4!	N×P

After 2. ..., B—K3 White wins more quickly. Now the knight obstructs the movement of his bishop.

3. B—B3!	B—K3
4. B—N4!	and wins.

In rook endings the motif of pinning can in like manner be combined with that of driving off. The next study demonstrates the underlying idea in two variations.

187.

V. and M. PLATOV, 1923.

White wins.

1. R—R3!!

White prefers to decoy Black's rook on to the closed QR file rather than to open that file imprudently by 1. R×P ch. In the latter case there would be no win for White 1. ..., K—N3 2. P—Q7, R—R6 ch 3. K—N2, R—R1 4. R—R5, K—B3 5. R—Q5, R—Q1 6. K—B3, K—B4! (Not ..., K—K3? 7. K—K4!)

1. ——   R—N3!

The sacrifice had to be refused, for though after 1. ..., R×R 2. P—Q7, R—R8 ch, 3. K—N2, R—R7 4. P—Q8 (Q), R×P ch 5. K—B3, K—N3 6. Q—K7, R—B6 ch 7. K—N4, R—K6! Black could save his pawns, he would jeopardize his king: 8. Q—Q6 ch, K—B2 9. K—B5! etc.

A version of driving off by pinning would have ensued after 1. ..., R—N2 2. R—R3 ch, K—N1 3. R—KN3!! and there would be no way of stopping White's QP.

The same manoeuvre is less effective now, because 2. R—R3 ch can be countered by 2. ..., K—N2! 3. R—KN3??, R×R 4. P—Q7, R—R6 ch! 5. K—N2, R—R1. Therefore White must operate with threats on the other wing.

2. P—Q7!   R—Q3
3. R×P!   K—N3 (R3)

There is no other defence against 4. P—Q8 (Q) ch, since in case of 3. ..., K—R1 (N1) White wins by 4. R—R8 ch and 5. P—Q8 (Q). But now White has recourse to driving off by pinning:

4. R—R6!   and wins.

* * *

Though we are concerned here with the various cases of driving off as a weapon for realizing a passed pawn, we propose to include an example which demonstrates that the same manoeuvre (driving off by pinning) is, strangely enough, also suitable for the neutralization of a pin. This motif may be called counter-pinning or—if you like it—cross-pinning.

(This manoeuvre is not to be confused with another which aims at the actual removal of an existing pin by a driving-off sacrifice. For instance, let us take this position: White's king on QN5, his queen on KB7 and his rook on KN5. Black's king on Black's KR1, his queen on KR2 and his rook on KN1. Now it would be wrong to pin Black by 1. R—R5? because of the possible unpinning and driving-off reply: 1. ..., R—N4 ch!)

188.

B. HORWITZ, 1873.

White wins.

Which of the two queens is doomed in this position?

1. R(6)×R   R×R(3)

After 1. . . ., Q×R(5)? 2. P—N6 ch Black cannot avert the mate.

2. P—N6 ch   K×P

2. . . ., K—N1? fails against 3. R—R8 ch, and 2. . . ., R×P? 3. Q×Q would also be in White's favour. For this reason White is willing to sacrifice a rook.

3. R—R6!   and wins,

because the counter-pin saves not only the life of the queen but also wins one of Black's chief officers.

BREAK-THROUGH

Thus far we have dealt with the driving off of various **pieces**. But in the end-game the driving off of **pawns** is also an important factor.

The driving off of pawns is aimed at **opening a line,** or more often, at **clearing a square** or **path.**

The driving-off operation for the establishment of a passed pawn, i. e. to remove the obstacle hindering its advance is called **break-through.** Let us see it in its simplest forms:

189.

SCHEME I.

I. 1. P—R6, K—Q3 2. P—N6! wins.

190.

SCHEME II.

II. 1. P—N6!, BP×P 2. P—R6!, P×P 3. P—B6 wins. Or:
1. P—N6!, RP×P 2. P—B6!, P×P 3. P—R6 wins.

Similar sacrifices purposing to establish a passed pawn can often be carried out in several phases. Sometimes we have to heap sacrifice on sacrifice in order to remove the obstacles. For example:

191.

SCHEME.

White wins.

Four pawns try to shoot forward in succession and it is the fifth that actually does the job.

1. P—R4!	P×P e.p.
2. P—N4!	P×P
3. P—B5!	P×P
4. P—Q6!	P×P
5. P—K7	and wins.

* * *

A break-through is of especial importance in the struggle between N and R pawns. An outside pawn is very rarely realizable and the opponent might also try and convert our NP—as we have seen in end-game No. 172—to a RP. An important tactical means of thwarting such an attempt is the break-through.

A typical instance of it is shown by this study:

192.

F. M. TEED, 1885.

White wins.

1. K—B7!   P—R4!

Forced, but seemingly good, for after 2. P×P? White will have only worthless outside pawns left, and in case of 2. K—B6?, P×P 3. P×P, K—R3 4. K—B5, K—R2 5. K×P, K—N2! Black can secure a draw by taking up the opposition.

Consequently only a break-through will bring us nearer the desired goal.*

2. P—R4!!   K—R3

The best, though it does not help either. After 2. ..., NP×P 3. P—N5! or 2. ..., RP×P 3. P×P White obtains a passed pawn with tempo. It is obvious now why White had to go precisely to KB7 on his first move.

3. K—B6!   NP×P

Nor is ..., RP×P 4. P×P ch, K—R4 5. P—N6, P—N6 6. P—N7, P—N7 7. P—N8 (Q) any better for Black.

4. P—N5 ch	K—R2
5. K—B7!	P—R6

* It is interesting that this example is very rarely to be found among end-game reproductions. Most theoretical books cite the Walker position (1841) as a textbook pattern. (White: king on KB8, pawns on KN5 and KR4. Black: king on his KR1, pawns on KN3 and KR2.) This position, however, is more artificial, moreover it meets neither the artistic nor the didactic requirements, since after 1. K—B7, P—R3 White can simply win also by playing 2. K×P, P×P 3. P×P!, KN1 4. K—R6!, etc. instead of 2. P—R5! as intended.

6. P—N6 ch	K—R3
7. P—N7	P—R7
8. P—N8 (Q)	P—R8 (Q)
9. Q—N6 ch	and mate.

These century-old examples show that the break-through has for a long time been a widely recognized and consciously applied tactical factor in end-games. Hence its frequent occurrence in over-the-board games which often produce study-like positions.

An example set by experienced grandmasters will throw light on the unpleasant consequences of ignoring the possibility of a break-through:

193.

STAHLBERG—TARTAKOWER, 1934.

White to play.

(This diagram is taken from a casual game played by the two Grandmasters in Budapest, after the Újpest International Tournament, 1934.)

In this losing position White made a bold gamble for a break-through, and it worked!

| 1. P—B4! | P×P?? |

Black had only the three united passed pawns in mind—which make a terrible force indeed—but overlooked the other break-through manoeuvre that was to start with the sudden onslaught of the RP. Instead of walking straight into the trap Black could have easily won by playing 1. ..., K—B3 and 2. ..., K×P, but now—however incredible it seems—he is hopelessly lost!

| 2. P—R4! | P—R4 |

2. ..., K—B4 3. P—R5, K—N4 4. P—Q5, K—B3 5. P—Q6, K—K3 6. P—R6! wins.

3. P—R5	P—R5
4. K—Q2!	P—N4
5. P—Q5 ch!	K—Q2

If 5. ..., K×P 6. P—R6! follows and the pawn is promoted with check.

| 6. P—R6! | |

There is no time to lose because after 6. K—B3?, P—R6! 7. P—R6, P—N5 ch! etc. Black recovers his breath.

6. — —	P—R6
7. K—B2!	P—N5
8. P×P	P—N6 ch
9. K—N1!	

After 9. K—B3?, P—R7 10. K—N2, P—B6 ch! 11. K—R1, P—B7

12. K—N2, P—R8 (Q) ch! Black would win.

9. — —	P—R7 ch
10. K—R1!!	P—B6
11. P—N8 (Q)	and wins.

* * *

An elaborate build-up for a break-through is demonstrated in this study:

194.

J. BEHTING, 1905.

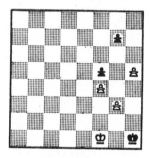

White wins.

In principle, White has two options here for capitalizing his extra pawn. The simple, technical way would be to exchange the NP for Black's BP, and march up with the king and the pawns; the tactical method to drive off the hostile pawns, i.e. effect a break-through.

But neither of these options is smooth going right from the outset. After 1. K—B2, K—R7 2. K—B3, K—R6 Black is just in time to prevent White's playing P—N4. After 1. P—N4?, P×P 2. P—P5, P—N6 Black's pawn will evidently outmarch White's.

With the text, a preparatory waiting move, White does not show his hand, keeping both irons in the fire.

| 1. K—K1!! | K—N7 |

In case of 2. . . ., K—R7 3. K—B2!, K—R6 4. K—B3, K—R7 White could proceed with a well-timed 5. P—N4. The text continuation, however, makes the break-through possible, since Black's king now obstructs his own pawn on the KN file.

2. P—N4!	P×P
3. P—B5	P—N6
4. P—B6!	

Green light for the RP to queen with check, should Black's king go to the KR file.

4. — —	P×P
5. P—R6	P—B4
6. P—R7	P—B5

Black has missed the boat, but only because White played K—K1! If instead K—K2? had been the first move, Black's BP could now advance with check, and White would not be able to win.

| 7. P—R8(Q) | P—B6 |
| 8. Q—R8! | and wins. |

As we have observed in these examples, the object of a break-through is to establish a passed pawn; in other words, to remove the obstacle barring the way of a blockaded (fixed) pawn. It is usually a case of pawns facing pawns, but it goes without saying that pieces may also take part in the struggle.

The sacrifice of a piece may serve either to drive off an obstructing hostile pawn or to annihilate it. An example of each to end this chapter:

195.

LUND—NIMZOVITCH, Oslo, 1921.

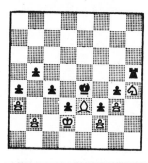

Black to play and win.

The blockade seems to be complete. Indeed it is only by a grandiose all-out break-through manoeuvre carried out along the whole breadth of the front that Black can prove the vulnerability of White's defences.

1. — —	P—N5!
2. P×P	R×N!
3. P×R	P—N6!
4. P×P	P—B6 ch
5. P×P	P—R6

—and Black wins. — In his textbook M. Czerniak describes the finish of

this end-game as an "orgy of sacrifices," and not without reason!

In the next end-game Black's doubled pawns are more than a match for a rook and a knight.

196.

ORTUETA—SANZ, Madrid, 1934.

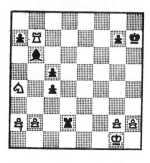

Black to play and win.

1. — —	R×QNP!!
2. N×R	P—B6

Threatening (after 3. N—Q1, N—R4 or N—B4) 3. . . ., P—B7 and 4. . . ., P—B8 (Q). 3. N—Q3 on the other hand would allow time for Black's other BP to intervene decisively with discovered check. E. g. 3. N—Q3?, P—B5 ch! 4. K—B1, P×N 5. K—K1, P—B7 6. K—Q2, B—K6 ch!, etc.; or: 4. N—B2, P—B7 etc.; or: 4. R×B, P×N! and the two pawns win against the rook. Nor would 3. R—K7 be any better for White in view of 3. . . ., P×N 4. R—K1, P—B5 ch! 5. K—B1, P—B6 etc.

Therefore White's only hope lies in returning the sacrifice.

3. R×B!   P—B5!!

In case of 3. . . ., P×R White could have continued with 4. N—Q3, P—B5 5. N—B1 etc. But now . . ., P—B7 is very dangerous again, since it cannot be parried by 4. R—QB6 on account of 4. . . ., P×N! and the pawn is promoted on the other file.

4. R—N4!   P—R4!!

A splendid additional threat! Now Black would counter 5. R—N8 or 5. N×P with 5. . . ., P—B7, while in the text the rook is unable to return to QN4.

5. R×P   P×N!
—and Black wins.

In this last example the breakthrough has been made possible by the **annihilation** of the obstacle—White's QNP—and not by the "driving-off" motif, yet the key to success lay in the driving on of the knight.

Having devoted this section to the subject of driving off, we have deliberately come back to the concept of driving on. The two motifs are, in fact, closely related, and may often occur together in the same combination.

We have examined them separately as tactical elements and now—in the following chapter—we propose to give a survey of both with particular stress on the relationship between them.

The tactical motifs we have discussed in the preceding chapters may also
occur together, in close interconnection. We have seen that, if we force
some hostile piece to an inconvenient
square, it is a case of driving off as
opposed to the driving-on manoeuvre
which consists in decoying a hostile
piece from a square favourable to the
opponent. In both cases we direct the
opponent's pieces by forcible means.

There are two instances when we
may speak of total direction. One is
when, as a result of our forcing move,
a hostile piece leaves a definite square
and lands on another definite square;
or, to put it more plainly, the "wherefrom" is just as important as the
"whereto?" Regarded from this angle
it is obvious that the motifs of driving off and driving on can be combined in a single move.

The other case of total direction is
when our combination is made up of
an alternation of driving-off and driving-on moves.

Let us demonstrate first the concept
of a one-move directing sacrifice.

In this position White's extra rook
seems to be amply offset by Black's
QN6 pawn. White has no winning
chance even if he can get both of
Black's NP's in exchange for the rook;

197.

Dr. G. KISSLING, 1921.

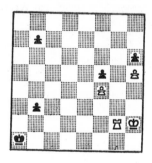

White wins.

what's more, after 1. R—N7, P—N7
2. R×P, P—N8 (Q) 3. R×Q, K×R
Black has a won end-game.

Still there is one hidden move that
turns the scales in White's favour.

1. R—N5!!

A total directing sacrifice since it
accomplishes not only the driving off
of Black's RP but also drives it precisely to its KN4, within convenient
slaying distance for White's BP.

1. — —   P×R

The acceptance of the sacrifice is forced, for after 1. ..., P—N7 2. R×P, P—N3 3. R—N5 or 2. ..., P—N8 (Q) 3. R—R5 ch, Q—R7! 4. R×Q ch, K×R White's BP is the first to queen.

2. P—R6 P—N7
3. P—R7 P—N8 (Q)

Black's queen is sooner or later to be exchanged off and then White's remaining pawn starts its triumphal march.

4. P—R8 (Q) ch K—R7
5. Q—R8 ch K—N7
6. Q×P ch K—B7
7. Q×Q ch K×Q
8. P×P and wins.

★ ★ ★

A directing sacrifice lays the foundation for the win also in the next rook ending in which, however, it does not lead straightaway to the winning position as was the case in the previous example.

198.

Dr. A. WOTAWA, 1951.

White wins.

1. P—N7! R×NP

If 1. ..., R—R1?, then 2. R×P, K—N3 3. R—N4 ch, etc. easily wins.

2. R—R3!!

It turns out that White's plan is not to realize his RP, but to launch a mating attack against Black's unhappily posted king. The directing move has in fact served a double purpose, namely **(a)** the hostile rook has been made to leave the QR file on which White's RP is a constant menace, and **(b)** the rook has occupied its KN2, the exact square where it indirectly bars the escape of its king (2. ..., K—N3? 3. R—N3 ch, etc. wins quickly.)

But why has White not captured Black's QRP? A fine instance of sparing the harmful pawn, for after 2. R×P? Black could have warded off the mating threat (P—N4) after R to the KN file by way of 2. ..., R—QR2! 3. R—KN4, R×P 4. R—N8, R—R6 ch.

But now White's threat is still in the air, the obstacle on the QR file frustrating the suggested line of defence

2. — — R—QB2
3. R—KN3 P—R6

Black is ready to parry the mating threat after 4. R—N8 by ..., R—B6 ch. Therefore another directing move is needed, the rook must be driven off from the open line and driven on to a closed one.

4. P—R7! R×P
5. R—N8! R—R5
6. P—N4 ch R×P

| 7. R×R | P—N4 |
| 8. R—N4! | and wins. |

In the next bishop ending the directing sacrifice brings about an exceptional drawing position in spite of the opponent's overwhelming superiority:

199.

A. A. TROITSKY, 1906.

Draw.

| 1. B—N4! | B—N4 |
| 2. B—Q2!! | |

The double purpose of the sacrifice is again very remarkable. It drives off the bishop from the Q8—KR4 diagonal and drives it on to the Q2 square. The driving off has cleared the way in front of White's pawn, the driving on restricts the mobility of Black's prospective queen. Though the sacrifice is not forcing, Black obviously cannot expect to win if he tolerates White's bishop on its QB—KR6 diagonal.

2. — —	B×B
3. P—K7	P—B8 (Q) ch
4. K—Q7	and draws,

because the interfering bishop prevents Black from giving more checks and White is free to queen.

* * *

Here follow some simple, classical examples of the combined application of chase, driving on and driving off, for bringing about the desired winning position.

200.

Dr. Em. LASKER, 1890.

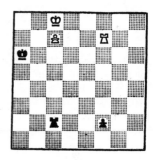

White wins.

1. K—N8	R—N7 ch
2. K—R8!	R—B7
3. R—B6 ch	K—R4

3. ..., K—N4? is unsound, since the QN file must be left open so that if need be the rook can harass White's king with checks.

4. K—N7	R—N7 ch
5. K—R7!	R—B7
6. R—B5 ch	K—R5
7. K—N7	R—N7 ch

Again and again Black is compelled to give another check, lest White should attain his R×P driving-off manoeuvre.

8. K—R6!	R—B7
9. R—B4 ch	K—R6
10. K—N6!	R—N7 ch
11. K—R5!	R—B7

White has completed his plan of gradually squeezing back the hostile king and now, after driving him to the second rank, White crowns it by a driving off with pinning.

12. R—B3 ch	K—R7
13. R×P!	and wins.

* * *

Occasionally we can also prevent the increase of the range of a hostile piece, for example the opening of a line, by way of direction.

201.

P. HEUÄCKER, 1930.

White wins.

The three elements of direction are presented here one by one and these three factors together combine to assure a gain of tempo needed for the eventual blockading of Black's harmful KP.

First, a try for driving off:

1. B—R7!	B—R8!

Now a little chase to bring the king nearer his goal on K4, to prevent the opening of the bishop's diagonal of course.

2. K—N1	B—B6
3. K—B2!	B—R8

And now a surprising driving-on manoeuvre to make the mountain come to Mohammed.

4. B—Q4!!	B×B

4. ..., P×B would indeed move the mountain, and Black would meekly resign himself to an immediate blockade by 5. K—Q3. Of course, the text continuation makes little difference.

5. K—Q3	B—R8

Unavoidable loss of tempo, because Black cannot play ..., P—K5 as long as the bishop is en prise. And he never does manage to play it after White's next move.

6. K—K4!	and wins,

because there is no cure against White's queening.

* * *

In the following example the directing manoeuvre leads to a Zugzwang position and eventually to Black's defeat.

202.

L. I. KUBBEL, 1929.

White wins.

1. P—Q4 ch!   K—K3

White threatened to rush ahead with P—N6 and N7 if either of his central pawns were captured.

2. P—Q5 ch   K—K4
3. P—N6!   N×P ch

The only way to overtake the NP leads via White's Q6. Even this line of defence has its drawback though: Black can't help "directing" White's king to a better place.

4. K—R4!   N—Q3

Things seem to be shaping out quite satisfactorily for Black: the NP cannot reach the promotion square. Indeed, Black's knight could easily

cope with the task, therefore we'd better shift it on to the king's shoulders.

5. B×N ch!   K×B
6. K—N5!

Zugzwang! The only reasonable knight move at Black's disposal also proves to be damaging because it immensely increases the effectiveness of a new driving-off sacrifice.

6. — —   N—K2
7. P—N7!   K—B2
8. P—Q6 ch!   and wins.

* * *

The above examples may have sufficed to throw light on the essentials of direction. We must point out, however, that direction is no longer a simple, elementary motif of tactical operations, but such a complex process of forcing as may enable us to tackle enormous, not to say impossible, tasks in both attack and defence.

This amounts to declaring that one who has, in his studies of technical subtleties, reached the point at which he consciously and purposefully utilizes the various motifs of direction is actually on the threshold of being able to find his way in the labyrinth of the most intricate combinations.

To cross that threshold he has to acquire abundant experience and develop both the **analytic** and **synthetic** methods of thought. In order to be able to perceive and understand the substance of an end-game with a view to drawing the correct conclusions, it is necessary to single out and to differentiate between certain characteristic features (analysis) and then to examine them in their interconnection and **unity** (synthesis). This is the process of logical thinking and creative imagination.

We propose to offer the reader a fund of practical experience by presenting here some of the finest-cut gems of artistic end-games. The reader is advised to enter into their deep analysis and follow up the thread of combinations in all detail.

It is advisable to re-examine the position after each move and then to play over the main variation again after the analysis.

203.

L. V. SALKIND, 1930.

White wins.

White's only winning chance lies in his QB6 pawn. For the rest, his pawns are isolated, his king badly posted and Black threatens to play ..., R—Q3—QB3. There is, therefore no time to lose.

1. P—B7	P—R4!

Threatening ..., K—B7 mate. Of course, we had to reckon with this danger in advance. What shall we do now? We have to drive off one or another of the enemy officers so as to provide some elbow-room for our king before it is too late.

2. R—Q4!!	R×P!

If 2. ..., R×R, White is free to promote his pawn for after 3. P—B8 (Q), R—Q6! 4. Q—N7!, K—B7 ch he can avert the danger by 5. Q—N3 ch! After 2. ..., K×R ch 3. K—N2! White is out of his predicament and is soon compensated by a queen for the sacrificed rook.

It would also be easy to stave off the mating danger in case of 2. ..., R—K6? 3. R—K4!, R×P (4. R—K2!). But now White would be led astray if he seized the alluring opportunity for a driving-off sacrifice. Though the play 3. R—Q2?!, K×R ch 4. K—N2 would put an end to the mating threat and even get a queen for White, Black would proceed with 4. ..., R—QB6! 5. P—B8 (Q), R—B7 ch, etc. and draw by perpetual check.

For the time being then, we must strive to drive off the rook, instead of the king.

3. R—B4!	R—N6!

We could easily find a defence now in 4. R—B2, but them Black's rook can prevent queening by 4 ..., R—N1 thanks to the open file. Let us deprive it of even that option..

4. R—N4!   R—R6!

To the open file, of course, otherwise Black could not guard the queening square after R—N2! We should also observe that Black can occupy his KR6 **only now** when White's rook is already closing the diagonal, otherwise White would promote his pawn with a double attack. This suggests to us the idea, even in our hurry, to drive off the rook that on the third rank there might be a square that is particularly suitable for the rook to be **driven on.**

5. R—R4!   R—N6
6. R—R3!!   and wins,

since after 6. . . ., R×R 7. P—B8 (Q), P—K3 8. Q—N7, K—B7 ch 9. Q—N3 ch!, R×Q ch 10. P×R the other QBP will also be promoted.

204.

O. DURAS, 1906.

White wins.

In bishop endings as we observed in Diagram No. 179, driving-off motifs are of particular importance. In this very difficult position the struggle is enlivened by driving on, square vacating and Zugzwang.

Our first conclusion is that we gain nothing by winning Black's bishop immediately in exchange for the NP, since after 1. P—N8 (Q), B×Q ch 2. K×B, P—B6!, etc., Black is first to queen. Obviously then our task is either to occupy the KN1—QR7 diagonal in order to prevent . . ., P—B7 or to drive off the hostile bishop from our KR2—QN8 diagonal and promote our QNP.

1. B—R3!   K—B5!
2. B—K7!   P—B6
3. B—Q8!   B×KRP

If 3. . . ., P—B7 4. B×B, P—B8 (Q) 5. P—N8 (Q) White's extra piece and pawn would decide the issue.

4. B—N6   K—N4!

Eliminates the threat 5. P—N8 (Q) which now fails on 5. . . ., B×Q ch 6. K×B, P—B7! 7. B×P, K×P.

5. P—R6!   P—N5
6. B—B2   B—B2

Threatening . . ., P—N6, and White's NP is harmless as long as it lacks the support of the QRP. Black seems to be getting the upper hand.

But now a remarkable "driving on" takes place: Black's bishop goes to the square it wants to, but gets imprisoned there.

| 7. P—N8 (Q)!! | B×Q ch |
| 8. K—N7!! | |

Of course White's king sticks to his RP which is a great power now. Black can only make tempo moves with his king behind the pawn, but he is soon deprived even of that possibility.

8. — —	K—R4
9. B—R4	K—N4
10. B—K1	P—N6

Forced, and just as bad as it would have been earlier.

11. B×P!	B×B
12. P—R7	P—B7
13. P—R8 (Q)	P—B8(Q)
14. Q—R6 ch	and wins.

* * *

Lest the difficult and intricate variations of the preceding examples should blur the clear uniform idea of direction in our mind, let us end this chapter with two apparently easy positions with a minimum of material, in which the pieces dance like graceful marionettes controlled by the invisible strings of creative imagination.

In both studies the single-track process of direction is crowned with a dramatic flourish: the concerted offensive of White's forces quite unexpectedly cuts short the life of Black's monarch.

205.

L. I. KUBBEL, 1922.

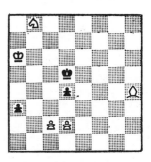

White wins.

To neutralize Black's dangerous passed pawn White must conquer the vital Q4 square.

| 1. N—B6! | K×N |

The best, for White would have countered 1. . . ., P—R7 with 2. N—N4 ch. For the rest, White threatened also to play N×P and B—B6 or N—N3. The driving-off manoeuvre has gained time for a new attack:

| 2. B—B6! | K—Q4! |

Not 2. . . ., K—B4? for fear of 3. B—K7 ch.

| 3. P—Q3! | P—R7 |
| 4. P—B4 ch! | K—B4 |

Forced move, otherwise either the QP falls or White wins easily by 4. . . ., P×P e. p. 5. B×P.

5. K—N7!!	P—R8(Q)
6. B—K7 ch	and mate!

206.

Dr. J. FRITZ, 1938.

White wins.

In this end-game both sides effectively direct each other's pieces by way of threats and attacks, and from the clash of the two lines of play a final picture emerges which could hardly be foreseen from the initial position.

It is worth noting how the threats are transformed and the plans modified as new targets for attack arise.

At any rate our first plan is the realization of the passed pawn.

1. K—N3!

Preventing ..., B—B5 ch and threatening P—B7, 1. N—K6? would not have the same effect, for after 1. ..., B—N7 or 1. ..., B—R6 Black's bishop could occupy its QN1—KR7 diagonal.

1. — —	N—N5!

Paving the way for a directing sacrifice by which Black will ultimately succeed in stealing White's cherished treasure.

Incidentally, there is no better continuation because if 1. ..., B—N7 or 1. ..., B—R6 White would continue with 2. N—B7 ch and 3. P—B7 since the knight guards both its Q6 and its K5.

2. P—B7	B—B5 ch!
3. K×B	N—Q4 ch
4. K—K5!	N×P

The pawn is lost, therefore we must change our plan. In addition to the piece sacrificed, Black has had to pay a heavy price for the pawn: White's king has become an active participant in the struggle while Black's knight is uncomfortably decentralized and as such a convenient target in White's second plan: the trapping of the knight.

5. K—Q6	N—K1 ch
6. K—K7!	N—N2

After 6. ..., N—B2 7. B—B4!, N—1 8. K—Q6!, N—N3 9. B—N3!, N—B1 ch 10. K—Q7, N—N3 ch (10. ..., N—R2 11. B—R4!) 11. K—B7, N—R1 ch 12. K—N7 White would have done it.

And now? Let us switch over to the third plan—a less obvious possibility, Zugzwang!

7. K—B8!!	N—R4
8. N—B7 ch	and mate!

THE FIGHTING KING

The motifs and elementary operations discussed in the previous chapters have invariably been accompanied by a factor which has made possible the efficient application of the principle of forcing. This factor is the direct or indirect effect of the **positions of both kings** upon the course of tactical operations.

The fact that in the overwhelming majority of end-games the king is in the open field, taking an active part in attack or defence, may often be conducive to greatly increasing the mobility and range of the hostile pieces. In open positions with few pieces a king, especially if posted near the middle of the board, is exposed to attack from several directions and offensive moves of every kind; every check given may count as a **gain of time** for the rapid deployment of the attacking piece. Practically speaking, the side that gives check can make two moves with the same piece at one go, thereby reaching without loss of time even such squares as were not originally under its direct control.

The group of squares within reach of a piece as it stands, including the square it occupies, is called the **range,** or scope, of that piece. Speaking of the range of a piece we generally think of its **primary range,** that is the group of squares it can reach **in one move.** But for a correct appraisal of the dynamic powers of a piece it is necessary that its **secondary range,** that is the group of squares it can occupy **in two moves,** should also be taken into consideration.

By giving check we can often extend the dynamic powers of a piece over a secondary range. Therefore the opponent's king very often becomes an indirect target, a springboard for the preparation of successful "skewers" or double attacks.

THE GEOMETRICAL MOTIF

A frequent objective of forcing and directing tactical operations is to achieve a position in which a king exposed to attack is placed on the line (diagonal) of another unsupported piece. In such cases we can capture the latter by giving check to the king. The target position which makes possible a dual attack (skewer) is called —on the strength of its spatial characteristics—geometrical position. Its tactical motif is the realization of the secondary range of the offensive piece whether queen, rook or bishop, intervening on the vulnerable line.

207.

A. A. TROITSKY, 1898.

White wins.

In this elementary example an energetic and meaningful sacrifice paves the way for forcing a geometrical position:

1. R—K6 ch!!

Opens a line for the queen, enforces self-interference on the long diagonal and drives Black's rook to its K3 to block a square. All this goes to the making of a successful chase.

| 1. — — | R×R |
| 2. Q—R6 ch | K—Q4 |

In case of 2. . . ., K—B (Q)2 the geometrical position is already arrived at and White wins by 3. Q—R7 ch, etc.

| 3. Q—B4 ch | K—Q3 |

After 3. . . ., K—K4, the secondary range of the queen is shifted to the diagonal: 4. Q—B3 ch, etc.

| 4. Q—B5 ch | K—Q2 |
| 5. Q—R7 ch | and wins. |

★ ★ ★

The range of the **queen** in a geometrical position is also demonstrated by the next examples. The existing queen paves the way for the action of her successor.

208.

L. van VLIET, 1888.

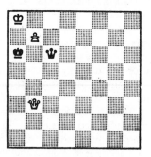

White wins.

| 1. Q—N4! | Q—R8! |

The longest move makes the game last longest. In case of 1. . . ., Q—Q4 (B6) 2. Q—R4 ch, K—N3 3. Q—N3 ch!! would force Black in a position in which a "skewer" by 4. P—N8 (Q) ch would be fatal. After 1. . . ., Q—N7 a similar geometrical position can be achieved by the continuation 2. Q—R3 ch, K—N3 3. Q—N2 ch!

| 2. Q—R3 ch | K—N3 |
| 3. Q—N2 ch! | K—B2 |

After 3. ..., K—R3 4. Q—R2 ch, K—N3 5. Q—N1 ch! the previous pattern would emerge. On 3. ..., K—B4 4. K—R7, Q—R2 5. Q—N6 ch, K—Q4 6. K—R6 wins.

Now the geometrical motif is realized by a diagonal driving-on manoeuvre.

| 4. Q—R2 ch!! | Q×Q |
| 5. P—N8 (Q) ch | and wins. |

* * *

The secondary range of the queen is of particular importance in end-games with mutual queening.

209.

N. D. GRIGORIEV, 1928.

White wins.

The extra tempo not only assures the timely promotion of White's pawn but also enables Black's prospective queen to be captured on any of the three available promotion squares.

1. P—Q4!	K—N4!
2. K—B7!	K—B4
3. P—Q5	K—K4
4. P—K4!	

Now Black may push forward with any of his three pawns, the result will ultimately be the same: a disastrous geometrical position:

A. 4. ..., P—QR4 5. K—K7, P—R5 6. P—Q6, P—R6 7. P—Q7, P—R7 8. P—Q8 (Q), P—R8 (Q) 9. Q—R8 ch—and wins.

B. 4. ..., P—N4 5. K—K7, P—N5 6. P—Q6, P—N6 7. P—Q7, P—N7 8. P—Q8 (Q), P—N8 (Q) 9. Q—Q6 ch, K×P 10. Q—N6 ch!—and wins.

C. 4. ..., P—KR4 5. K—K7, P—R5 6. P—Q6, P—R6 7. P—Q7, P—R7 8. P—Q8 (Q), P—R8 (Q) 9. Q—Q6 ch, K×P 10. Q—B6 ch—and wins.

* * *

The secondary range of the **rook** is also a frequent and well-known motif of end-game tactics. Thus far, the rook "skewer" as an efficient tactical weapon has appeared in the main or subvariations of the following end-games: Nos. 79, 124, 128, 131, 133, 148 and 160.

For the sake of completeness, we include one more example here. In this it is the recognition of the simplest and most characteristic geometrical position that leads us to the solution, but—as we shall see—the correct solution will result only from the correct recognition.

210.

N. D. GRIGORIEV, 1933.

White wins.

1. K—B6!

1. P—R7?, R—KR7 2. R—R6 (threatening mate) fails against the interpolated 2. ..., R—R3 ch! and ..., R×P.

1. — —	P—R6
2. P—R7	R—KR7
3. K—N7	P—R7

It seems that White's natural continuation is 4. R—QR6, nevertheless the following move is a very important interpolation.

It is worth noting that the sound continuation after 3. ..., K—K2 is 4. R—QN6!, and R—QR6! should be played only on Black's 4. ..., P—R7 so that in case of 5. ..., R—N7 ch 6. K—R6, R—R7 ch 7. K—N6, R—N7 ch 8. K—B5, R—R7 White could play 9. R×P! with tempo, attacking the hostile rook at the same time.

4. R—K ch!	K—Q2
5. R—QR6!	R—N7 ch
6. K—B6	R—B7 ch
7. K—K5	R—K7 ch
8. K—B4	R—R7

And now a driving-off attempt, since White's pawn is taboo on account of Black's badly posted king:

9. R×P!   and wins,

because the rook will be lost after 9. ..., R×P 10. R—R7 ch, or 9. ..., R—(anywhere) 10. R—R8!, It would make no difference if Black's king had gone to his Q1 on the fourth move. It was important, however, not to tolerate him on his K1, since he could then rush to the defence of the rook: 9. ..., R×P 10. R—R8 ch, K—B2! 11. R—R7 ch, K—N3 etc.

* * *

In end-games Nos. 67, 101, 102, 130, 138, 139, and 162 we saw many examples of the realization of a **bishop's** secondary range. Therefore it is enough to stress the importance of playing them over again. These, together with the examples of queen "skewers"—on files, ranks or diagonal —(Nos. 107, 108, 125, 158, 165) offer an adequate background for the study of the relationships between various simple tactical motifs and the geometrical motif.

THE RANGE OF THE KNIGHT

Unlike "line-pieces," the knight controls individual squares on the board, and as such is not suitable for launching attacks of the "skewer" type; but it is a most formidable fighter when it comes to simultaneous attacks launched in several directions.

From each of the 16 central squares of the board the knight, like the queen, exercises its direct effect in eight directions; therefore even its primary range is not to be underrated. By intermediate checks the area within its reach can be considerably extended.

because the secondary range of the knight extends over the whole route of the bishop's escape, due to the possible checks on QB5 and KB6.

It is remarkable that a knight's effectiveness in its secondary range can allow it to intervene almost like a bishop, that is diagonally. An especially striking illustration of this is seen in the next example.

211.

L. PROKES, 1951.

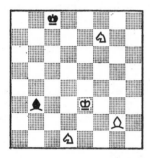

White wins.

Both knights are in peril; how are they to defend each other? The one at the edge of the board is little help, but the one that can reach the centre will be exceedingly valuable!

1. N—Q6 ch	K—Q2

If 1. . . ., K—B2 White can establish contact between the knights by 2. N—N5 ch and 3. N—B3.

2. N—K4!	B×N
3. K—Q2!	wins,

212.

L. I. KUBBEL, 1908.

White wins.

1. N—K6!

Directly preventing the bishop from going to the long diagonal and also threatening P—R7. It is not sufficient, however, to guard Q4 alone, control must be extended also to K5 and KB6.

1. — —	K—N6
2. N—Q4 ch!!	K—B5
3. N—B3!	and wins,

because the knight not only prevents . . ., B—K4, but also thwarts B—B7—

Q5, B—R5—B3 or B—K8—B6. That is one alternative. And the other?

1. — —	B—R5
2. N—B5 ch!	K—B5
3. N—K4!	and wins again,

since the roads from Black's KR5 and K8 are blocked, and an approach via KN6 or KB7 is prevented; thus Black cannot stop White's pawn.

The whole area from White's K1 to KR4 and from QB3 to KB6 is in the range of the knight!

The only disadvantage of the knight is that it is a "short-range" piece, which is why it often cannot catch up with a pawn running towards the queening square. Therefore, confronted with a king and a pawn, we can generally expect results to come not from its direct defensive effect, but from its indirect dual threats.

213.

F. J. PROKOP, 1927.

Draw.

White cannot stand idly waiting for Black to play ... P—N6 (when N—R3 would make the defence easy), because Black is seriously threatening to repel the knight.

For instance: 1. K—N3?, K—B5! 2. N—B7, P—N6! or 2. N—R7, K—B4! or 2. N—K6 ch, K—K4 3. N—B8, K—B4! and the promotion cannot be prevented. This must be forestalled by voluntary retreat.

| 1. N—R7!! | K—B6! |

1. ..., P—N6? 2. N—N5! and White has free access to KR3. If 1. ..., K—B5?, White captures the dangerous pawn by 2. N—B6!, P—N6 3. N—R5 ch. 1. ..., K—K5? would allow a double attack by N—B6 ch.

But now Black threatens ..., P—N6 and, after N—N5, ..., K—N5!, depriving White of his last hope. Therefore new efforts must be made!

2. N—B8!	P—N6
3. N—N6	K—N5
4. N—K5 ch	and draws,

because the centrally posted knight has better chances of controlling KN2 and KN1.

* * *

Usually it is rather difficult to recognize the geometrical relationships which make such "devilish" knight manoeuvres possible. But if the reader takes the trouble to study the examples Nos. 64, 65, 70, 123, 128, 134 and 181 over and over again from this viewpoint (of course not at one go!), he will get some idea of how to spot a chance if there is one, and how to wield the tactical weapons that make a knight "big."

CONCERTED ACTION

We have seen that a hostile king, as a direct target, and another piece or square in close geometrical relation to him, as an indirect target, may go a long way towards increasing the range of our pieces.

Very often the piece singled out for effecting a "skewer" or a dual attack must rely on the literally "self-sacrificing" help of one or more of its fellows. One prepares the ground for the favourable position, the other exploits it. This is what we call **concerted action**.

In the general evaluation of pieces three light officers are equivalent to a queen. But if these light pieces can go into harmonious concerted action, their combined powers multiply.

214.

H. RINCK, 1928.

White wins.

1. B—B2 ch   K—Q4

1. ..., K—K5? 2. N—Q6 ch wins the queen.

2. B—B4 ch!   K—B3
3. B—N5 ch!   K×B
4. N—Q6 ch   and wins.

A double attack has emerged from the simple chase and driving off, like the contours of a familiar face after some skilful strokes of the pencil. In fact, no more than a two-move "petite combinaison" but it contains the very essence of tactics. Let us see the same idea expressed in a more colourful example:

215.

H. RINCK, 1903.

White wins.

1. R—R8!   Q—R7!

1. ..., Q×R or 1. ..., Q—Q4 would have permitted the bishop to launch a double attack by 2. B—B3. After 1. ..., Q—K3 or 1. ..., Q—B5 the rook could have done the same (2. R—R6 ch or 2. R—B8 ch).

2. R×P!   **Q—N1**

There is nothing better again, because the rook is defended by the "range" of the bishop (2. ..., Q×R? 3. B—K8 ch).

3. R—R8!   **Q—R2**

Thus far the rook has paved the way for the bishop; now they change parts.

4. B—N6   **Q×B**
5. R—R6 ch   **and wins.**

* * *

The next end-game is a classical beauty exemplifying the concerted action of a bishop and a knight.

216.

V. and M. PLATOV, 1909.

White wins.

1. B—B6   **P—Q5**
2. N—K2!   **P—R8 (Q)**

It has not been difficult to discover the antidote of line interference (1. ..., P—Q5) in the attempted driving off (2. N—K2); though we might raise the question: "Why not play 2. N—B3? Then we could win the queen in the same way (3. B×P ch) as in the text continuation, could we not?"

Yes, indeed, but this primitive concerted action would lead only to a draw after 3. B×P ch, Q×B 4. N×Q, K×N 5. K—B4, K×P 6. K—N5, K—K5 7. K—R6, K—B4 8. K×P, K—B3! Therefore we have to fulfil taller orders!

3. N—B1!!

Threatening 4. B—N5 mate (!), while the knight is indirectly defended by the bishop.

3. — —   **Q—R4**

Apparently the best, for after 3. ..., P—R3 4. B—K5! the mate can be averted only by 4. ..., Q×N or 4. ..., K—Q7, but the first alternative would bring the queen within range of the bishop, and the second within that of the knight. The latter motif can be enforced even now.

4. B×P ch!   **K×B (K—Q7)**
5. N—N3 ch   **and wins.**

DOUBLE THREAT

The king has, as we have seen, a considerable part in increasing the range of some pieces and in giving scope to their concerted action. The question arises now whether the range of the king himself can be extended at all.

It is unthinkable that one king should give a direct check to the other, because two kings never stand on adjacent squares. He can, however, give a **discovered** check, i. e. he can take part in double attacks springing from the opening of lines or in "threatening attacks." (See Fundamental Concepts, Diagrams No. 6. and 7.)

Besides these, a king's movement also has a spatial (geometrical) quality which may be consciously utilized for the increase of his dynamic powers. From the fact that a king can move not only on ranks and files but also on diagonals, we can draw the important conclusion that the king is **able to approach two targets in different directions at the same time.**

For instance, if we want to bring our king from K1 to K7, the geometrically shortest way leads via K2—K3—K4, etc. and it requires six moves to make. Yet the **same number** of moves is enough even if we choose a diagonal route via Q2—QB3—QN4 or KB2—KN3—KR4. This means that, e. g. K—B2, will bring us **closer** to QB5—N6 as well as to KR4 lying in the opposite direction.

Consequently, the diagonal movement of a king may be utilized for bringing about simultaneous double threats. By its help we may discover surprising exceptions to the general rules, as for example the stopping of an "unstoppable" pawn.

217.

R. RÉTI, 1928.

Draw.

1. K—N6	K—N3

The driving-off attempt 1. . . ., P—B4 or 1. . . ., P—R4 would be followed by 2. K×NP!, P—B5 (R5) 3. K—B6! etc. (As in the main variation or if 3. . . ., P—B6 (R6) 4. K—K6!, P—B7 (R7) 5. P—B7!, K—N2 6. K—Q7! queening.)

2. K×P!	P—B4

After 2. . . ., K×P 3. K×BP the RP will also be lost; if 2. . . ., P—R4 the draw would be secured by 3. K×P, P—R5 4. K—K5! threatening both Q6 and KB4.

3. K—B6!	P—B5
4. K—K5!	

This bi-directional approach gives Black the Hobsons' choice of either allowing his pawn to be captured or permitting the opponent also to promote his pawn!

4. — —	P—B6
5. K—Q6!	P—B7
6. P—B7!	and draws.*

In the following end-game a round-about approach of White's king combined with an intermediate attack wins a tempo which enables him to catch up with Black's "unstoppable" pawn:

218.

R. RÉTI, 1928.

Draw.

* In another well-known end-game Grandmaster Réti presents this idea with a minimum amount of material: White's king on KR8, pawn on QB6; Black's king on his QR3, pawn on KR3. The stipulation: Black to move and White to draw. Solution: 1. ..., P—R4 2. K—N7, P—R5 3. K—B6!, K—N3 4. K—K5 etc. The idea originates from an over-the-board game: Marco— Schlechter, 1895. In that position— White's king on QR4, pawn on QB5, Black's king on his QR3, pawn on KR3— White hammers out a double threat by 1. K—N4, P—R4 2. P—B6!, K—N3 3. K—B4, P—R5 4. K—Q5!; in case of 4. ..., P—R6 White's reply, 5. K—Q6 assures the promotion of the BP, while after 4. ..., K—B2 5. K—K4 Black's RP will be overhauled.

1. K—K7!

With one eye on the pawn and the other on QB5 where he will attack the bishop which is to be driven on to QN5. After 1. K—N7 (B7)?, P—N4 or 1. P—K7?, B—N4 White would be hopelessly lost.

1. — —	P—N4
2. K—Q6!	P—N5
3. P—K7!	

It is necessary to fire off this threat now, when the bishop—on account of the NP's line-interfering effect—can control his K1 only from QN4.

| 3. — — | B—N4 |
| 4. K—B5! | B—Q2 |

4. ..., P—N6 5. K×B and White will also queen his pawn. But now White can not only overtake Black's NP, but annihilate it by driving off the hostile bishop.

| 5. K—Q4! | K—N3 |

5. ..., P—N6 6. K—K3, B—B3 would offer a short-lived defence owing to 7. P—K8 (Q)!, B×Q 8. K—B3 and 9. K×P.

6. K—K4	K—B3
7. K—B4	K—Q3
8. P—K8 (Q)!	B×Q
9. K×P	draw.

219.

M. G. KLIATSKIN, 1925.

White wins.

Two light pieces left to themselves would be no match for Black's pawns marching forward on both wings. But the king's intervention, however purposeless it seems, saves the situation.

1. K—N7!	P—QR4!
2. K—R6!	P—R5
3. K—R5!	P—R6
4. K—R4!	P—R7

Where is the king heading for? It soon turns out that his ultimate aim is by no means a mere hopeless chase after the pawn.

5. K—N3!	P—R8 (Q)
6. N—K6 ch	and mate!

This is the main variation. In case of any deviation White has sufficient time to turn his material advantage to account.

We have seen similar examples of concerted action in end-games Nos. 98, 99, 142 and 206.

Many examples have proved that in the attack against a king the extension of range by an intermediate check is a characteristic time-gaining factor. Also the active intervention of a king—in the form of a double attack—has been seen to result in a gain of time.

All this must have made the idea of gaining time sufficiently clear. Nevertheless, in discussing the roles of the kings, we have to bring up the subject once more, if only to point out the reverse of the medal, Zugzwang!

220.

R. RÉTI, 1922.

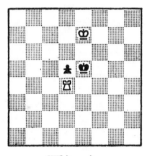

White wins.

White's rook must obviously leave its Q4, permitting Black's pawn to advance. Thereupon White needs to rush his king round to the rook's aid, but, the approach being barred, he can't help wasting a move.

The point is that the "wasted" waiting move must not be damaging, nor facilitate the progress of the hostile king.

1. R—Q2!! P—Q5
2. R—Q1!!

Now Black is forced to give ground and **now** too the rook is at a favourable distance from the advancing enemy.

2. — — K—Q4!
3. K—Q7! K—K5

If 3. . . ., K—B5 White's king would break in on the other side.

4. K—B6 K—K6
5. K—B5 P—Q6
6. K—B4 P—Q7
7. K—B3 and wins.

The exacting problem fan will probably take exception to this study from an "artistic" point of view, seeing that **(a)** 1. R—Q3 is just as good a key as 1. R—Q2, **(b)** White's second and third moves may be transposed and **(c)** White's king could (on the fourth and fifth moves) just as well walk up the Q file. All that is quite true. But the **idea** expressed here—a gain of tempo by **sacrificing a tempo** —is nevertheless very fascinating, delightful and instructive.

The next end-game illustrates the prevention and counter-imposition of Zugzwang by way of sacrifice. The author of the study selects a very interesting motif of an end-game type which was comprehensively and systematically analysed by the first Hungarian master of international fame, József Szén.

221.

J. BEHTING, 1929.

White wins.

1. K—N1!

Any other move would lose outright. In similar positions—as proved by Szén—a symmetrical situation is equivalent to Zugzwang. For example, after 1. P—R6?, P—N6! the side to move loses.

1. — — K—B (R) 2

In case of a pawn move White's king would face up to the advancing pawn, sooner or later enforcing a move by the hostile monarch. For instance: 1. . . ., P—N6 2. K—N2! or 1. . . ., P—R6 2. K—R2!, P—B6 3. K—N3!

—2. P—N8 (Q) ch!!

This sacrifice paralyses the king and establishes Zugzwang. 2. P—R6?, K—N1!, however, would lead to an exactly opposite situation.

2. — — K×Q
3. P—R6! P—B6

4. K—B2!	P—R6
5. K—N3!	P—R7
6. K×P	P—B7
7. K—N2	P—N6
8. K—B1!	and wins,

because White picks up the adverse pawns one by one and queens his own as soon as Black moves his king.

CLOSE-RANGE FIGHTING

Very frequent motifs in skirmishing round the king are the pin, the unpin and the flight from the pin. The space and time elements defining the range of the pieces are never so much in evidence as during a close-range fight, with attack and counter-attack swiftly alternating in the framework of a single combination.

222.

L. I. KUBBEL, 1934.

White wins.

To realize his extra pawn White must either increase his material superiority, or liquidate to a favourable pawn ending. The introductory move points to the first alternative—and achieves the second.

1. R—R4!	R—QR6!

White threatened 2. R×B and 3. B—K1 (pinning) or in case of 1. . . ., R—B (KR) 6 2. B—K1! winning a piece.

Black's counter-attack amounts to giving up a piece, but only, after 2. R×R?, B×R ch 3. K×B, K—B6!—in exchange for the powerful pawn.

2. R×B ch!	K×R
3. B—K1 ch!	

3. B—B5 ch?, K×B 4. K×R would secure the pawn, but give away the win, there being no chance of its promotion.

3. — —	K—R5
4. B—B3!	and wins,

since the encircled rook most soon perish on account of Zugzwang; and after 4. . . ., R×B 5. K×R White's king can comfortably escort the pawn to the queening square.

223.

T. B. GORGIEV, 1929.

White wins.

White is the exchange to the good, but this alone is not enough for victory. He must try and increase his material advantage, which calls for some heated close-range fighting. Black's king puts up a valiant resistance, but ultimately, a reluctant yet convenient target, finds himself playing into White's hands.

1. B—B6 ch	K—R2
2. R—N7 ch	K—R3
3. R—B7!	K—N3

If ..., N—B3?, then 4. B×B, N×B 5. R—Q7!, N—K3 6. R—Q6 (pin) wins.

4. R—B8	N—B3!

Forced, otherwise Black loses more quickly.

5. B×B	K—N2!
6. R—K8	K—B2

This appears to chase the rook away and recover the bishop. While White's rook is indeed of little use in defence, it is the more valuable in counter-attack, pulling off an exchange manoeuvre based on its secondary range.

7. R—R8!	K—N2
8. B—B6 ch!	K×B
9. R—R6 ch	and wins.

* * *

The next two examples demonstrate how, after the subsidence of tactical skirmishes, the wider range of the active piece is crystallized in a gain of space.

224.

S. M. KAMINER, 1926.

White wins.

Black threatens both ..., B—B3 and ..., P—K8 (Q), so White's first move is forced.

1. R—K5	N—Q7!

Threatening ..., B—B3 ch and ..., N—B6 ch.

2. R×P	P—R8 (Q) ch!
3. K×Q	N—K5!

The knight is invulnerable on account of the pin ..., B—B3, and threatens both ..., N×B and ..., N—N3 ch.

4. B—B2	B—Q8!

By energetic play Black manages to liquidate to a "theoretical" draw, but, unhappily for him, the ensuing position is a rare exception to the rule.

5. R—K1	N×B ch
6. K—N2	N—Q6
7. R×B	N×P

This is the "most" Black could hope for. But the knight posted on its N7 is trapped by the easily centralized rook.

8. R—Q4!	K—K3
9. K—B2	K—K4
10. K—K3!	and wins.

225.

M. S. LIBURKIN, 1931.

White wins.

The battle centres round QB6; both sides throw in all their tactical weapons.

1. R—B7 ch	K—N1!
2. R—N7 ch	K—R1
3. B—K8!	

Not 3. R×P?? owing to . . ., N—Q4 ch. Should the attacked knight move away now, White would have safeguarded his pawn.

| 3. — — | N×P |
| 4. R×P | |

The matter seems to be settled. White now threatens both B×N and R—R6 ch. 4. . . ., K—R2 fails against 5. R—N1 and 6. R—QR1.

But a surprising line opening—threat with scope-extension—holds out new hopes for Black.

| 4. — — | N—N5!! |

Counter-attacking the offensive bishop, guarding against R—R6 ch and threatening . . ., N—Q4 ch.

| 5. B—B7! | B—K1!! |

Another beautiful counterplay! The underlying motif: driving off to permit . . ., N—Q4 ch. If White's bishop makes another detour, Black can solve his problem by . . ., N—B3. But White plays:

| 6. K×N | B×B |
| 7. R—R6!! | |

Demonstrating the superiority of the rook's range to that of the bishop. White threatens R—R8 ch and R—R7. If 7. . . ., B—R7 8. R—R6 ch would be fatal. The attempt to escape lands the king in a mess.

7. — —	B—Q4
8. K—B5!	B—N7
9. K—N6	and wins.

ATTACK AGAINST A DEFENDING PIECE

The dynamic power and range of a piece is influenced, apart from the time and space factors, also by the extent to which it is burdened with defensive duties. Obviously the complete freedom of movement of a piece presupposes that it is not called upon to defend its companions or keep certain squares under its corporal or control effect.

A piece burdened with defensive obligations is restricted in its activity; therefore, any attack against it will also threaten the piece protected by it. An attack launched against a defending piece can often be as effective as a double attack in disrupting the concerted action of the defensive forces.

226.

M. HAVEL, 1924.

White wins.

The knight defending the bishop is a convenient target here. Though after 1. K—K7?, N—B4 ch or 1. K—B7?, N—K8 ch Black could somehow extricate himself from the danger, he is powerless against the joint onslaught of king and rook.

1. R—N6!	N—B2 ch
2. K—K7	B—B5
3. R—KB6!	N—K4!

After 3. ..., B—N6? 4. R—B3, B—Q4 5. R—B5!, B—N6 Black could not sacrifice either of his pieces for White's advancing pawn.

4. R—B5	N—N3 ch
5. K—B6	B—Q6
6. R—Q5!	N—B5

The defensive position is repeating itself, with Black losing ground inch by inch.

7. R—Q4	N—R4 ch
8. K—N5	B—K7

This does not help either, because White can now liquidate by a double attack. The outcome is decided by the difference between the scope of the two kings.

9. R—R4 ch!	K—N7
10. R×N	and wins.

Relentless chase, as seen in the previous example, is only one of the many forcing tactical methods that may be resorted to in order to harass a defending piece. A fairly frequent motif is the directing sacrifice with a view to driving off the defending piece and decoying it into the range of the attacker.

227.

S. M. KAMINER, 1925.

White wins.

1. R—B4!!	R—Q7 ch

If 1. ..., R×R?, White would get the rook back with a bonus (2. B×N ch). A subvariation, along more or less the same lines as the text, likewise works out to White's advantage: ..., R—B5 ch 2. K—N1!, R—B4 3. P—N4, R—N4 4. P—R4, R—K4 5. R—K4!

2. K—K1	R—Q6
3. K—K2	R—K6 ch
4. K—Q2	R—K4
5. R—K4!	R—N4

5. ..., R—B (R) is followed by 6. P—N4 and P—R4 etc.

6. R—KN4!	R×R
7. B×N ch	and wins.

A notable motif at the finish was the beneficial intermediate check, typically exploiting a momentary gap in the defence.

* * *

228.

JENŐ BÁN, 1943.

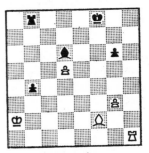

White wins.

1. B—B5	R—R1 ch

1. ..., K—K2? fails against 2. R—R7 ch leading to the loss of Black's rook. This is equally the case after ..., R—Q1?, 2. R—R8 ch.

2. K—N2!

2. K—N3?, R—R6 ch 3. K×P, B×B ch 4. K×B, R×P would result in a draw. After the tempting 2. K—N1 Black would find a defence in 2. ..., R—R3 3. R—B1 ch, K—K2! 4. R—K1 ch, K—Q2 5. R—K6, R—B3! This "by-play" is apt to divert our attention from a hidden, but actually very simple point:

2. — —	R—R3

Protecting the bishop and parrying the threat of R—R8 ch. But the defending rook has not yet weathered the strom.

3. R—R1!	and wins,

for against 3. . . ., R×R the interpolated 4. B×B ch wins a piece, while after 3. . . ., B×B 4. R×R White's material superiority is slowly but surely realized.

* * *

Another characteristic example demonstrates how a piece burdened by defensive obligations can be "out-attacked."

229.

A. MANDLER and E. KÖNIG, 1924.

White wins.

By a driving-on manoeuvre White forces the pinning of Black's KR, then, putting more pressure on the defending piece, manages to capture its "protégé."

1. P—B7!	K—N2
2. P—B8 (Q) ch!	K×Q
3. R—B1 ch	K—N2

After 3. . . ., K—K2 White reaches his desired end by playing 4. R (B1)—

K1. In case of 3. . . ., R—B6 he would double the vigour of the attack by 4. R (K2)—KB2!

| 4. R—N2 ch | K—R3 |

Against 4. . . ., R—N6 follows 5. R(B1)—KN1 according to the previous pattern.

| 5. R—R1 ch | R—R6 |
| 6. R(N2)—R2!! | |

Black is now out-attacked. "Spite-checks" keep the rook alive only two more moves.

6. — —	R—B6 ch
7. K—N4!	R—N6 ch
8. K—R4	and wins.

THE KING AS A DIRECT TARGET

In the last phase of the struggle the weaker side's king suddenly finds himself in the focus of events. In most end-games of a tactical type, the actual mate is, as a rule, not the crowning act of the last decisive battle, but rather its colourless and grim aftermath, a dreary "punishing expedition" against a helpless opponent. A king rarely dies a "hero's death" in the heat of battle; he is usually taken prisoner when the fight is over.

Nevertheless in a high percentage of combinations the mating threat, as a tactical weapon of forcing, plays an important part. This was the case in end-games Nos. 85, 86, 87, 90, 91, 98, 110, 145, 146, 147, 151, 153, 154, 156.

We then only stressed the particular tactical motif being illustrated; now we propose to give a brief survey of how those motifs are interwoven in the web of a mating combination.

From simple examples we shall proceed to more complicated ones, and we trust that the reader will find joy and gratification in the gradually widening scope of the combinations which, however colourful and ramified they may be, are invariably built up of the fundamental tactical bricks that have been the subject of the preceding chapters.

A glance at the two diagrams below will convince you again that it is not material balance, but the difference in efficiency between active and passive pieces that matters in all tactical operations. This truth is borne out by many an unexpected mating attack.

230.

H. RINCK, 1921.

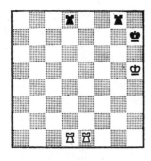

White wins.

| 1. R—K7 ch | K—R1 |
| 2. K—R6! | R (N1)—K1 |

Necessary, because White threatened R—R7 mate. After 2. . . ., R(N1) —B1 the king would likewise perish for lack of air. (3. R—R7 ch, K—N1 4. R—N1 mate.)

3. R(1)—Q7!   and wins,

because Black's KR blocks its king's route of escape, e. g. . . ., K—N1, 4. R—N7 ch, K—R1 5. R—R7 ch, K— N1 6. QR—N7 ch, K—B1 7. R—R8 mate.

231.

R. RÉTI, 1925.

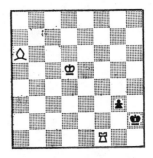

White wins.

White's bishop has to obtain control of the KN2 square before the pawn "gets tough." It is possible? Yes, provided we discover the only mating chance hidden in the position!

1. R—B3!	P—N7
2. B—B1!!	P—N8 (Q)
3. R—R3 ch	and mate!

* * *

Mate with a minimum of material usually requires the hostile king to be at the edge of the board, or, still better, in the corner. To bring about such a favourable situation it is well worth sacrificing the rest of our forces, retaining only the bare minimum needed to give mate.

"Single-track" mating combinations are few and far between. Usually the mating chance is linked with the possibility of liquidation to a technically simple winning position.

232.

W. STEINITZ, 1862.

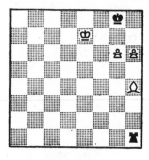

White wins.

A bishop and two pawns are worth more than a rook, but by playing 1. B—N5 White would only reach deadlock, since Black could safely sacrifice his rook whenever White advances his RP. The win is achieved by a forcing mating threat.

1. P—R7 ch	K—N2!
2. P—R8 (Q) ch!	K×Q
3. K—B7!	R—B8 ch

The best, since after 3. . . ., R×B, 4. P—N7 ch, etc. Black is lost in a few moves, while 3. . . ., R—KN8 leads to an immediate mate. (4. B—B6 ch.) Now the threat results in a favourable liquidation.

4. B—B6 ch	R×B ch
5. K×R	K—N1
6. P—N7	and wins.

233.

A. A. TROITSKY, 1895.

White wins.

By trying to hang on to his solitary pawn White runs the risk of stalemate, but behind a stalemate there always gleams the hope of mate.

| 1. B—R6 ch | K—N1 |
| 2. P—N7 | K—B2 |

2. . . ., P—K3 ch?! 3. K—Q6!, K—B2 4. K—K5, K—N1 5. K—B6, P—K4 6. K—K6!, P—K5 7. K—B6!, P—K6 8. B×P etc. and White wins. But now, playing 3. K—K5?, White could keep his pawn only at the cost of stalemate (3. . . ., P—K3 4. K—Q6,

P—K4! 5. K×P, K—N1.) Therefore:

3. P—N8 (Q) ch!   K×Q
4. K—K6

Zugzwang. Black is forced into the corner where, thanks to the presence of the two harmful pawns, even a solitary bishop is able to deliver the fatal blow.

4. — —   K—R1
5. K—B7   P—K3
6. B—N7 ch   and mate!

234.

J. GUNST, 1922.

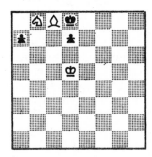

White wins.

This theme is closely related to the previous one, the stress being laid, however, not upon the driving-on manoeuvre but upon gaining the tempo that creates the Zugzwang.

1. B—N7!!

After the natural 1. B—R6, K—B2, White ought to make a waiting move to bring about the former mating pattern, but after 2. K—B5 Black can interpolate 2. . . ., P—Q3 ch! and the pawn can no longer be blockaded.

1. — —   K—B2

Any other move would allow White to save both pieces.

2. B—R6!   K×N

If 2. . . ., P—Q3 3. N—B6 and the struggle is drawn out into a "more prosaic" knight-bishop mate.

3. K—Q6   K—R1
4. K—B7   P—Q3
5. B—N7 ch   and mate!

* * *

Let us now watch a gallant fight by the cavalry with queenly assistance:

235.

L. I. KUBBEL, 1925.

White wins.

1. N—K3 ch!   K—N6
2. Q—N4 ch   K—B7
3. Q—B4 ch   K—K7 (8)

There was no other way out; after any deviation from the text a quick mate would have followed. Now the precarious position of Black's queen allows White to pursue the chase under the protection of his unprotected knight.

4. Q—B1 ch!   K—Q7

The knight must not be touched on account of 5. Q—K1 ch winning the queen.

5. Q—Q1 ch   K—B6
6. Q—B2 ch   K—N5

6. . . ., K—Q5? fails against 7. N—B5 ch.

7. Q—N2 ch   N—N6

7. . . ., K—R4 8. N—B4 ch, K—R3 9. Q—N6 mate. But the knight move has drawbacks: (a) it has opened the diagonal onto the queen, and (b) it blocks a square in the proximity of the king. This brings us to a splendid finale.

8. Q—R3 ch!   K×Q
9. N—B2 ch   and mate!

1. Q—Q4 ch   K—N4!
2. Q—B6 ch   K—N5
3. Q—B3 ch   K—N4
4. Q—N3 ch   B—N5

4. . . ., K—B4? would lose to 5. Q—Q3 ch, winning the queen. But as a result of the square block in a restricted area, Black's king gets entangled in a mating net. (The mating position is very much like the one in Diagram No. 2.)

5. Q—R4 ch!!   K×Q
6. B—B6 ch   and mate!

Of course Black is not compelled to put his head into the noose right away, but to escape he has to pay with his queen: 5. . . ., K—B5 6. Q—B2 ch, B—B6 ch 7. Q×B ch, K—N4 8. Q—N3 ch, K—B4 9. Q—Q3 ch, etc. Have these been a bit artificial? Well, let us now look at a game-like position, with a natural, self-evident sequence of moves:

236.

A. A. TROITSKY, 1916.

White wins.

237.

M. S. LIBURKIN, 1935.

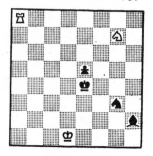

White wins.

To get the upper hand, White must win one of Black's pieces. He can do so rather easily.

   1. R—R2   B—N8

   1. . . ., N—B8 2. K—K1 and White wins.

   2. R—KN2   K—B6
   3. R×B   K—B7
   4. R—K1   P—K5

Are there any two chess players worthy of the name who would not have made the same moves, White or Black, in an over-the-board game? And who would not find it perfectly natural to bring the idle knight to help secure the K2 square and round up Black's surviving forces?

   5. N—K6   P—K6

And it is "obvious" now, isn't it, that White must continue with 6. N—Q4 or 6. N—B4 to ward off the threatened . . ., P—K7 ch?

But what happens if Black nevertheless plays 6. . . ., P—K7 ch and counters 7. N×P with 7. . . ., N—B8!?

The imprisoned rook cannot move and there is no medicine against perpetual check (3. . . ., N—K6—B8 ch). In short, White cannot realize his extra rook!

In that case how can we stave off the loss of the rook after 6. . . ., P—K7 ch 7. K—Q2, N—K5 (B8) ch? We can't. But why be a rook up and draw, if mate can be enforced without it? For mate with a solitary knight does not only occur in fairy tales or over-complicated positions, but some-

times even in an ordinary game if the king is forced to the edge of the board and his pieces block a couple of squares around him.

Now perhaps we can see the solution.

   6. N—B5!!   P—K7 ch
   7. K—Q2   N—B8 ch
   8. K—B1!   K×R
   9. N—Q3 ch   and mate!

If Black refuses to take the rook, White will realize his material superiority by **accurate** play: 8. . . ., K—K6 9. K—B2!, N—Q7 10. N—Q3!, N—B6 11. R—QN1!! (against the harassing . . ., N—Q5 ch and N—N4 ch).

* * *

The substance of the following artistic composition is accentuated by the active share taken by the offensive king in spinning a mating net round his royal opponent. In the analysis we have laid special stress on the tactical motifs that make up the winning combination.

238.

A. A. TROITSKY, 1924.

White wins.

Black is a piece ahead and threatens to deprive White of all winning chances by ..., B—B4 and ..., R×P, or ..., R—N4 ch and ..., R×P. The situation brooks no delay; White must act at once, judiciously applying the **principle of forcing** based on the heaping of **threat upon threat.**

1. P—R7!

The dangerous pawn forcingly **directs** the movement of the rook. On the one hand it **drives off** the rook from its fifth rank, putting a stop to the direct attack against the NP; on the other, it **drives it on** to its fourth rank to prevent any further harassing checks.

1. — —   R—N4 ch

Black **chases** the king where he was wanting to go anyway; hence White **gains time** for an opportune intervention by his king.

2. K×P   R×P
3. K—B7!

Sparing Black's momentarily **harmful bishop,** whose corporal effect now manifests itself in **line interference,** because Black cannot ward off the **mating threat** by way of ..., R×P ch. (Owing to the former driving-on manoeuvre he cannot even give check on the QB file.)

3. — —   B—K3!

Active defence, since it not only guards Black's QR7, but also renews the threat ..., R×P ch by a **line opening.**

4. K—N8

Gain of space and **concerted action** of rook and king expressed by the mate threat.

4. — —   B—Q4

This **line interference** is the only defence against R—Q6 mate. It does not seem to help either, but there is more finesse in it than meets the eye.

5. R×B

Driving-off sacrifice in the interest of promotion.

5. — —   R×R!

Though dictated by necessity, this move still demands caution, since Black lays a **stalemate-trap** for us. If 6. P—R8 (Q)? a driving-on move, 6. ..., R—Q1 ch! would lead to stalemate after 7. Q×R.

6. P—R8 (R)!!

Averting the stalemate by underpromotion and threatening mate again (R—R6!). Therefore Black's rook is forcibly **driven on** to Q6.

6. — —   R—Q3
7. K—B7!

Line opening and attack combined with threat. The fourth mating threat (R—R8) can only be warded off by leaving the rook en prise. **White wins.**

* * *

As the last example of our short summary we introduce one of the liveliest mating combinations:

239.

A. A. SELETSKY, 1933.

1. Q—N5!   K—K3 ch

At first sight it would be more natural to prevent queening by 1. . . ., B×P. Then, however, 2. N—B4! would decide the issue on account of the mating threat 3. B—R5. For instance: 2. . . ., Q—Q3 3. B—B4 ch, K—K1 4. Q—N8 ch, Q—B1 5. B—B7 ch!, K—K2 6. N—N6 ch; or 2. . . ., Q—QN1 3. B—R5 ch, K—B1 4. Q—B6 ch, K—N1 5. Q—B7 ch, K—R1 6. N—N6 mate; or 2. . . ., Q—N2 3. B—B4 ch, K—B1 4. Q—Q8 ch, B—K1 5. N—K6 ch etc.

2. K—N1!

It will turn out later that this is the only square on which the king is safe from the harassing checks of Black's queen.

2. — —   K×P

2. . . ., B×P? 3. B—N4 ch, K—Q3 4. Q—B5 ch, or 3. . . ., K—B2 4. B—R5 ch, K—K3 5. Q—K5 ch in either case resulting in a mate in the centre of the board.

3. N—B5 ch   K—B1

3. . . ., K—Q3 4. Q—N3 ch!, K—Q4 (4. . . ., K×N? 5. Q—R3 ch!) 5. B—B4 ch!, K×B 6. Q—N3 ch and White wins the queen (N—K6 ch or Q—R3 ch).

4. B—R6 ch   K—N1
5. Q—N3 ch   K—R1

Black's king is cornered. By way of two energetic driving-on sacrifices he will be walled in completely.

6. B—N7 ch!!   B×B
7. N—Q7!!   Q—Q1

Black must defend his QN3. But he can't hold out long!

8. Q—QN8 ch!   Q×Q
9. N—N6 ch   and mate!

240.

SCHEME.

"A miracle on the chessboard!"—this is how that master of composition, Dr. György Páros, describes this final position in his work "Wonders on the Chessboard" (1940).

The boundless empire of tactical possibilities in chess play is indeed marvellously rich and variegated. But even miracles are governed by the laws of Nature. Chess play too has its own natural laws and its particular phenomena deriving from them. We only have to discover them.

He who has arrived from Damiano's smothered mate (No. 13) through Troitsky's smothered mate (145) at Seletsky's smothered mate (239), and who has perceived the eternal familiar motifs beneath the ever-changing multicoloured garments of brilliant combinations not only with an amazed but also with a critical eye, will certainly have made some progress on the road towards that discovery.

INDEX

(The numerals indicate the serial number of the end-games.)

213

A CATALOG OF SELECTED
DOVER BOOKS
IN ALL FIELDS OF INTEREST

A CATALOG OF SELECTED DOVER
BOOKS IN ALL FIELDS OF INTEREST

CONCERNING THE SPIRITUAL IN ART, Wassily Kandinsky. Pioneering work by father of abstract art. Thoughts on color theory, nature of art. Analysis of earlier masters. 12 illustrations. 80pp. of text. 5⅜ x 8½. 23411-8 Pa. $3.95

ANIMALS: 1,419 Copyright-Free Illustrations of Mammals, Birds, Fish, Insects, etc., Jim Harter (ed.). Clear wood engravings present, in extremely lifelike poses, over 1,000 species of animals. One of the most extensive pictorial sourcebooks of its kind. Captions. Index. 284pp. 9 x 12. 23766-4 Pa. $12.95

CELTIC ART: The Methods of Construction, George Bain. Simple geometric techniques for making Celtic interlacements, spirals, Kells-type initials, animals, humans, etc. Over 500 illustrations. 160pp. 9 x 12. (USO) 22923-8 Pa. $9.95

AN ATLAS OF ANATOMY FOR ARTISTS, Fritz Schider. Most thorough reference work on art anatomy in the world. Hundreds of illustrations, including selections from works by Vesalius, Leonardo, Goya, Ingres, Michelangelo, others. 593 illustrations. 192pp. 7⅛ x 10¼. 20241-0 Pa. $9 95

CELTIC HAND STROKE-BY-STROKE (Irish Half-Uncial from "The Book of Kells"): An Arthur Baker Calligraphy Manual, Arthur Baker. Complete guide to creating each letter of the alphabet in distinctive Celtic manner. Covers hand position, strokes, pens, inks, paper, more. Illustrated. 48pp. 8¼ x 11. 24336-2 Pa. $3.95

EASY ORIGAMI, John Montroll. Charming collection of 32 projects (hat, cup, pelican, piano, swan, many more) specially designed for the novice origami hobbyist. Clearly illustrated easy-to-follow instructions insure that even beginning papercrafters will achieve successful results. 48pp. 8¼ x 11. 27298-2 Pa. $2.95

THE COMPLETE BOOK OF BIRDHOUSE CONSTRUCTION FOR WOODWORKERS, Scott D. Campbell. Detailed instructions, illustrations, tables. Also data on bird habitat and instinct patterns. Bibliography. 3 tables. 63 illustrations in 15 figures. 48pp. 5¼ x 8½. 24407-5 Pa. $2.50

BLOOMINGDALE'S ILLUSTRATED 1886 CATALOG: Fashions, Dry Goods and Housewares, Bloomingdale Brothers. Famed merchants' extremely rare catalog depicting about 1,700 products: clothing, housewares, firearms, dry goods, jewelry, more. Invaluable for dating, identifying vintage items. Also, copyright-free graphics for artists, designers. Co-published with Henry Ford Museum & Greenfield Village. 160pp. 8¼ x 11. 25780-0 Pa. $9.95

HISTORIC COSTUME IN PICTURES, Braun & Schneider. Over 1,450 costumed figures in clearly detailed engravings—from dawn of civilization to end of 19th century. Captions. Many folk costumes. 256pp. 8⅜ x 11¾. 23150-X Pa. $12.95

STICKLEY CRAFTSMAN FURNITURE CATALOGS, Gustav Stickley and L. & J. G. Stickley. Beautiful, functional furniture in two authentic catalogs from 1910. 594 illustrations, including 277 photos, show settles, rockers, armchairs, reclining chairs, bookcases, desks, tables. 183pp. 6½ x 9¼. 23838-5 Pa. $9.95

AMERICAN LOCOMOTIVES IN HISTORIC PHOTOGRAPHS: 1858 to 1949, Ron Ziel (ed.). A rare collection of 126 meticulously detailed official photographs, called "builder portraits," of American locomotives that majestically chronicle the rise of steam locomotive power in America. Introduction. Detailed captions. xi + 129pp. 9 x 12. 27393-8 Pa. $12.95

AMERICA'S LIGHTHOUSES: An Illustrated History, Francis Ross Holland, Jr. Delightfully written, profusely illustrated fact-filled survey of over 200 American lighthouses since 1716. History, anecdotes, technological advances, more. 240pp. 8 x 10¾. 25576-X Pa. $12.95

TOWARDS A NEW ARCHITECTURE, Le Corbusier. Pioneering manifesto by founder of "International School." Technical and aesthetic theories, views of industry, economics, relation of form to function, "mass-production split" and much more. Profusely illustrated. 320pp. 6⅛ x 9¼. (USO) 25023-7 Pa. $9.95

HOW THE OTHER HALF LIVES, Jacob Riis. Famous journalistic record, exposing poverty and degradation of New York slums around 1900, by major social reformer. 100 striking and influential photographs. 233pp. 10 x 7⅞. 22012-5 Pa. $10.95

FRUIT KEY AND TWIG KEY TO TREES AND SHRUBS, William M. Harlow. One of the handiest and most widely used identification aids. Fruit key covers 120 deciduous and evergreen species; twig key 160 deciduous species. Easily used. Over 300 photographs. 126pp. 5⅜ x 8½. 20511-8 Pa. $3.95

COMMON BIRD SONGS, Dr. Donald J. Borror. Songs of 60 most common U.S. birds: robins, sparrows, cardinals, bluejays, finches, more—arranged in order of increasing complexity. Up to 9 variations of songs of each species. Cassette and manual 99911-4 $8.95

ORCHIDS AS HOUSE PLANTS, Rebecca Tyson Northen. Grow cattleyas and many other kinds of orchids—in a window, in a case, or under artificial light. 63 illustrations. 148pp. 5⅜ x 8½. 23261-1 Pa. $4.95

MONSTER MAZES, Dave Phillips. Masterful mazes at four levels of difficulty. Avoid deadly perils and evil creatures to find magical treasures. Solutions for all 32 exciting illustrated puzzles. 48pp. 8¼ x 11. 26005-4 Pa. $2.95

MOZART'S DON GIOVANNI (DOVER OPERA LIBRETTO SERIES), Wolfgang Amadeus Mozart. Introduced and translated by Ellen H. Bleiler. Standard Italian libretto, with complete English translation. Convenient and thoroughly portable—an ideal companion for reading along with a recording or the performance itself. Introduction. List of characters. Plot summary. 121pp. 5¼ x 8½. 24944-1 Pa. $2.95

TECHNICAL MANUAL AND DICTIONARY OF CLASSICAL BALLET, Gail Grant. Defines, explains, comments on steps, movements, poses and concepts. 15-page pictorial section. Basic book for student, viewer. 127pp. 5⅜ x 8½. 21843-0 Pa. $4.95

BRASS INSTRUMENTS: Their History and Development, Anthony Baines. Authoritative, updated survey of the evolution of trumpets, trombones, bugles, cornets, French horns, tubas and other brass wind instruments. Over 140 illustrations and 48 music examples. Corrected and updated by author. New preface. Bibliography. 320pp. 5⅜ x 8½. 27574-4 Pa. $9.95

HOLLYWOOD GLAMOR PORTRAITS, John Kobal (ed.). 145 photos from 1926-49. Harlow, Gable, Bogart, Bacall; 94 stars in all. Full background on photographers, technical aspects. 160pp. 8⅜ x 11¼. 23352-9 Pa. $11.95

MAX AND MORITZ, Wilhelm Busch. Great humor classic in both German and English. Also 10 other works: "Cat and Mouse," "Plisch and Plumm," etc. 216pp. 5⅜ x 8½. 20181-3 Pa. $6.95

THE RAVEN AND OTHER FAVORITE POEMS, Edgar Allan Poe. Over 40 of the author's most memorable poems: "The Bells," "Ulalume," "Israfel," "To Helen," "The Conqueror Worm," "Eldorado," "Annabel Lee," many more. Alphabetic lists of titles and first lines. 64pp. 5$\frac{3}{16}$ x 8¼. 26685-0 Pa. $1.00

PERSONAL MEMOIRS OF U. S. GRANT, Ulysses Simpson Grant. Intelligent, deeply moving firsthand account of Civil War campaigns, considered by many the finest military memoirs ever written. Includes letters, historic photographs, maps and more. 528pp. 6⅛ x 9¼. 28587-1 Pa. $11.95

AMULETS AND SUPERSTITIONS, E. A. Wallis Budge. Comprehensive discourse on origin, powers of amulets in many ancient cultures: Arab, Persian Babylonian, Assyrian, Egyptian, Gnostic, Hebrew, Phoenician, Syriac, etc. Covers cross, swastika, crucifix, seals, rings, stones, etc. 584pp. 5⅜ x 8½. 23573-4 Pa. $12.95

RUSSIAN STORIES/PYCCKNE PACCKA3bl: A Dual-Language Book, edited by Gleb Struve. Twelve tales by such masters as Chekhov, Tolstoy, Dostoevsky, Pushkin, others. Excellent word-for-word English translations on facing pages, plus teaching and study aids, Russian/English vocabulary, biographical/critical introductions, more. 416pp. 5⅜ x 8½. 26244-8 Pa. $8.95

PHILADELPHIA THEN AND NOW: 60 Sites Photographed in the Past and Present, Kenneth Finkel and Susan Oyama. Rare photographs of City Hall, Logan Square, Independence Hall, Betsy Ross House, other landmarks juxtaposed with contemporary views. Captures changing face of historic city. Introduction. Captions. 128pp. 8¼ x 11. 25790-8 Pa. $9.95

AIA ARCHITECTURAL GUIDE TO NASSAU AND SUFFOLK COUNTIES, LONG ISLAND, The American Institute of Architects, Long Island Chapter, and the Society for the Preservation of Long Island Antiquities. Comprehensive, well-researched and generously illustrated volume brings to life over three centuries of Long Island's great architectural heritage. More than 240 photographs with authoritative, extensively detailed captions. 176pp. 8¼ x 11. 26946-9 Pa. $14.95

NORTH AMERICAN INDIAN LIFE: Customs and Traditions of 23 Tribes, Elsie Clews Parsons (ed.). 27 fictionalized essays by noted anthropologists examine religion, customs, government, additional facets of life among the Winnebago, Crow, Zuni, Eskimo, other tribes. 480pp. 6⅛ x 9¼. 27377-6 Pa. $10.95

FRANK LLOYD WRIGHT'S HOLLYHOCK HOUSE, Donald Hoffmann. Lavishly illustrated, carefully documented study of one of Wright's most controversial residential designs. Over 120 photographs, floor plans, elevations, etc. Detailed perceptive text by noted Wright scholar. Index. 128pp. 9¼ x 10¾. 27133-1 Pa. $11.95

THE MALE AND FEMALE FIGURE IN MOTION: 60 Classic Photographic Sequences, Eadweard Muybridge. 60 true-action photographs of men and women walking, running, climbing, bending, turning, etc., reproduced from rare 19th-century masterpiece. vi + 121pp. 9 x 12. 24745-7 Pa. $10.95

1001 QUESTIONS ANSWERED ABOUT THE SEASHORE, N. J. Berrill and Jacquelyn Berrill. Queries answered about dolphins, sea snails, sponges, starfish, fishes, shore birds, many others. Covers appearance, breeding, growth, feeding, much more. 305pp. 5¼ x 8¼. 23366-9 Pa. $8.95

GUIDE TO OWL WATCHING IN NORTH AMERICA, Donald S. Heintzelman. Superb guide offers complete data and descriptions of 19 species: barn owl, screech owl, snowy owl, many more. Expert coverage of owl-watching equipment, conservation, migrations and invasions, etc. Guide to observing sites. 84 illustrations. xiii + 193pp. 5⅜ x 8½. 27344-X Pa. $8.95

MEDICINAL AND OTHER USES OF NORTH AMERICAN PLANTS: A Historical Survey with Special Reference to the Eastern Indian Tribes, Charlotte Erichsen-Brown. Chronological historical citations document 500 years of usage of plants, trees, shrubs native to eastern Canada, northeastern U.S. Also complete identifying information. 343 illustrations. 544pp. 6½ x 9¼. 25951-X Pa. $12.95

STORYBOOK MAZES, Dave Phillips. 23 stories and mazes on two-page spreads: Wizard of Oz, Treasure Island, Robin Hood, etc. Solutions. 64pp. 8¼ x 11. 23628-5 Pa. $2.95

NEGRO FOLK MUSIC, U.S.A., Harold Courlander. Noted folklorist's scholarly yet readable analysis of rich and varied musical tradition. Includes authentic versions of over 40 folk songs. Valuable bibliography and discography. xi + 324pp. 5⅜ x 8½. 27350-4 Pa. $7.95

MOVIE-STAR PORTRAITS OF THE FORTIES, John Kobal (ed.). 163 glamor, studio photos of 106 stars of the 1940s: Rita Hayworth, Ava Gardner, Marlon Brando, Clark Gable, many more. 176pp. 8⅜ x 11¼. 23546-7 Pa. $12.95

BENCHLEY LOST AND FOUND, Robert Benchley. Finest humor from early 30s, about pet peeves, child psychologists, post office and others. Mostly unavailable elsewhere. 73 illustrations by Peter Arno and others. 183pp. 5⅜ x 8½. 22410-4 Pa. $6.95

YEKL and THE IMPORTED BRIDEGROOM AND OTHER STORIES OF YIDDISH NEW YORK, Abraham Cahan. Film Hester Street based on Yekl (1896). Novel, other stories among first about Jewish immigrants on N.Y.'s East Side. 240pp. 5⅜ x 8½. 22427-9 Pa. $6.95

SELECTED POEMS, Walt Whitman. Generous sampling from *Leaves of Grass*. Twenty-four poems include "I Hear America Singing," "Song of the Open Road," "I Sing the Body Electric," "When Lilacs Last in the Dooryard Bloom'd," "O Captain! My Captain!"–all reprinted from an authoritative edition. Lists of titles and first lines. 128pp. 5³⁄₁₆ x 8¼. 26878-0 Pa. $1.00

THE BEST TALES OF HOFFMANN, E. T. A. Hoffmann. 10 of Hoffmann's most important stories: "Nutcracker and the King of Mice," "The Golden Flowerpot," etc. 458pp. 5⅜ x 8½. 21793-0 Pa. $9.95

FROM FETISH TO GOD IN ANCIENT EGYPT, E. A. Wallis Budge. Rich detailed survey of Egyptian conception of "God" and gods, magic, cult of animals, Osiris, more. Also, superb English translations of hymns and legends. 240 illustrations. 545pp. 5⅜ x 8½. 25803-3 Pa. $11.95

FRENCH STORIES/CONTES FRANÇAIS: A Dual-Language Book, Wallace Fowlie. Ten stories by French masters, Voltaire to Camus: "Micromegas" by Voltaire; "The Atheist's Mass" by Balzac; "Minuet" by de Maupassant; "The Guest" by Camus, six more. Excellent English translations on facing pages. Also French-English vocabulary list, exercises, more. 352pp. 5⅜ x 8½. 26443-2 Pa. $8.95

CHICAGO AT THE TURN OF THE CENTURY IN PHOTOGRAPHS: 122 Historic Views from the Collections of the Chicago Historical Society, Larry A. Viskochil. Rare large-format prints offer detailed views of City Hall, State Street, the Loop, Hull House, Union Station, many other landmarks, circa 1904-1913. Introduction. Captions. Maps. 144pp. 9⅜ x 12¼. 24656-6 Pa. $12.95

OLD BROOKLYN IN EARLY PHOTOGRAPHS, 1865-1929, William Lee Younger. Luna Park, Gravesend race track, construction of Grand Army Plaza, moving of Hotel Brighton, etc. 157 previously unpublished photographs. 165pp. 8⅞ x 11¾. 23587-4 Pa. $13.95

THE MYTHS OF THE NORTH AMERICAN INDIANS, Lewis Spence. Rich anthology of the myths and legends of the Algonquins, Iroquois, Pawnees and Sioux, prefaced by an extensive historical and ethnological commentary. 36 illustrations. 480pp. 5⅜ x 8½. 25967-6 Pa. $8.95

AN ENCYCLOPEDIA OF BATTLES: Accounts of Over 1,560 Battles from 1479 B.C. to the Present, David Eggenberger. Essential details of every major battle in recorded history from the first battle of Megiddo in 1479 B.C. to Grenada in 1984. List of Battle Maps. New Appendix covering the years 1967-1984. Index. 99 illustrations. 544pp. 6½ x 9¼. 24913-1 Pa. $14.95

SAILING ALONE AROUND THE WORLD, Captain Joshua Slocum. First man to sail around the world, alone, in small boat. One of great feats of seamanship told in delightful manner. 67 illustrations. 294pp. 5⅜ x 8½. 20326-3 Pa. $5.95

ANARCHISM AND OTHER ESSAYS, Emma Goldman. Powerful, penetrating, prophetic essays on direct action, role of minorities, prison reform, puritan hypocrisy, violence, etc. 271pp. 5⅜ x 8½. 22484-8 Pa. $6.95

MYTHS OF THE HINDUS AND BUDDHISTS, Ananda K. Coomaraswamy and Sister Nivedita. Great stories of the epics; deeds of Krishna, Shiva, taken from puranas, Vedas, folk tales; etc. 32 illustrations. 400pp. 5⅜ x 8½. 21759-0 Pa. $10.95

BEYOND PSYCHOLOGY, Otto Rank. Fear of death, desire of immortality, nature of sexuality, social organization, creativity, according to Rankian system. 291pp. 5⅜ x 8½. 20485-5 Pa. $8.95

A THEOLOGICO-POLITICAL TREATISE, Benedict Spinoza. Also contains unfinished Political Treatise. Great classic on religious liberty, theory of government on common consent. R. Elwes translation. Total of 421pp. 5⅜ x 8½. 20249-6 Pa. $9.95

MY BONDAGE AND MY FREEDOM, Frederick Douglass. Born a slave, Douglass became outspoken force in antislavery movement. The best of Douglass' autobiographies. Graphic description of slave life. 464pp. 5⅜ x 8½. 22457-0 Pa. $8.95

FOLLOWING THE EQUATOR: A Journey Around the World, Mark Twain. Fascinating humorous account of 1897 voyage to Hawaii, Australia, India, New Zealand, etc. Ironic, bemused reports on peoples, customs, climate, flora and fauna, politics, much more. 197 illustrations. 720pp. 5⅜ x 8½. 26113-1 Pa. $15.95

THE PEOPLE CALLED SHAKERS, Edward D. Andrews. Definitive study of Shakers: origins, beliefs, practices, dances, social organization, furniture and crafts, etc. 33 illustrations. 351pp. 5⅜ x 8½. 21081-2 Pa. $8.95

THE MYTHS OF GREECE AND ROME, H. A. Guerber. A classic of mythology, generously illustrated, long prized for its simple, graphic, accurate retelling of the principal myths of Greece and Rome, and for its commentary on their origins and significance. With 64 illustrations by Michelangelo, Raphael, Titian, Rubens, Canova, Bernini and others. 480pp. 5⅜ x 8½. 27584-1 Pa. $9.95

PSYCHOLOGY OF MUSIC, Carl E. Seashore. Classic work discusses music as a medium from psychological viewpoint. Clear treatment of physical acoustics, auditory apparatus, sound perception, development of musical skills, nature of musical feeling, host of other topics. 88 figures. 408pp. 5⅜ x 8½. 21851-1 Pa. $10.95

THE PHILOSOPHY OF HISTORY, Georg W. Hegel. Great classic of Western thought develops concept that history is not chance but rational process, the evolution of freedom. 457pp. 5⅜ x 8½. 20112-0 Pa. $9.95

THE BOOK OF TEA, Kakuzo Okakura. Minor classic of the Orient: entertaining, charming explanation, interpretation of traditional Japanese culture in terms of tea ceremony. 94pp. 5⅜ x 8½. 20070-1 Pa. $3.95

LIFE IN ANCIENT EGYPT, Adolf Erman. Fullest, most thorough, detailed older account with much not in more recent books, domestic life, religion, magic, medicine, commerce, much more. Many illustrations reproduce tomb paintings, carvings, hieroglyphs, etc. 597pp. 5⅜ x 8½. 22632-8 Pa. $11.95

SUNDIALS, Their Theory and Construction, Albert Waugh. Far and away the best, most thorough coverage of ideas, mathematics concerned, types, construction, adjusting anywhere. Simple, nontechnical treatment allows even children to build several of these dials. Over 100 illustrations. 230pp. 5⅜ x 8½. 22947-5 Pa. $7.95

DYNAMICS OF FLUIDS IN POROUS MEDIA, Jacob Bear. For advanced students of ground water hydrology, soil mechanics and physics, drainage and irrigation engineering, and more. 335 illustrations. Exercises, with answers. 784pp. 6⅛ x 9¼. 65675-6 Pa. $19.95

SONGS OF EXPERIENCE: Facsimile Reproduction with 26 Plates in Full Color, William Blake. 26 full-color plates from a rare 1826 edition. Includes "TheTyger," "London," "Holy Thursday," and other poems. Printed text of poems. 48pp. 5¼ x 7. 24636-1 Pa. $4.95

OLD-TIME VIGNETTES IN FULL COLOR, Carol Belanger Grafton (ed.). Over 390 charming, often sentimental illustrations, selected from archives of Victorian graphics—pretty women posing, children playing, food, flowers, kittens and puppies, smiling cherubs, birds and butterflies, much more. All copyright-free. 48pp. 9¼ x 12¼. 27269-9 Pa. $5.95

PERSPECTIVE FOR ARTISTS, Rex Vicat Cole. Depth, perspective of sky and sea, shadows, much more, not usually covered. 391 diagrams, 81 reproductions of drawings and paintings. 279pp. 5⅜ x 8½. 22487-2 Pa. $6.95

DRAWING THE LIVING FIGURE, Joseph Sheppard. Innovative approach to artistic anatomy focuses on specifics of surface anatomy, rather than muscles and bones. Over 170 drawings of live models in front, back and side views, and in widely varying poses. Accompanying diagrams. 177 illustrations. Introduction. Index. 144pp. 8⅜ x11¼. 26723-7 Pa. $8.95

GOTHIC AND OLD ENGLISH ALPHABETS: 100 Complete Fonts, Dan X. Solo. Add power, elegance to posters, signs, other graphics with 100 stunning copyright-free alphabets: Blackstone, Dolbey, Germania, 97 more–including many lower-case, numerals, punctuation marks. 104pp. 8⅛ x 11. 24695-7 Pa. $8.95

HOW TO DO BEADWORK, Mary White. Fundamental book on craft from simple projects to five-bead chains and woven works. 106 illustrations. 142pp. 5⅜ x 8. 20697-1 Pa. $4.95

THE BOOK OF WOOD CARVING, Charles Marshall Sayers. Finest book for beginners discusses fundamentals and offers 34 designs. "Absolutely first rate . . . well thought out and well executed."–E. J. Tangerman. 118pp. 7¾ x 10⅝. 23654-4 Pa. $6.95

ILLUSTRATED CATALOG OF CIVIL WAR MILITARY GOODS: Union Army Weapons, Insignia, Uniform Accessories, and Other Equipment, Schuyler, Hartley, and Graham. Rare, profusely illustrated 1846 catalog includes Union Army uniform and dress regulations, arms and ammunition, coats, insignia, flags, swords, rifles, etc. 226 illustrations. 160pp. 9 x 12. 24939-5 Pa. $10.95

WOMEN'S FASHIONS OF THE EARLY 1900s: An Unabridged Republication of "New York Fashions, 1909," National Cloak & Suit Co. Rare catalog of mail-order fashions documents women's and children's clothing styles shortly after the turn of the century. Captions offer full descriptions, prices. Invaluable resource for fashion, costume historians. Approximately 725 illustrations. 128pp. 8⅜ x 11¼. 27276-1 Pa. $11.95

THE 1912 AND 1915 GUSTAV STICKLEY FURNITURE CATALOGS, Gustav Stickley. With over 200 detailed illustrations and descriptions, these two catalogs are essential reading and reference materials and identification guides for Stickley furniture. Captions cite materials, dimensions and prices. 112pp. 6½ x 9¼. 26676-1 Pa. $9.95

EARLY AMERICAN LOCOMOTIVES, John H. White, Jr. Finest locomotive engravings from early 19th century: historical (1804–74), main-line (after 1870), special, foreign, etc. 147 plates. 142pp. 11⅜ x 8¼. 22772-3 Pa. $10.95

THE TALL SHIPS OF TODAY IN PHOTOGRAPHS, Frank O. Braynard. Lavishly illustrated tribute to nearly 100 majestic contemporary sailing vessels: Amerigo Vespucci, Clearwater, Constitution, Eagle, Mayflower, Sea Cloud, Victory, many more. Authoritative captions provide statistics, background on each ship. 190 black-and-white photographs and illustrations. Introduction. 128pp. 8⅞ x 11¾. 27163-3 Pa. $13.95

THE INFLUENCE OF SEA POWER UPON HISTORY, 1660–1783, A. T. Mahan. Influential classic of naval history and tactics still used as text in war colleges. First paperback edition. 4 maps. 24 battle plans. 640pp. 5⅜ x 8½.   25509-3 Pa. $12.95

THE STORY OF THE TITANIC AS TOLD BY ITS SURVIVORS, Jack Winocour (ed.). What it was really like. Panic, despair, shocking inefficiency, and a little heroism. More thrilling than any fictional account. 26 illustrations. 320pp. 5⅜ x 8½.
20610-6 Pa. $8.95

FAIRY AND FOLK TALES OF THE IRISH PEASANTRY, William Butler Yeats (ed.). Treasury of 64 tales from the twilight world of Celtic myth and legend: "The Soul Cages," "The Kildare Pooka," "King O'Toole and his Goose," many more. Introduction and Notes by W. B. Yeats. 352pp. 5⅜ x 8½.   26941-8 Pa. $8.95

BUDDHIST MAHAYANA TEXTS, E. B. Cowell and Others (eds.). Superb, accurate translations of basic documents in Mahayana Buddhism, highly important in history of religions. The Buddha-karita of Asvaghosha, Larger Sukhavativyuha, more. 448pp. 5⅜ x 8½.   25552-2 Pa. $9.95

ONE TWO THREE . . . INFINITY: Facts and Speculations of Science, George Gamow. Great physicist's fascinating, readable overview of contemporary science: number theory, relativity, fourth dimension, entropy, genes, atomic structure, much more. 128 illustrations. Index. 352pp. 5⅜ x 8½.   25664-2 Pa. $8.95

ENGINEERING IN HISTORY, Richard Shelton Kirby, et al. Broad, nontechnical survey of history's major technological advances: birth of Greek science, industrial revolution, electricity and applied science, 20th-century automation, much more. 181 illustrations. ". . . excellent . . ."–*Isis.* Bibliography. vii + 530pp. 5⅜ x 8¼.
26412-2 Pa. $14.95

DALÍ ON MODERN ART: The Cuckolds of Antiquated Modern Art, Salvador Dalí. Influential painter skewers modern art and its practitioners. Outrageous evaluations of Picasso, Cézanne, Turner, more. 15 renderings of paintings discussed. 44 calligraphic decorations by Dalí. 96pp. 5⅜ x 8½. (USO)   29220-7 Pa. $4.95

ANTIQUE PLAYING CARDS: A Pictorial History, Henry René D'Allemagne. Over 900 elaborate, decorative images from rare playing cards (14th–20th centuries): Bacchus, death, dancing dogs, hunting scenes, royal coats of arms, players cheating, much more. 96pp. 9¼ x 12¼.   29265-7 Pa. $11.95

MAKING FURNITURE MASTERPIECES: 30 Projects with Measured Drawings, Franklin H. Gottshall. Step-by-step instructions, illustrations for constructing handsome, useful pieces, among them a Sheraton desk, Chippendale chair, Spanish desk, Queen Anne table and a William and Mary dressing mirror. 224pp. 8⅛ x 11¼.
29338-6 Pa. $13.95

THE FOSSIL BOOK: A Record of Prehistoric Life, Patricia V. Rich et al. Profusely illustrated definitive guide covers everything from single-celled organisms and dinosaurs to birds and mammals and the interplay between climate and man. Over 1,500 illustrations. 760pp. 7½ x 10⅛.   29371-8 Pa. $29.95

Prices subject to change without notice.

Available at your book dealer or write for free catalog to Dept. GI, Dover Publications, Inc., 31 East 2nd St., Mineola, N.Y. 11501. Dover publishes more than 500 books each year on science, elementary and advanced mathematics, biology, music, art, literary history, social sciences and other areas.